THIS FIERY TRIAL

Abraham Lincoln in 1858
(Illinois State Historical Society)

THIS FIERY TRIAL

The Speeches and Writings

of Abraham Lincoln

EDITED BY

WILLIAM E. GIENAPP

OXFORD
UNIVERSITY PRESS

2002

OXFORD
UNIVERSITY PRESS

Oxford   New York

Athens Auckland Bangkok Bogotá Buenos Aires
Cape Town Chennai Dar es Salaam Delhi Florence Hong Kong Istanbul
Karachi Kolkata Kuala Lumpur Madrid Melbourne Mexico City Mumbai
Nairobi Paris São Paulo Shanghai Singapore Taipei Tokyo Toronto Warsaw

and associated companies in
Berlin Ibadan

Published by Oxford University Press, Inc.
198 Madison Avenue, New York, New York 10016

Oxford is a registered trademark of Oxford University Press

Library of Congress Cataloging-in-Publication Data
Lincoln, Abraham, 1809–1865
This fiery trial : the speeches and writings of Abraham Lincoln /
[compiled] by William E. Gienapp.
p. cm.
Includes bibliographical references (p.).
ISBN 0-19-515106-2   ISBN 0-19-515101-1 (pbk.)
1. United States—Politics and government—1815–1861—Sources.
2. United States—Politics and government—1861–1865—Sources.
3. Illinois—Politics and government—To 1865—Sources.
4. Lincoln, Abraham, 1809–1865—Political and social views.
I. Gienapp, William E.   II. Title
E457.92 2001 973.7′092—dc21   2001050005

Book design and composition by Mark McGarry, Texas Type & Book Works, Inc.
Set in Monotype Dante

1 3 5 7 9 8 6 4 2
Printed in the United States of America
on acid-free paper

For the memory of my wife's parents,
Frank E. and Dorothy L. Kilian

Like Abraham Lincoln, they believed
education was a priceless gift

Fellow-citizens, *we* cannot escape history. . . . The fiery trial through which we pass, will light us down, in honor or dishonor, to the latest generation.

ABRAHAM LINCOLN, 1862

CONTENTS

II. "HALF *SLAVE* AND HALF *FREE*," 1854–1860

III. "THE PERPETUITY OF POPULAR GOVERNMENT," 1860–1861

IV. "*WE* CANNOT ESCAPE HISTORY," 1862

V. "A NEW BIRTH OF FREEDOM," 1863

VI. "EVENTS HAVE CONTROLLED ME," 1863–1864

VII. "TO BIND UP THE NATION'S WOUNDS," 1864–1865

PREFACE

THOUGH he was largely self-educated, Abraham Lincoln's literary ability was extraordinary. There are many reasons historians are attracted to Lincoln, but one certainly is the elegance and power of his language. The most eloquent president in our history, he possessed a literary style that at times was almost poetic. Indeed, he is the one American president whose writings could be considered literature.

Lincoln's writings reflected the influence of certain classic works that he read as a young man and knew well, particularly the Bible, Shakespeare's plays, Burns's poetry, and John Bunyan's *The Pilgrim's Progress*. His images, on the other hand, often were drawn from his rural frontier upbringing and his interactions with ordinary people as a politician and lawyer. He combined these two influences into a distinctive literary style that set him apart from other political leaders of his time.

In this volume, I have sought to include many of the most important documents from the much larger body of Lincoln's writings and speeches. Except for his 1859 autobiography, which is the first document, the selections are organized chronologically from his entry into politics until the end of his presidency. Most are public rather than private in nature. Few of Lincoln's private letters survive, and those available are not especially revealing. Even among friends and associates, he rarely discussed his family or marriage and disclosed little about his private life or feelings. Lincoln was preeminently a public person, his main interest was politics, and it was his public career that accounts for his historical significance.

This collection is limited to Lincoln's writings and speeches, which provide the most direct record of his ideas. Virtually all of the letters printed in this volume are complete; in only a few cases have I made minor deletions. Most of the speeches and proclamations have necessarily been abridged, but I have reproduced extensive selections from most of these documents to give the reader a fuller flavor of Lincoln's arguments. In some cases, because of its importance, the entire document has been included.

The texts for the documents in this collection are taken from *The Collected Works of Abraham Lincoln*, edited by Roy P. Basler. I wish to thank Thomas Schwartz and the Abraham Lincoln Association for permission to reproduce these documents. I have not corrected Lincoln's sometimes erratic spelling or used *sic* to indicate errors. When Lincoln inadvertently repeated a word, I have silently corrected this mistake. The beginning of each document has been standardized, but any changes have been indicated in the text. In a few cases, when several versions of a document exist, I have used what seems to me the best text. The brief introductions are intended to place the documents in the context of Lincoln's career and direct the reader to certain key points, but I have not attempted to provide a summary of Lincoln's life in these opening comments.

While an independent work that can be read on its own, this volume complements my biographical study, *Abraham Lincoln and Civil War America*. This collection is designed to illustrate some of the main themes developed in my biography: primarily, Lincoln's qualities of leadership, his maturation as president, the evolution of his thought regarding slavery and emancipation, and his expansion of the powers of the presidency, as well as his moderation and flexibility, his determination in the face of defeat or criticism, and his strong belief in opportunity, equality, and democracy. Thus the chronological divisions in this work correspond to the chapters in my biography.

This project was conceived in collaboration with Chris Rogers and subsequently edited by Peter Coveney, both of Oxford University Press. One could not ask for more supportive editors. Joellyn Ausanka smoothly and efficiently guided the manuscript through the production process. Several scholars have generously answered my inquiries about particular documents. I wish in particular to thank Rodney Davis, Thomas Schwartz, and Douglas Wilson.

Finally, I would like to acknowledge the contributions of my family. My older son, Bill, previously assembled some of the materials used in this volume for another project, while my younger son, Jonathan, helped with the research and copying for this volume. My wife, Erica, has her own interests but was always willing to put them aside to help me in many ways, large and small.

JUNE 2001   WILLIAM E. GIENAPP

THIS FIERY TRIAL

PROLOGUE

"Not much of me"

Autobiography, December 20, 1859

Late in 1859, Jesse Fell, an Illinois newspaperman, forwarded to Abraham Lincoln a letter from a Pennsylvania editor requesting information about his life. Interest in Lincoln as a possible presidential candidate was growing, and the editor intended to publish a biographical article that would make him better known in the East. In sending Fell a "little sketch" of his life, the would-be candidate explained that "there is not much of it" because "there is not much of me." Lincoln, whom his law partner called the most "shut-mouthed man" he ever knew, was never one to reveal much about himself, and in this autobiographical account he barely went beyond the mundane facts of his early life and offered only an occasional glimpse into his character. In fact, the sketch never mentioned his wife or children and offered not a single particular of his public life since 1854. Even the physical description Lincoln provided lacked much detail.

I was born Feb. 12, 1809, in Hardin County, Kentucky. My parents were both born in Virginia, of undistinguished families—second families, perhaps I should say. My mother, who died in my tenth year, was of a family of the name of Hanks, some of whom now reside in Adams, and others in Macon counties, Illinois. My paternal grandfather, Abraham

Lincoln, emigrated from Rockingham County, Virginia, to Kentucky, about 1781 or 2, where, a year or two later, he was killed by indians, not in battle, but by stealth, when he was laboring to open a farm in the forest. His ancestors, who were quakers, went to Virginia from Berks County, Pennsylvania. An effort to identify them with the New-England family of the same name ended in nothing more definite, than a similarity of Christian names in both families, such as Enoch, Levi, Mordecai, Solomon, Abraham, and the like.

My father, at the death of his father, was but six years of age; and he grew up, litterally without education. He removed from Kentucky to what is now Spencer county, Indiana, in my eighth year. We reached our new home about the time the State came into the Union. It was a wild region, with many bears and other wild animals still in the woods. There I grew up. There were some schools, so called; but no qualification was ever required of a teacher, beyond *"readin, writin, and cipherin,"* to the Rule of Three. If a straggler supposed to understand latin, happened to sojourn in the neighborhood, he was looked upon as a wizzard. There was absolutely nothing to excite ambition for education. Of course when I came of age I did not know much. Still somehow, I could read, write, and cipher to the Rule of Three; but that was all. I have not been to school since. The little advance I now have upon this store of education, I have picked up from time to time under the pressure of necessity.

I was raised to farm work, which I continued till I was twenty two. At twenty one I came to Illinois, and passed the first year in Illinois—Macon county. Then I got to New-Salem, (at that time in Sangamo, now in Menard county[)], where I remained a year as a sort of Clerk in a store. Then came the Black-Hawk war; and I was elected a Captain of Volunteers—a success which gave me more pleasure than any I have had since. I went the campaign, was elated, ran for the Legislature the same year (1832) and was beaten—the only time I have been beaten by the people. The next, and three succeeding biennial elections, I was elected to the Legislature. I was not a candidate afterwards. During this Legislative period I had studied law, and removed to Springfield to practice it. In 1846 I was once elected to the lower House of Congress. Was not a candidate for re-election. From 1849 to 1854, both inclusive, practiced law more assiduously than ever before. Always a whig in politics, and generally on the whig electoral tickets, making active canvasses. I was losing interest in politics, when the repeal of the Missouri Compromise aroused me again. What I have done since then is pretty well known.

If any personal description of me is thought desirable, it may be said, I am, in height, six feet, four inches, nearly; lean in flesh, weighing, on an average, one hundred and eighty pounds; dark complexion, with coarse black hair, and grey eyes—no other marks or brands recollected.

I

"PECULIAR AMBITION"

1831–1853

"I am young and unknown"

Communication to the People of Sangamo County, March 9, 1832

In 1831 Abraham Lincoln left home and settled in the small village of New Salem on the Sangamo River. He took a variety of jobs in the town, but his main interest soon became politics, and less than a year after his arrival, Lincoln announced his candidacy for the legislature. He was twenty-three years old. He had only a limited education and no political experience, but he was ambitious and had made many friends. Lacking any powerful patrons, he brought his name forward in a letter published in the Sangamo Journal *on March 15, 1832. Lincoln soon volunteered to serve in the Black Hawk War and returned to New Salem only a couple of weeks before the election. With little time to campaign, he was defeated in his first political race, the only time, he later recalled, that he was beaten by a direct vote of the people. Still, he won 277 of the 300 votes cast in New Salem, testimony to his great popularity among his neighbors.*

To the People of Sangamo County

FELLOW-CITIZENS: Having become a candidate for the honorable office of one of your representatives in the next General Assembly of this state, in accordance with an established custom, and the principles of true republicanism, it becomes my duty to make known to you—the people whom I propose to represent—my sentiments with regard to local affairs.

Time and experience have verified to a demonstration, the public utility of internal improvements. That the poorest and most thinly populated countries would be greatly benefitted by the opening of good roads, and in the clearing of navigable streams within their limits, is what no person will deny. . . .

With respect to the county of Sangamo, some more easy means of communication than we now possess, for the purpose of facilitating the task of exporting the surplus products of its fertile soil, and importing necessary articles from abroad, are indispensably necessary. . . . However desirable an object the construction of a rail road through our country may be . . . the probable cost of this contemplated rail road is estimated at $290,000;—the bare statement of which, in my opinion, is sufficient to justify the belief, that the improvement of Sangamo river is an object much better suited to our infant resources.

. . . Upon the subject of education, not presuming to dictate any plan or system respecting it, I can only say that I view it as the most important subject which we as a people can be engaged in. That every man may receive at least, a moderate education, and thereby be enabled to read the histories of his own and other countries, by which he may duly appreciate the value of our free institutions, appears to be an object of vital importance, even on this account alone, to say nothing of the advantages and satisfaction to be derived from all being able to read the scriptures and other works, both of a religious and moral nature, for themselves. For my part, I desire to see the time when education, and by its means, morality, sobriety, enterprise and industry, shall become much more general than at present, and should be gratified to have it in my power to contribute something to the advancement of any measure which might have a tendency to accelerate the happy period. . . .

. . . Upon the subjects of which I have treated, I have spoken as I thought. I may be wrong in regard to any or all of them; but holding it a sound maxim, that it is better to be only sometimes right, than at all times wrong, so soon as I discover my opinions to be erroneous, I shall be ready to renounce them.

Every man is said to have his peculiar ambition. Whether it be true or not, I can say for one that I have no other so great as that of being truly esteemed of my fellow men, by rendering myself worthy of their esteem. How far I shall succeed in gratifying this ambition, is yet to be developed. I am young and unknown to many of you. I was born and have ever remained in the most humble walks of life. I have no wealthy or popular relations to recommend me. My case is thrown exclusively upon the independent voters of this county, and if elected they will have conferred a favor upon me, for which I shall be unremitting in my labors to compensate. But if the good people in their wisdom shall see fit to keep me in the background, I have been too familiar with disappointments to be very much chagrined. Your friend and fellow-citizen,

"I shall be governed by their will"

Letter to the Editor of the *Sangamo Journal*, June 13, 1836

Lincoln was elected to the legislature in 1834. Two years later, in a public letter that was considerably shorter than his initial declaration four years earlier, he announced his candidacy for reelection. Lincoln's announcement downplayed party questions, but in the last paragraph he endorsed the presidential candidate of the anti-Jackson party in Illinois. In this communication, he advocated several traditional Whig policies, including the distribution of the proceeds from federal land sales to the states to fund internal improvements, and the idea that representatives should follow the will of their constituents. In contrast to his earlier statement, the tone of this declaration was much more self-confident, and indeed in the election, Lincoln ran ahead of all other candidates in the county.

To the Editor of the Journal: New Salem

In your paper of last Saturday, I see a communication over the signature of "Many Voters," in which the candidates who are announced in the Journal, are called upon to "show their hands." Agreed. Here's mine!

I go for all sharing the privileges of the government, who assist in bearing its burthens. Consequently I go for admitting all whites to the right of suffrage, who pay taxes or bear arms, (by no means excluding females.)

If elected, I shall consider the whole people of Sangamo my constituents, as well those that oppose, as those that support me.

While acting as their representative, I shall be governed by their will, on all subjects upon which I have the means of knowing what their will is; and upon all others, I shall do what my own judgment teaches me will best advance their interests. Whether elected or not, I go for distributing the proceeds of the sales of the public lands to the several states, to enable our state, in common with others, to dig canals and construct rail roads, without borrowing money and paying interest on it.

If alive on the first Monday in November, I shall vote for Hugh L. White for President. Very respectfully,

"Founded on both injustice and bad policy"

Protest in the Illinois Legislature on Slavery, March 3, 1837

Although Lincoln once declared that he could not remember when he did not oppose slavery, it was not an overriding issue for him in his early political career. Nevertheless, Lincoln and fellow representative Dan Stone entered a formal protest in the state legislature in 1837 condemning the institution of slavery while also criticizing the abolitionist movement for hurting the antislavery cause. Their protest was a response to resolutions recently passed by the legislature that censured abolitionist societies and asserted that the Constitution protected slavery. Abolitionism was distinctly unpopular in Illinois and also in Lincoln's own county, which had a large southern-born population, and he had nothing to gain politically by publicly condemning slavery. In this context, Lincoln's first public declaration against slavery was a politically courageous act.

Resolutions upon the subject of domestic slavery having passed both branches of the General Assembly at its present session, the undersigned hereby protest against the passage of the same.

They believe that the institution of slavery is founded on both injustice and bad policy; but that the promulgation of abolition doctrines tends rather to increase than to abate its evils.

They believe that the Congress of the United States has no power, under the constitution, to interfere with the institution of slavery in the different States.

They believe that the Congress of the United States has the power, under the constitution, to abolish slavery in the District of Columbia; but that that power ought not to be exercised unless at the request of the people of said District.

The difference between these opinions and those contained in the said resolutions, is their reason for entering this protest.

DAN STONE,

A. LINCOLN,

Representatives from the county of Sangamo.

"Cold, calculating, unimpassioned reason"

Speech to the Young Men's Lyceum of Springfield, January 27, 1838

The Young Men's Lyceum of Springfield sponsored public lectures as a means to disseminate information and enhance the cultural life of the community. In January 1838 Lincoln delivered an address under the organization's auspices. While his speech was an interesting effort, especially for someone under the age of thirty, more nonsense has been written about the Lyceum Address than any speech Lincoln ever delivered. Several scholars have suggested that Lincoln was projecting himself into the role of the tyrant who would threaten American liberties. In reality, his argument derived from the traditional Whig fear that a lawless executive threatened the Republic. More important was Lincoln's emphasis on the discipline of reason, his condemnation of mob violence, and his upholding of the forces of law and order. As such, the speech expressed the middle class's fear of unrestrained passion and the need for self-control, concerns that were central to Lincoln's own maturing character and personality.

As a subject for the remarks of the evening, *the perpetuation of our political institutions*, is selected:

In the great journal of things happening under the sun, we, the American People, find our account running, under date of the nineteenth century of the Christian era. We find ourselves in the peaceful possession, of the fairest portion of the earth, as regards extent of territory, fertility of soil, and salubrity of climate. We find ourselves under the government of a system of political institutions, conducing more essentially to the ends of civil and religious liberty, than any of which the history of former times tells us. We, when mounting the stage of existence, found ourselves the legal inheritors of these fundamental blessings. We toiled not in the acquirement or establishment of them— they are a legacy bequeathed us, by a *once* hardy, brave, and patriotic, but *now* lamented and departed race of ancestors. Their's was the task . . . to possess themselves, and through themselves, us, of this goodly land; and to uprear upon its hills and its valleys, a political edifice of liberty and equal rights; 'tis ours only, to transmit these . . . to the latest generation that fate shall permit the world to know. . . .

How, then, shall we perform it? At what point shall we expect the approach of danger? By what means shall we fortify against it? Shall we expect some transatlantic military giant, to step the Ocean, and crush us at a blow? Never! All the armies of Europe, Asia and Africa combined, with all the treasure of the earth (our own excepted) in their military chest; with a Buonaparte for a commander, could not by force, take a drink from the Ohio, or make a track on the Blue Ridge, in a trial of a thousand years.

At what point then is the approach of danger to be expected? I answer, if it ever reach us, it must spring up amongst us. It cannot come from abroad. If destruction be our lot, we must ourselves be its author and finisher. As a nation of freemen, we must live through all time, or die by suicide.

I hope I am over wary; but if I am not, there is, even now, something of ill-omen amongst us. I mean the increasing disregard for law which pervades the country; the growing disposition to substitute the wild and furious passions, in lieu of the sober judgement of Courts; and the worse than savage mobs, for the executive ministers of justice. This disposition is awfully fearful in any community; and that it now exists in ours, though grating to our feelings to admit, it would be a violation of truth, and an insult to our intelligence, to deny. Accounts of outrages committed by mobs, form the every-day news of the times. . . .

But you are, perhaps, ready to ask, "What has this to do with the perpetuation of our political institutions?" I answer, it has much to do with it. Its direct consequences are, comparatively speaking, but a small evil; and much of its danger consists, in the proneness of our minds, to regard its direct, as its only consequences. . . . When men take it in their

heads to day, to hang gamblers, or burn murderers, they should recollect, that, in the confusion usually attending such transactions, they will
be as likely to hang or burn some one, who is neither a gambler nor a
murderer as one who is; and that, acting upon the example they set, the
mob of to-morrow, may, and probably will, hang or burn some of
them, by the very same mistake. And not only so; the innocent, those
who have ever set their faces against violations of law in every shape,
alike with the guilty, fall victims to the ravages of mob law; and thus it
goes on, step by step, till all the walls erected for the defence of the persons and property of individuals, are trodden down, and disregarded.
. . . By the operation of this mobocratic spirit, which all must admit, is
now abroad in the land, the strongest bulwark of any Government, and
particularly of those constituted like ours, may effectually be broken
down and destroyed—I mean the *attachment* of the People. . . .

I know the American People are *much* attached to their Government;
—I know they would suffer *much* for its sake;—I know they would
endure evils long and patiently, before they would ever think of
exchanging it for another. Yet, notwithstanding all this, if the laws be
continually despised and disregarded, if their rights to be secure in their
persons and property, are held by no better tenure than the caprice of a
mob, the alienation of their affections from the Government is the natural consequence; and to that, sooner or later, it must come.

Here then, is one point at which danger may be expected.

The question recurs "how shall we fortify against it?" The answer is
simple. Let every American, every lover of liberty, every well wisher to
his posterity, swear by the blood of the Revolution, never to violate in
the least particular, the laws of the country; and never to tolerate their
violation by others. As the patriots of seventy-six did to the support of
the Declaration of Independence, so to the support of the Constitution
and Laws, let every American pledge his life, his property, and his sacred
honor;—let every man remember that to violate the law, is to trample
on the blood of his father, and to tear the character of his own, and his
children's liberty. Let reverence for the laws, be breathed by every
American mother, to the lisping babe, that prattles on her lap—let it be
taught in schools, in seminaries, and in colleges;—let it be written in
Primmers, spelling books, and in Almanacs;—let it be preached from
the pulpit, proclaimed in legislative halls, and enforced in courts of jus-

tice. And, in short, let it become the *political religion* of the nation; and let the old and the young, the rich and the poor, the grave and the gay, of all sexes and tongues, and colors and conditions, sacrifice unceasingly upon its altars.

While ever a state of feeling, such as this, shall universally, or even, very generally prevail throughout the nation, vain will be every effort, and fruitless every attempt, to subvert our national freedom. . . .

But, it may be asked, why suppose danger to our political institutions? Have we not preserved them for more than fifty years? And why may we not for fifty times as long?

We hope there is no *sufficient* reason. We hope all dangers may be overcome; but to conclude that no danger may ever arise, would itself be extremely dangerous. . . . It is to deny, what the history of the world tells us is true, to suppose that men of ambition and talents will not continue to spring up amongst us. And, when they do, they will as naturally seek the gratification of their ruling passion, as others have *so* done before them. The question then, is, can that gratification be found in supporting and maintaining an edifice that has been erected by others? Most certainly it cannot. Many great and good men sufficiently qualified for any task they should undertake, may ever be found, whose ambition would aspire to nothing beyond a seat in Congress, a gubernatorial or a presidential chair; *but such belong not to the family of the lion, or the tribe of the eagle.* What! think you these places would satisfy an Alexander, a Caesar, or a Napoleon? Never! Towering genius disdains a beaten path. It seeks regions hitherto unexplored. It sees *no distinction* in adding story to story, upon the monuments of fame, erected to the memory of others. It *denies* that it is glory enough to serve under any chief. It *scorns* to tread in the footsteps of *any* predecessor, however illustrious. It thirsts and burns for distinction; and, if possible, it will have it, whether at the expense of emancipating slaves, or enslaving freemen. Is it unreasonable then to expect, that some man possessed of the loftiest genius, coupled with ambition sufficient to push it to its utmost stretch, will at some time, spring up among us? And when such a one does, it will require the people to be united with each other, attached to the government and laws, and generally intelligent, to successfully frustrate his designs. . . .

Here then, is a probable case, highly dangerous, and such a one as could not have well existed heretofore.

Another reason which *once was*; but which, to the same extent, is *now no more*, has done much in maintaining our institutions thus far. I mean the powerful influence which the interesting scenes of the revolution had upon the *passions* of the people as distinguished from their judgment. . . .

But this state of feeling *must fade, is fading, has faded*, with the circumstances that produced it.

I do not mean to say, that the scenes of the revolution *are now* or *ever will be* entirely forgotten; but that like every thing else, they must fade upon the memory of the world, and grow more and more dim by the lapse of time. In history, we hope, they will be read of, and recounted, so long as the bible shall be read;—but even granting that they will, their influence *cannot be* what it heretofore has been. . . .

They* *were* the pillars of the temple of liberty; and now, that they have crumbled away, that temple must fall, unless we, their descendants, supply their places with other pillars, hewn from the solid quarry of sober reason. Passion has helped us; but can do so no more. It will in future be our enemy. Reason, cold, calculating, unimpassioned reason, must furnish all the materials for our future support and defence. Let those materials be moulded into *general intelligence, sound morality* and, in particular, *a reverence for the constitution and laws*; and, that we improved to the last; that we remained free to the last; that we revered his name to the last; that, during his long sleep, we permitted no hostile foot to pass over or desecrate his resting place; shall be that which to learn the last trump shall awaken our WASHINGTON.

Upon these let the proud fabric of freedom rest, as the rock of its basis; and as truly as has been said of the only greater institution, *"the gates of hell shall not prevail against it."*

"Bow to it I never will"

Speech on the Subtreasury, December 26, 1839

As a fervent Whig, Lincoln believed in the use of government power to promote economic development, and he was a strong advocate of a national bank and a well-regulated paper currency. In the following

*The Founders

speech, he attacked the Democratic proposal to create a subtreasury that would hold federal funds but would not make loans or issue any bank notes (paper money). Lincoln's economic reasoning was respectable, but the speech is most interesting for its ornate style and exaggerated rhetoric. Such oratory was standard fare at this time, but the speech stands in sharp contrast to the simple style and keen logic of his later speeches. Lincoln was still finding his way as a public speaker and had not yet risen above the prevailing partisan culture.

Many free countries have lost their liberty; and *ours may* lose hers; but if she shall, be it my proudest plume, not that I was the *last* to desert, but that I *never* deserted her. I know that the great volcano at Washington, aroused and directed by the evil spirit that reigns there, is belching forth the lava of political corruption, in a current broad and deep, which is sweeping with frightful velocity over the whole length and breadth of the land, bidding fair to leave unscathed no green spot or living thing, while on its bosom are riding like demons on the waves of Hell, the imps of that evil spirit, and fiendishly taunting all those who dare resist its destroying course, with the hopelessness of their effort; and knowing this, I cannot deny that all may be swept away. Broken by it, I, too, may be; bow to it I never will. The *probability* that we may fall in the struggle *ought not* to deter us from the support of a cause we believe to be just; it *shall not* deter me. If ever I feel the soul within me elevate and expand to those dimensions not wholly unworthy of its Almighty Architect, it is when I contemplate the cause of my country, deserted by all the world beside, and I standing up boldly and alone and hurling defiance at her victorious oppressors. Here, without contemplating consequences, before High Heaven, and in the face of the world, I swear eternal fidelity to the just cause, as I deem it, of the land of my life, my liberty and my love. And who, that thinks with me, will not fearlessly adopt the oath that I take. Let none faulter, who thinks he is right, and we may succeed. But, if after all, we shall fail, be it so. We still shall have the proud consolation of saying to our consciences, and to the departed shade of our country's freedom, that the cause approved of our judgment, and adored of our hearts, in disaster, in chains, in torture, in death, we NEVER faultered in defending.

"The most miserable man living"

Letter to John T. Stuart, January 23, 1841

Sometime around New Year's, 1841, Lincoln broke off his engagement to Mary Todd. Overcome by a sense of guilt, he quickly experienced a very severe bout of depression that greatly alarmed his friends and required the care of a physician. He temporarily ceased attending legislative sessions and conceded that he had made "a discreditable exhibition of myself." In a letter to his law partner, who was serving in Congress, Lincoln concentrated on political news but near the end noted his mental condition without elaborating on the cause. Such personal comments are unusual in Lincoln's correspondence, and he apparently said very little even to friends about his broken engagement. Two years later, the couple resumed their courtship and were married.

Dear Stuart: Springfield, Ills.

Yours of the 3rd. Inst. is recd. & I proceed to answer it as well as I can, tho' from the deplorable state of my mind at this time I fear I shall give you but little satisfaction. About the matter of the congressional election, I can only tell you, that there is a bill now before the Senate adopting the General Ticket system, but whether the party have fully determined on it's adoption is yet uncertain. There is no sign of opposition to you among our friends, and none that I can learn among our enemies; tho', of course, there will be, if the Genl. Ticket be adopted. The Chicago American, Peoria Register, & Sangamo Journal, have already hoisted your flag upon their own responsibility; & the other whig papers of the District are expected to follow immediately. On last evening there was a meeting of our friends at Butler's, and I submitted the question to them & found them unanamously in favour of having you announced as a candidate. A few of us this morning, however, concluded, that as you were already being announced in the papers, we would delay announcing you, *as by your own authority* for a week or two. We thought that to appear too keen about it might spur our opponents on about their Genl. Ticket project. Upon the whole, I think I may say with certainty, that your reelection is sure, if it be in the power of the whigs to make it so.

For not giving you a general summary of news, you *must* pardon me; it is not in my power to do so. I am now the most miserable man living. If what I feel were equally distributed to the whole human family, there would not be one cheerful face on the earth. Whether I shall ever be better I can not tell; I awfully forebode I shall not. To remain as I am is impossible; I must die or be better, it appears to me. The matter you speak of on my account, you may attend to as you say, unless you shall hear of my condition forbidding it. I say this, because I fear I shall be unable to attend to any bussiness here, and a change of scene might help me. If I could be myself, I would rather remain at home with Judge Logan. I can write no more. Your friend, as ever—

"An *evil* tree can not bring forth *good* fruit"

Letter to Williamson Durley, October 3, 1845

Lincoln vigorously campaigned for Henry Clay, the Whig presidential candidate in 1844, his "ideal of a statesman." In their frustration following Clay's defeat, Whigs lashed out at Liberty party voters, who refused to vote for Clay because he was a slaveholder and thereby helped elect James K. Polk, the Democratic candidate and an aggressive expansionist. In the following letter to an Illinois politician, Lincoln rebuked political abolitionists for aiding the annexation of Texas. Subsequent events would shatter Lincoln's faith, expressed in this letter, that slavery would die a natural death.

Friend Durley: Springfield

When I saw you at home, it was agreed that I should write to you and your brother Madison. Until I then saw you, I was not aware of your being what is generally called an abolitionist, or, as you call yourself, a Liberty-man; though I well knew there were many such in your country. I was glad to hear you say that you intend to attempt to bring about, at the next election in Putnam, a union of the whigs proper, and such of the liberty men, as are whigs in principle on all questions save only that of slavery. So far as I can perceive, by such union, neither party need yield any thing, on *the* point in difference between them. If the whig abolitionists of New York had voted with us last fall, Mr. Clay would now be president, whig principles in the ascendent, and Texas not annexed; whereas by the division, all that either had at stake in the contest, was lost. And, indeed, it was extremely probable, beforehand, that such would be the result. As I always understood, the Liberty-men deprecated the annexation of Texas extremely; and, this being so, why they should refuse to so cast their votes as to prevent it, even to me, seemed wonderful. What was their process of reasoning, I can only judge from what a single one of them told me. It was this: "We are not to do *evil* that *good* may come." This general, proposition is doubtless correct; but did it apply? If by your votes you could have prevented the *extention,* &c. of slavery, would it not have been *good* and not *evil* so to have used your votes, even though it involved the casting of them for a slaveholder? By the *fruit* the tree is to be known. An *evil* tree can not bring forth *good* fruit. If the fruit of electing Mr. Clay would have been to prevent the extension of slavery, could the act of electing have been *evil*?

But I will not argue farther. I perhaps ought to say that individually I never was much interested in the Texas question. I never could see much good to come of annexation; inasmuch, as they were already a free republican people on our own model; on the other hand, I never could very clearly see how the annexation would augment the evil of slavery. It always seemed to me that slaves would be taken there in about equal numbers, with or without annexation. And if more *were* taken because of annexation, still there would be just so many the fewer left, where they were taken from. It is possibly true, to some extent, that with annexation, some slaves may be sent to Texas and continued in slavery, that otherwise might have been liberated. To whatever extent this may be true, I think annexation an evil. I hold it to be a paramount duty of us in the free states, due to the Union of the states, and perhaps to liberty itself (paradox though it may seem) to let the slavery of the other states alone; while, on the other hand, I hold it to be equally clear, that we should never knowingly lend ourselves directly or indirectly, to prevent that slavery from dying a natural death—to find new places for it to live in, when it can no longer exist in the old. Of course I am not now considering what would be our duty, in cases of insurrection among the slaves.

To recur to the Texas question, I understand the Liberty men to have viewed annexation as a much greater evil than I ever did; and I, would like to convince you if I could, that they could have prevented it, without violation of principle, if they had chosen.

I intend this letter for you and Madison together; and if you and he or either shall think fit to drop me a line, I shall be pleased.

Yours with respect

"I am not a member of any . . . Church"

Handbill Addressed to the Voters of the
Seventh Congressional District, July 31, 1846

In 1846 Lincoln won the Whig nomination for Congress in the Seventh District. His opponent was Peter Cartwright, the famous Methodist preacher. During the campaign, Cartwright apparently spread the rumor that his opponent was an infidel, which prompted Lincoln to issue a handbill discussing his religious beliefs. This document is the most extensive statement Lincoln ever made about his religious outlook. It was very carefully phrased to neutralize this issue and appeal to the church-going voters in the district, yet it left much unsaid about his religious views. Throughout his life, Lincoln never joined a church and remained uncomfortable with organized religion. Nevertheless, his district was reliably Whig, and he was handily elected to Congress

FELLOW CITIZENS:

A charge having got into circulation in some of the neighborhoods of this District, in substance that I am an open scoffer at Christianity, I have by the advice of some friends concluded to notice the subject in this form. That I am not a member of any Christian Church, is true; but I have never denied the truth of the Scriptures; and I have never spoken with intentional disrespect of religion in general, or of any denomination of Christians in particular. It is true that in early life I was inclined to believe in what I understand is called the "Doctrine of Necessity"— that is, that the human mind is impelled to action, or held in rest by some power, over which the mind itself has no control; and I have sometimes (with one, two or three, but never publicly) tried to maintain this opinion in argument. The habit of arguing thus however, I have, entirely left off for more than five years. And I add here, I have always understood this same opinion to be held by several of the Christian denominations. The foregoing, is the whole truth, briefly stated, in relation to myself, upon this subject.

I do not think I could myself, be brought to support a man for office, whom I knew to be an open enemy of, and scoffer at, religion. Leaving the higher matter of eternal consequences, between him and his Maker, I still do not think any man has the right thus to insult the feelings, and injure the morals, of the community in which he may live. If, then, I was guilty of such conduct, I should blame no man who should condemn me for it; but I do blame those, whoever they may be, who falsely put such a charge in circulation against me.

"*No one man* should hold the power"

Letter to William Herndon, February 15, 1848

Lincoln was slow to recognize the importance of the territorial issue, but when he took his seat in Congress in 1847, he quickly joined other Whigs in blaming James K. Polk for the war with Mexico. He also consistently voted in favor of proposals to bar slavery from any territory acquired from Mexico as the result of a war that he believed was unnecessary and deliberately provoked. From the party's beginning, Whigs had condemned unbridled executive power, and in this letter to his law partner, William Herndon, Lincoln argued that it was constitutionally dangerous for a president, without consulting Congress, to involve the nation in a war. Lincoln's letter was written in response to Herndon's worry that he was politically damaging himself back home by his opposition to the war. Lincoln, however, was careful to vote for all military supply bills and also recognized that some territorial acquisition was inevitable, positions that largely undercut opposition in his district.

Dear William: Washington

Your letter of the 29th. Jany. was received last night. Being exclusively a constitutional argument, I wish to submit some reflections upon it in the same spirit of kindness that I know actuates you. Let me first state what I understand to be your position. It is, that if it shall become *necessary, to repel invasion*, the President may, without violation of the Constitution, cross the line, and *invade* the teritory of another country; and that whether such *necessity* exists in any given case, the President is to be the *sole* judge.

Before going further, consider well whether this is, or is not your position. If it is, it is a position that neither the President himself, nor any friend of his, so far as I know, has ever taken. Their only positions are first, that the soil was *ours* where hostilities commenced, and second, that whether it was rightfully *ours* or not, *Congress had annexed it*, and the President, for that reason was bound to defend it, both of which are as clearly proved to be false in fact, as you can prove that your house is not mine. That soil was not ours; and Congress did not annex or attempt to annex it. But to return to your position: Allow the President to invade a neighboring nation, whenever *he* shall deem it necessary to repel an invasion, and you allow him to do so, *whenever he may choose to say* he deems it necessary for such purpose—and you allow him to make war at pleasure. Study to see if you can fix *any limit* to his power in this respect, after you have given him so much as you propose. If, today, he should choose to say he thinks it necessary to invade Canada, to prevent the British from invading us, how could you stop him? You may say to him, "I see no probability of the British invading us" but he will say to you "be silent; I see it, if you dont."

The provision of the Constitution giving the war-making power to Congress, was dictated, as I understand it, by the following reasons. Kings had always been involving and impoverishing their people in wars, pretending generally, if not always, that the good of the people was the object. This, our Convention understood to be the most oppressive of all Kingly oppressions; and they resolved to so frame the Constitution that *no one man* should hold the power of bringing this oppression upon us. But your view destroys the whole matter, and places our President where kings have always stood. Write soon again. Yours truly,

"I like the letters very much"

Letter to Mary Todd Lincoln, April 16, 1848

Very few of Lincoln's family letters survive. Unlike most congressional wives, Mary Lincoln accompanied her husband to Washington in 1847, but she soon grew tired of boardinghouse life, and after a few months she took their two sons, Bob and Eddy, and went to Kentucky to visit her family. Lincoln's letter to his absent wife is filled with mundane commentary, and as such contrasts sharply with the more focused content and vigorous prose of his political letters. An intensely private individual, Lincoln did not find it easy to express his intimate emotions, and his stilted, awkward family letters are most revealing for what they do not say.

Dear Mary: Washington

In this troublesome world, we are never quite satisfied. When you were here, I thought you hindered me some in attending to business; but now, having nothing but business—no variety—it has grown exceedingly tasteless to me. I hate to sit down and direct documents, and I hate to stay in this old room by myself. You know I told you in last sunday's letter, I was going to make a little speech during the week; but the week has passed away without my getting a chance to do so; and now my interest in the subject has passed away too. Your second and third letters have been received since I wrote before. Dear Eddy thinks father is *"gone tapila*[.]" Has any further discovery been made as to the breaking into your grand-mother's house? If I were she, I would not remain there alone. You mention that your uncle John Parker is likely to be at Lexington. Dont forget to present him my very kindest regards.

I went yesterday to hunt the little plaid stockings, as you wished; but found that McKnight has quit business, and Allen had not a single pair of the description you give, and only one plaid pair of any sort that I thought would fit "Eddy's dear little feet." I have a notion to make another trial to-morrow morning. If I could get them, I have an excellent chance of sending them. Mr. Warrick Tunstall, of St. Louis is here. He is to leave early this week, and to go by Lexington. He says he knows you, and will call to see you; and he voluntarily asked, if I had not some package to send to you.

I wish you to enjoy yourself in every possible way; but is there no danger of wounding the feelings of your good father, by being so openly intimate with the Wickliffe family?

Mrs. Broome has not removed yet; but she thinks of doing so tomorrow. All the house—or rather, all with whom you were on decided good terms—send their love to you. The others say nothing.

Very soon after you went away, I got what I think a very pretty set of shirt-bosom studs—modest little ones, jet, set in gold, only costing 50 cents a piece, or 1.50 for the whole.

Suppose you do not prefix the "Hon" to the address on your letters to me any more. I like the letters very much, but I would rather they should not have that upon them. It is not necessary, as I suppose you have thought, to have them to come free.

And you are entirely free from head-ache? That is good—good—considering it is the first spring you have been free from it since we were acquainted. I am afraid you will get so well, and fat, and young, as to be wanting to marry again. Tell Louisa I want her to watch you a little for me. Get weighed, and write me how much you weigh.

I did not get rid of the impression of that foolish dream about dear Bobby till I got your letter written the same day. What did he and Eddy think of the little letters father sent them? Dont let the blessed fellows forget father. . . .

Most affectionately

"Resolve to be honest"

Notes for a law lecture, July 1, 1850?

These notes, which apparently were intended for a lecture on the law that was never delivered, outline Lincoln's legal attitudes. The date of this document is uncertain, and it may have been written later in the 1850s. For Lincoln, who had learned the law without any formal guidance, diligence and careful study were the keys to legal success. Like most attorneys, Lincoln took whatever cases came his way, but his associates in the bar testified that he was not particularly effective when he did not firmly believe in his client's case.

I am not an accomplished lawyer. I find quite as much material for a lecture in those points wherein I have failed, as in those wherein I have been moderately successful. The leading rule for the lawyer, as for the man of every other calling, is diligence. Leave nothing for to-morrow which can be done to-day. Never let your correspondence fall behind. Whatever piece of business you have in hand, before stopping, do all the labor pertaining to it which can then be done. When you bring a common-law suit, if you have the facts for doing so, write the declaration at once. If a law point be involved, examine the books, and note the authority you rely on upon the declaration itself, where you are sure to find it when wanted. The same of defenses and pleas. In business not likely to be litigated,—ordinary collection cases, foreclosures, partitions, and the like,—make all examinations of titles, and note them, and even draft orders and decrees in advance. This course has a triple advantage; it avoids omissions and neglect, saves your labor when once done, performs the labor out of court when you have leisure, rather than in court when you have not. Extemporaneous speaking should be practised and cultivated. It is the lawyer's avenue to the public. However able and faithful he may be in other respects, people are slow to bring him business if he cannot make a speech. And yet there is not a more fatal error to young lawyers than relying too much on speech-making. If any one, upon his rare powers of speaking, shall claim an exemption from the drudgery of the law, his case is a failure in advance.

Discourage litigation. Persuade your neighbors to compromise whenever you can. Point out to them how the nominal winner is often a real loser—in fees, expenses, and waste of time. As a peacemaker the lawyer has a superior opportunity of being a good man. There will still be business enough.

Never stir up litigation. A worse man can scarcely be found than one who does this. Who can be more nearly a fiend than he who habitually overhauls the register of deeds in search of defects in titles, whereon to stir up strife, and put money in his pocket? A moral tone ought to be infused into the profession which should drive such men out of it.

The matter of fees is important, far beyond the mere question of bread and butter involved. Properly attended to, fuller justice is done to both lawyer and client. An exorbitant fee should never be claimed. As a general rule never take your whole fee in advance, nor any more than a small retainer. When fully paid beforehand, you are more than a common mortal if you can feel the same interest in the case, as if something was still in prospect for you, as well as for your client. And when you lack interest in the case the job will very likely lack skill and diligence in the performance. Settle the amount of fee and take a note in advance. Then you will feel that you are working for something, and you are sure to do your work faithfully and well. Never sell a fee note—at least not before the consideration service is performed. It leads to negligence and dishonesty—negligence by losing interest in the case, and dishonesty in refusing to refund when you have allowed the consideration to fail.

There is a vague popular belief that lawyers are necessarily dishonest. I say vague, because when we consider to what extent confidence and honors are reposed in and conferred upon lawyers by the people, it appears improbable that their impression of dishonesty is very distinct and vivid. Yet the impression is common, almost universal. Let no young man choosing the law for a calling for a moment yield to the popular belief—resolve to be honest at all events; and if in your own judgment you cannot be an honest lawyer, resolve to be honest without being a lawyer. Choose some other occupation, rather than one in the choosing of which you do, in advance, consent to be a knave.

"More painful than pleasant"

Letter to John D. Johnston, January 12, 1851

Lincoln addressed this letter to his stepbrother when informed by a relative that his father was dying. Lincoln felt a deep estrangement from his father, a feeling that had only deepened in the years since he had left home, and he mustered only a series of feeble excuses for not coming to see him. Unwilling to make a pretense of affection, Lincoln resorted to a series of religious platitudes that were hollow and unconvincing. Thomas Lincoln died less than a week later; his son did not attend the funeral.

Dear Brother: Springfield

On the day before yesterday I received a letter from Harriett, written at Greenup. She says she has just returned from your house; and that Father is very low, and will hardly recover. She also says you have written me two letters; and that although you do not expect me to come now, you wonder that I do not write. I received both your letters, and although I have not answered them, it is not because I have forgotten them, or been uninterested about them—but because it appeared to me I could write nothing which could do any good. You already know I desire that neither Father or Mother shall be in want of any comfort either in health or sickness while they live; and I feel sure you have not failed to use my name, if necessary, to procure a doctor, or any thing else for Father in his present sickness. My business is such that I could hardly leave home now, if it were not, as it is, that my own wife is sick-abed. (It is a case of baby-sickness, and I suppose is not dangerous.) I sincerely hope Father may yet recover his health; but at all events tell him to remember to call upon, and confide in, our great, and good, and merciful Maker; who will not turn away from him in any extremity. He notes the fall of a sparrow, and numbers the hairs of our heads; and He will not forget the dying man, who puts his trust in Him. Say to him that if we could meet now, it is doubtful whether it would not be more painful than pleasant; but that if it be his lot to go now, he will soon have a joyous meeting with many loved ones gone before; and where the rest of us, through the help of God, hope ere-long to join them.

Write me again when you receive this. Affectionately

II

"HALF *SLAVE* AND HALF *FREE*"
1854–1860

"The legitimate object of government"

Fragment on government, July 1, 1854?

The exact date Lincoln wrote this statement about the role of government is unknown. Like other Whigs, Lincoln believed that government played a positive role in society, which had to be balanced with the American ideal of individual liberty. Indeed, he believed that government was indispensable in any organized society.

The legitimate object of government, is to do for a community of people, whatever they need to have done, but can not do, *at all,* or can not, *so well do,* for themselves—in their separate, and individual capacities.

In all that the people can individually do as well for themselves, government ought not to interfere.

The desirable things which the individuals of a people can not do, or can not well do, for themselves, fall into two classes: those which have relation to *wrongs,* and those which have not. Each of these branch off into an infinite variety of subdivisions.

The first—that in relation to wrongs—embraces all crimes, misdemesnors, and non-performance of contracts. The other embraces all which, in its nature, and without wrong, requires combined action, as public roads and highways, public schools, charities, pauperism, orphanage, estates of the deceased, and the machinery of government itself.

From this it appears that if all men were just, there still would be *some,* though not *so much,* need of government.

"Our republican robe is soiled"
Speech at Peoria, October 16, 1854

Following his retirement from Congress in 1849, Lincoln took only a limited interest in politics. In 1854, however, the Kansas–Nebraska Act roused Lincoln's moral indignation and his smoldering political ambition. Drafted by Senator Stephen A. Douglas of Illinois, this statute repealed the Missouri Compromise and, under the doctrine of popular sovereignty, which allowed the people of a territory to determine the status of slavery, opened the new territories of Kansas and Nebraska to slavery. Taking to the stump in the 1854 campaign, Lincoln subjected Douglas and the principle of popular sovereignty to withering criticism. Lincoln delivered this speech on the Kansas–Nebraska Act at Springfield, and then repeated it at Peoria in reply to Douglas, who spoke earlier. Beginning in 1854, slavery became the central issue in Lincoln's political career, and his public statements possessed a new moral earnestness at the same time that his language became more crisp and lean. The earlier rhetorical flourishes and hyperbole were conspicuously absent as he appealed for the restoration of what he considered the policy of the Founding Fathers on slavery. The Peoria Address also marked the emergence in Lincoln's thought of the importance of the Declaration of Independence in defining American ideals.

The repeal of the Missouri Compromise, and the propriety of its restoration, constitute the subject of what I am about to say. . . .

And, as this subject is no other, than part and parcel of the larger general question of domestic-slavery, I wish to MAKE and to KEEP the distinction between the EXISTING institution, and the EXTENSION of it, so broad, and so clear, that no honest man can misunderstand me, and no dishonest one, successfully misrepresent me. . . .

. . . We have before us, the chief material enabling us to correctly judge whether the repeal of the Missouri Compromise is right or wrong.

I think, and shall try to show, that it is wrong; wrong in its direct effect, letting slavery into Kansas and Nebraska—and wrong in its prospective principle, allowing it to spread to every other part of the wide world, where men can be found inclined to take it.

This *declared* indifference, but as I must think, covert *real* zeal for the spread of slavery, I can not but hate. I hate it because of the monstrous injustice of slavery itself. I hate it because it deprives our republican example of its just influence in the world—enables the enemies of free institutions, with plausibility, to taunt us as hypocrites—causes the real friends of freedom to doubt our sincerity, and especially because it forces so many really good men amongst ourselves into an open war with the very fundamental principles of civil liberty—criticising the Declaration of Independence, and insisting that there is no right principle of action but *self-interest*.

Before proceeding, let me say I think I have no prejudice against the Southern people. They are just what we would be in their situation. If slavery did not now exist amongst them, they would not introduce it. If it did now exist amongst us, we should not instantly give it up. This I believe of the masses north and south. Doubtless there are individuals, on both sides, who would not hold slaves under any circumstances; and others who would gladly introduce slavery anew, if it were out of existence. We know that some southern men do free their slaves, go north, and become tip-top abolitionists; while some northern ones go south, and become most cruel slave-masters.

When southern people tell us they are no more responsible for the origin of slavery, than we; I acknowledge the fact. When it is said that the institution exists; and that it is very difficult to get rid of it, in any satisfactory way, I can understand and appreciate the saying. I surely will not blame them for not doing what I should not know how to do myself. If all earthly power were given me, I should not know what to do, as to the existing institution. My first impulse would be to free all the slaves, and send them to Liberia,—to their own native land. But a moment's reflection would convince me, that whatever of high hope, (as I think there is) there may be in this, in the long run, its sudden execution is impossible. If they were all landed there in a day, they would all perish in the next ten days; and there are not surplus shipping and surplus money enough in the world to carry them there in many times ten days. What then? Free them all, and keep them among us as underlings? Is it quite certain that this betters their condition? I think I would not hold one in slavery, at any rate; yet the point is not clear enough for me to denounce people upon. What next? Free them, and make them politically and socially, our equals? My own feelings will not admit of this; and if mine would, we well know that those of the great mass of white people will not. Whether this feeling accords with justice and sound judgment, is not the sole question, if indeed, it is any part of it. A universal feeling, whether well or ill-founded, can not be safely disregarded. We can not, then, make them equals. It does seem to me that systems of gradual emancipation might be adopted; but for their tardiness in this, I will not undertake to judge our brethren of the south. . . .

Let me here drop the main argument, to notice what I consider rather an inferior matter. It is argued that slavery will not go to Kansas and Nebraska, *in any event*. This is a *palliation*—a *lullaby*. I have some hope that it will not; but let us not be too confident. As to climate, a glance at the map shows that there are five slave States—Delaware, Maryland, Virginia, Kentucky, and Missouri—and also the District of Columbia, all north of the Missouri compromise line. The census returns of 1850 show that, within these, there are 867,276 slaves—being more than one-fourth of all the slaves in the nation.

It is not climate, then, that will keep slavery out of these territories. . . . No peculiarity of the country will—nothing in *nature* will. Will the disposition of the people prevent it? Those nearest the scene, are all in favor of the extension. The yankees, who are opposed to it may be more numerous; but in military phrase, the battle-field is too far from *their* base of operations.

But it is said, there now is *no* law in Nebraska on the subject of slavery; and that, in such case, taking a slave there, operates his freedom. That *is* good book-law; but is not the rule of actual practice. Wherever slavery is, it has been first introduced without law. The oldest laws we find concerning it, are not laws introducing it; but *regulating* it, as an already existing thing. A white man takes his slave to Nebraska now; who will inform the negro that he is free? Who will take him before court to test the question of his freedom? In ignorance of his legal emancipation, he is kept chopping, splitting and plowing. Others are brought, and move on in the same track. At last, if ever the time for voting comes, on the question of slavery, the institution already in fact exists in the country, and cannot well be removed. The facts of its presence, and the difficulty of its removal will carry the vote in its favor. Keep it out until a vote is taken, and a vote in favor of it, can not be got in any population of forty thousand, on earth, who have been drawn together by the ordinary motives of emigration and settlement. To get slaves into the country simultaneously with the whites, in the incipient stages of settlement, is the precise stake played for, and won in this Nebraska measure. . . .

But one great argument in the support of the repeal of the Missouri Compromise, is still to come. That argument is "the sacred right of self government." It seems our distinguished Senator* has found great difficulty in getting his antagonists, even in the Senate to meet him fairly on this argument—some poet has said

"Fools rush in where angels fear to tread."

At the hazzard of being thought one of the fools of this quotation, I meet that argument—I rush in, I take that bull by the horns.

I trust I understand, and truly estimate the right of self-government. My faith in the proposition that each man should do precisely as he pleases with all which is exclusively his own, lies at the foundation of the sense of justice there is in me. I extend the principles to communities of men, as well as to individuals. I so extend it, because it is politically wise, as well as naturally just: politically wise, in saving us from broils about matters which do not concern us. Here, or at Washington, I would not trouble myself with the oyster laws of Virginia, or the cranberry laws of Indiana.

The doctrine of self government is right—absolutely and eternally right—but it has no just application, as here attempted. Or perhaps I should rather say that whether it has such just application depends upon whether a negro is *not* or *is* a man. If he is *not* a man, why in that case, he who *is* a man may, as a matter of self-government, do just as he pleases with him. But if the negro *is* a man, is it not to that extent, a total destruction of self-government, to say that he too shall not govern *himself*? When the white man governs himself that is self-government; but when he governs himself, and also governs *another* man, that is *more* than self-government—that is despotism. If the negro is a *man*, why

*Stephen A. Douglas.

then my ancient faith teaches me that "all men are created equal;" and that there can be no moral right in connection with one man's making a slave of another.

Judge Douglas* frequently, with bitter irony and sarcasm, paraphrases our argument by saying "The white people of Nebraska are good enough to govern themselves, *but they are not good enough to govern a few miserable negroes!!*"

Well I doubt not that the people of Nebraska are, and will continue to be as good as the average of people elsewhere. I do not say the contrary. What I do say is, that no man is good enough to govern another man, *without that other's consent*. I say this is the leading principle—the sheet anchor of American republicanism. Our Declaration of Independence says:

"We hold these truths to be self evident: that all men are created equal; that they are endowed by their Creator with certain inalienable rights; that among these are life, liberty and the pursuit of happiness. That to secure these rights, governments are instituted among men, DERIVING THEIR JUST POWERS FROM THE CONSENT OF THE GOVERNED."

I have quoted so much at this time merely to show that according to our ancient faith, the just powers of governments are derived from the consent of the governed. Now the relation of masters and slaves is, PRO TANTO, a total violation of this principle. The master not only governs the slave without his consent; but he governs him by a set of rules altogether different from those which he prescribes for himself. Allow ALL the governed an equal voice in the government, and that, and that only is self government.

Let it not be said I am contending for the establishment of political and social equality between the whites and blacks. I have already said the contrary. I am not now combating the argument of NECESSITY, arising from the fact that the blacks are already amongst us; but I am combating what is set up as MORAL argument for allowing them to be taken where they have never yet been—arguing against the EXTENSION of a bad thing, which where it already exists, we must of necessity, manage as we best can. . . .

---

*Douglas had served on the Illinois Supreme Court, so Lincoln habitually referred to him as Judge.

I particularly object to the NEW position which the avowed principle of this Nebraska law gives to slavery in the body politic. I object to it because it assumes that there CAN be MORAL RIGHT in the enslaving of one man by another. I object to it as a dangerous dalliance for a few [free?] people—a sad evidence that, feeling prosperity we forget right—that liberty, as a principle, we have ceased to revere. I object to it because the fathers of the republic eschewed, and rejected it. The argument of "Necessity" was the only argument they ever admitted in favor of slavery; and so far, and so far only as it carried them, did they ever go. . . . But this is not all. The earliest Congress, under the constitution, took the same view of slavery. They hedged and hemmed it in to the narrowest limits of necessity. . . .

. . . The plain unmistakable spirit of that age, towards slavery, was hostility to the PRINCIPLE, and toleration, ONLY BY NECESSITY.

But NOW it is to be transformed into a "sacred right." Nebraska brings it forth, places it on the high road to extension and perpetuity; and, with a pat on its back, says to it, "Go, and God speed you." Henceforth it is to be the chief jewel of the nation—the very figure-head of the ship of State. Little by little, but steadily as man's march to the grave, we have been giving up the OLD for the NEW faith. Near eighty years ago we began by declaring that all men are created equal; but now from that beginning we have run down to the other declaration, that for SOME men to enslave OTHERS is a "sacred right of self-government." These principles can not stand together. They are as opposite as God and mammon; and whoever holds to the one, must despise the other. . . .

Let no one be deceived. The spirit of seventy-six and the spirit of Nebraska, are utter antagonisms; and the former is being rapidly displaced by the latter.

Fellow countrymen—Americans south, as well as north, shall we make no effort to arrest this? Already the liberal party throughout the world, express the apprehension "that the one retrograde institution in America, is undermining the principles of progress, and fatally violating the noblest political system the world ever saw." This is not the taunt of enemies, but the warning of friends. Is it quite safe to disregard it—to despise it? Is there no danger to liberty itself, in discarding the earliest practice, and first precept of our ancient faith? In our greedy chase to make profit of the negro, let us beware, lest we "cancel and tear to pieces" even the white man's charter of freedom.

Our republican robe is soiled, and trailed in the dust. Let us repurify it. Let us turn and wash it white, in the spirit, if not the blood, of the Revolution. Let us turn slavery from its claims of "moral right," back upon its existing legal rights, and its arguments of "necessity." Let us return it to the position our fathers gave it; and there let it rest in peace. Let us re-adopt the Declaration of Independence, and with it, the practices, and policy, which harmonize with it. Let north and south—let all Americans—let all lovers of liberty everywhere—join in the great and good work. If we do this, we shall not only have saved the Union; but we shall have so saved it, as to make, and to keep it, forever worthy of the saving. We shall have so saved it, that the succeeding millions of free happy people, the world over, shall rise up, and call us blessed, to the latest generations.

"Where I now stand"

Letter to Joshua Speed, August 24, 1855

Joshua Speed was the only close friend Lincoln had in his adult life. As young men they had lived together in Springfield, but Speed had eventually returned to his native Kentucky. By 1855, as he explained in a long letter to Speed, Lincoln found himself politically adrift. He made it clear, however, that he did not sympathize with the Know Nothing party, which called for restrictions on the rights of immigrants and Catholics. Aware of the Know Nothings' strength in Illinois and that no strong opposition party to the Democrats could be organized without their support, Lincoln confined his criticism to private letters. In less than a year, he would join the new Republican party.

Dear Speed: Springfield

You know what a poor correspondent I am. Ever since I received your very agreeable letter of the 22nd. of May I have been intending to write you in answer to it. You suggest that in political action now, you and I would differ. I suppose we would; not quite as much, however, as you may think. You know I dislike slavery; and you fully admit the abstract wrong of it. So far there is no cause of difference. But you say that sooner than yield your legal right to the slave—especially at the bidding of those who are not themselves interested, you would see the Union dissolved. I am not aware that *any one* is bidding you to yield that right; very certainly *I* am not. I leave that matter entirely to yourself. I also acknowledge *your* rights and *my* obligations, under the constitution, in regard to your slaves. I confess I hate to see the poor creatures hunted down, and caught, and carried back to their stripes, and unrewarded toils; but I bite my lip and keep quiet. In 1841 you and I had together a tedious low-water trip, on a Steam Boat from Louisville to St. Louis. You may remember, as I well do, that from Louisville to the mouth of the Ohio there were, on board, ten or a dozen slaves, shackled together with irons. That sight was a continual torment to me; and I see something like it every time I touch the Ohio, or any other slave-border. It is hardly fair for you to assume, that I have no interest in a thing which has, and continually exercises, the power of making me miserable. You ought rather to appreciate how much the great body of the Northern people do crucify their feelings, in order to maintain their loyalty to the constitution and the Union.

I do oppose the extension of slavery, because my judgment and feelings so prompt me; and I am under no obligation to the contrary. If for this you and I must differ, differ we must. You say if you were President, you would send an army and hang the leaders of the Missouri outrages upon the Kansas elections; still, if Kansas fairly votes herself a slave state, she must be admitted, or the Union must be dissolved. But how if she votes herself a slave state *unfairly*—that is, by the very means for which you say you would hang men? Must she still be admitted, or the Union be dissolved? That will be the phase of the question when it first becomes a practical one. In your assumption that there may be a *fair* decision of the slavery question in Kansas, I plainly see you and I would differ about the Nebraska-law. I look upon that enactment not as a *law*, but as *violence* from the beginning. It was conceived in violence, passed in violence, is maintained in violence, and is being executed in violence. I say it was *conceived* in violence, because the destruction of the Missouri Compromise, under the circumstances, was nothing less than violence. It was *passed* in violence, because it could not have passed at all but for the votes of many members, in violent disregard of the known will of their constituents. It is *maintained* in violence because the elections since, clearly demand it's repeal, and this demand is openly disregarded. *You* say men ought to be hung for the way they are executing that law; and *I* say the way it is being executed is quite as good as any of its antecedents. It is being executed in the precise way which was intended from the first; else why does no Nebraska man express astonishment or condemnation? . . .

That Kansas will form a Slave constitution, and, with it, will ask to be admitted into the Union, I take to be an already settled question; and so settled by the very means you so pointedly condemn. By every principle of law, ever held by any court, North or South, every negro taken to Kansas is free; yet in utter disregard of this—in the spirit of violence merely—that beautiful Legislature gravely passes a law to hang men who shall venture to inform a negro of his legal rights. This is the substance, and real object of the law. . . .

In my humble sphere, I shall advocate the restoration of the Missouri Compromise, so long as Kansas remains a territory; and when, by all these foul means, it seeks to come into the Union as a Slave-state, I shall oppose it. I am very loth, in any case, to withhold my assent to the enjoyment of property *acquired*, or *located*, in good faith; but I do not admit that *good faith*, in taking a negro to Kansas, to be held in slavery, is a *possibility* with any man. Any man who has sense enough to be the controller of his own property, has too much sense to misunderstand the outrageous character of this whole Nebraska business. But I digress. In my opposition to the admission of Kansas I shall have some company; but we may be beaten. If we are, I shall not, on that account, attempt to dissolve the Union. On the contrary, if we succeed, there will be enough of us to take care of the Union. I think it probable, however, we shall be beaten. Standing as a unit among yourselves, you can, directly, and indirectly, bribe enough of our men to carry the day—as you could on an open proposition to establish monarchy. Get hold of some man in the North, whose position and ability is such, that he can make the support of your measure—whatever it may be—a *democratic party necessity*, and the thing is done. . . .

You say if Kansas fairly votes herself a free state, as a christian you will rather rejoice at it. All decent slave-holders *talk* that way; and I do not doubt their candor. But they never *vote* that way. Although in a private letter, or conversation, you will express your preference that Kansas shall be free, you would vote for no man for Congress who would say the same thing publicly. No such man could be elected from any district in any slave-state. You think Stringfellow & Co* ought to be hung; and yet, at the next presidential election you will vote for the exact type and representative of Stringfellow. The slave-breeders and slave-traders, are a small, odious and detested class, among you; and yet in politics, they dictate the course of all of you, and are as completely your masters, as you are the masters of your own negroes.

You enquire where I now stand. That is a disputed point. I think I am a whig; but others say there are no whigs, and that I am an abolitionist. When I was at Washington I voted for the Wilmot Proviso as good as forty times, and I never heard of any one attempting to unwhig me for that. I now do no more than oppose the *extension* of slavery.

I am not a Know-Nothing. That is certain. How could I be? How can any one who abhors the oppression of negroes, be in favor of degrading classes of white people? Our progress in degeneracy appears to me to be pretty rapid. As a nation, we began by declaring that *"all men are created equal."* We now practically read it "all men are created equal, *except negroes.*" When the Know-Nothings get control, it will read "all men are created equal, except negroes, *and foreigners, and catholics.*" When it comes to this I should prefer emigrating to some country where they make no pretence of loving liberty—to Russia, for instance, where despotism can be taken pure, and without the base alloy of hypocracy.

. . . My kindest regards to Mrs. Speed. On the leading subject of this letter, I have more of her sympathy than I have of yours.

And yet let [me] say I am   Your friend forever

"Can we not come together, for the future"

Speech at a Republican banquet, December 10, 1856

In 1856 Lincoln campaigned strenuously for the Republican ticket in Illinois. The party did remarkably well in the state in its first campaign, electing its gubernatorial candidate and only narrowly losing in the

*Benjamin F. Stringfellow was a proslavery leader in Kansas.

presidential contest. With the opposition divided between the Republicans and the Americans (Know Nothings), however, the Democrats prevailed nationally and elected James Buchanan president. At a banquet in Chicago a month after the election, Lincoln encouraged party members to continue the battle and emphasized the necessity of union among anti-Democratic forces.

Our government rests in public opinion. Whoever can change public opinion, can change the government, practically just so much. Public opinion, or [on?] any subject, always has a *"central idea,"* from which all its minor thoughts radiate. That "central idea" in our political public opinion, at the beginning was, and until recently has continued to be, "the equality of men." And although it was always submitted patiently to whatever of inequality there seemed to be as matter of actual necessity, its constant working has been a steady progress towards the practical equality of all men. The late Presidential election was a struggle, by one party, to discard that central idea, and to substitute for it the opposite idea that slavery is right, in the abstract, the workings of which, as a central idea, may be the perpetuity of human slavery, and its extension to all countries and colors. Less than a year ago, the Richmond *Enquirer*, an avowed advocate of slavery, regardless of color, in order to favor his views, invented the phrase, "State equality," and now the President, in his Message, adopts the *Enquirer's* catch-phrase, telling us the people "have asserted the constitutional equality of each and all of the States of the Union as States." The President flatters himself that the new central idea is completely inaugurated; and so, indeed, it is, so far as the mere fact of a Presidential election can inaugurate it. To us it is left to know that the majority of the people have not yet declared for it, and to hope that they never will.

All of us who did not vote for Mr. Buchanan, taken together, are a majority of four hundred thousand. But, in the late contest we were divided between Fremont and Fillmore. Can we not come together, for the future. Let every one who really believes, and is resolved, that free society is not, *and shall not be,* a failure, and who can conscientiously declare that in the past contest he has done only what he thought best— let every such one have charity to believe that every other one can say as much. Thus let bygones be bygones. Let past differences, as nothing be;

and with steady eye on the real issue, let us reinaugurate the good old "central ideas" of the Republic. We *can* do it. The human heart *is* with us—God is with us. We shall again be able not to declare, that "all States as States, are equal," nor yet that "all citizens as citizens are equal," but to renew the broader, better declaration, including both these and much more, that "all *men* are created equal."

"All the powers of earth seem rapidly combining against him"

Speech in Springfield, June 26, 1857

Shortly after Buchanan assumed office in 1857, the Supreme Court issued its decision in the case of a Missouri slave named Dred Scott. The Dred Scott decision was one of the most controversial rulings that the high court has ever issued in its history. The primary opinion, written by Chief Justice Roger Taney, declared that blacks could not be citizens of the United States and decreed that Congress could not prohibit slavery from the territories, thereby negating the most important principle of the Republican party. In response to Douglas, who gave a speech in Springfield defending the decision, Lincoln dissected the court's reasoning and justified Republican opposition to the ruling. In his address, Lincoln devoted more attention to the race question than he had previously.

We believe, as much as Judge Douglas, (perhaps more) in obedience to, and respect for the judicial department of government. We think its decisions on Constitutional questions, when fully settled, should control, not only the particular cases decided, but the general policy of the country, subject to be disturbed only by amendments of the Constitution as provided in that instrument itself. More than this would be revolution. But we think the Dred Scott decision is erroneous. We know the court that made it, has often over-ruled its own decisions, and we shall do what we can to have it to over-rule this. We offer no *resistance* to it.

Judicial decisions are of greater or less authority as precedents, according to circumstances. That this should be so, accords both with common sense, and the customary understanding of the legal profession.

If this important decision had been made by the unanimous concurrence of the judges, and without any apparent partisan bias, and in accordance with legal public expectation, and with the steady practice of the departments throughout our history, and had been in no part, based on assumed historical facts which are not really true; or, if wanting in some of these, it had been before the court more than once, and had there been affirmed and re-affirmed through a course of years, it then might be, perhaps would be, factious, nay, even revolutionary, to not acquiesce in it as a precedent. . . .

. . . The Chief Justice does not directly assert, but plainly assumes, as a fact, that the public estimate of the black man is more favorable *now* than it was in the days of the Revolution. This assumption is a mistake. In some trifling particulars, the condition of that race has been ameliorated; but, as a whole, in this country, the change between then and now is decidedly the other way; and their ultimate destiny has never appeared so hopeless as in the last three or four years. In two of the five States—New Jersey and North Carolina—that then gave the free negro the right of voting, the right has since been taken away; and in a third—New York—it has been greatly abridged; while it has not been extended, so far as I know, to a single additional State, though the number of the States has more than doubled. In those days, as I understand, masters could, at their own pleasure, emancipate their slaves; but since then, such legal restraints have been made upon emancipation, as to amount almost to prohibition. In those days, Legislatures held the unquestioned power to abolish slavery in their respective States; but now it is becoming quite fashionable for State Constitutions to withhold that power from the Legislatures. In those days, by common consent, the spread of the black man's bondage to new countries was prohibited; but now, Congress decides that it *will* not continue the prohibition, and the Supreme Court decides that it *could* not if it would. In those days, our Declaration of Independence was held sacred by all, and thought to include all; but now, to aid in making the bondage of the negro universal and eternal, it is assailed, and sneered at, and construed, and hawked at, and torn, till, if its framers could rise from their graves, they could not at all recognize it. All the powers of earth seem rapidly combining against him. Mammon is after him; ambition follows, and philosophy follows, and the Theology of the day is fast joining the cry. They have him in his prison house; they have searched his person, and left no prying instrument with him. One after another they have closed the heavy iron doors upon him, and now they have him, as it were, bolted in with a lock of a hundred keys, which can never be unlocked without the concurrence of every key; the keys in the hands of a hundred different men, and they scattered to a hundred different and distant places; and they stand musing as to what invention, in all the dominions of mind and matter, can be produced to make the impossibility of his escape more complete than it is. . . .

There is a natural disgust in the minds of nearly all white people, to the idea of an indiscriminate amalgamation of the white and black races; and Judge Douglas evidently is basing his chief hope, upon the chances of being able to appropriate the benefit of this disgust to himself. If he can, by much drumming and repeating, fasten the odium of that idea upon his adversaries, he thinks he can struggle through the storm. . . . He finds the Republicans insisting that the Declaration of Independence includes ALL men, black as well as white; and forthwith he boldly denies that it includes negroes at all, and proceeds to argue gravely that all who contend it does, do so only because they want to vote, and eat, and sleep, and marry with negroes! He will have it that they cannot be consistent else. Now I protest against that counterfeit logic which concludes that, because I do not want a black woman for a *slave* I must necessarily want her for a *wife*. I need not have her for either, I can just leave her alone. In some respects she certainly is not my equal; but in her natural right to eat the bread she earns with her own hands without asking leave of any one else, she is my equal, and the equal of all others.

Chief Justice Taney, in his opinion in the Dred Scott case, admits that the language of the Declaration is broad enough to include the whole human family, but he and Judge Douglas argue that the authors of that instrument did not intend to include negroes, by the fact that they did not at once, actually place them on an equality with the whites. Now this grave argument comes to just nothing at all, by the other fact, that they did not at once, *or ever afterwards*, actually place all white people on an equality with one or another. And this is the staple argument of both the Chief Justice and the Senator, for doing this obvious violence to the plain unmistakable language of the Declaration. I think the authors of that notable instrument intended to include *all* men, but they did not intend to declare all men equal *in all respects*. They did not mean to say all were equal in color, size, intellect, moral developments, or social capacity. They defined with tolerable distinctness, in what respects they did consider all men created equal—equal in "certain inalienable rights, among which are life, liberty, and the pursuit of happiness." This they said, and this [they] meant. They did not mean to assert the obvious untruth, that all were then actually enjoying that equality, nor yet, that they were about to confer it immediately upon them. In fact they had no power to confer such a boon. They meant simply to declare the *right*, so that the *enforcement* of it might follow as fast as circumstances should permit. They meant to set up a standard maxim for free society, which should be familiar to all, and revered by all; constantly looked to, constantly labored for, and even though never perfectly attained, constantly approximated, and thereby constantly spreading and deepening its influence, and augmenting the happiness and value of life to all people of all colors everywhere. . . .

"A question of *interest*"

Fragment on slavery, 1857–1858?

The date of this fragment is unknown. While his secretaries speculated Lincoln wrote this in 1854, it seems much more likely to come from later in the decade.

If A. can prove, however conclusively, that he may, of right, enslave B.— why may not B. snatch the same argument, and prove equally, that he may enslave A?—

You say A. is white, and B. is black. It is *color*, then; the lighter, having the right to enslave the darker? Take care. By this rule, you are to be slave to the first man you meet, with a fairer skin than your own.

You do not mean *color* exactly?—You mean the whites are *intellectually* the superiors of the blacks, and, therefore have the right to enslave them? Take care again. By this rule, you are to be slave to the first man you meet, with an intellect superior to your own.

But, say you, it is a question of *interest*; and, if you can make it your *interest*, you have the right to enslave another. Very well. And if he can make it his interest, he has the right to enslave you.

"A house divided"

Speech to the Republican state convention, June 16, 1858

In 1858 the Republican state convention took the unusual step of designating Lincoln as the party's candidate to oppose Stephen A. Douglas, who was running for reelection to the Senate. That evening Lincoln delivered what was essentially an acceptance speech outlining the issues of his forthcoming campaign. Douglas's recent political course put Lincoln in a difficult position. When the Buchanan administration endorsed Kansas's admission under the proslavery Lecompton Constitution, Douglas broke with the Democratic leadership and helped defeat the bill. Douglas's action ruptured the Democratic party, but it also weakened Lincoln's earlier charge that he was a proponent of slavery's expansion. In order to destroy Douglas's antislavery credentials, Lincoln gave renewed emphasis to the moral issue of slavery and called for the eventual end of slavery in the Republic. But the main thrust of his speech was the claim that Douglas and other Democratic leaders were part of a conspiracy to make slavery a national institution. A number of advisers worried about the radical tenor of Lincoln's language, and while his speech generated immense enthusiasm among the Republican delegates, he was on the defensive for the remainder of the campaign. Nevertheless, the House Divided speech marked the beginning of Lincoln's emergence as a national political figure.

Mr. President and Gentlemen of the Convention.

If we could first know *where* we are, and *whither* we are tending, we could then better judge *what* to do, and *how* to do it.

We are now far into the *fifth* year, since a policy was initiated, with the *avowed* object, and *confident* promise, of putting an end to slavery agitation.

Under the operation of that policy, that agitation has not only, *not ceased*, but has *constantly augmented*.

In *my* opinion, it *will* not cease, until a *crisis* shall have been reached, and passed.

"A house divided against itself cannot stand."

I believe this government cannot endure, permanently half *slave* and half *free*.

I do not expect the Union to be *dissolved*—I do not expect the house to *fall*—but I *do* expect it will cease to be divided.

It will become *all* one thing, or *all* the other.

Either the *opponents* of slavery, will arrest the further spread of it, and place it where the public mind shall rest in the belief that it is in course of ultimate extinction; or its *advocates* will push it forward, till it shall become alike lawful in *all* the States, *old* as well as *new*—*North* as well as *South*.

Have we no *tendency* to the latter condition?

Let any one who doubts, carefully contemplate that now almost complete legal combination—piece of *machinery* so to speak—compounded of the Nebraska doctrine, and the Dred Scott decision. Let him consider not only *what work* the machinery is adapted to do, and *how well* adapted; but also, let him study the *history* of its construction, and trace, if he can, or rather *fail*, if he can, to trace the evidences of design, and concert of action, among its chief bosses, from the beginning.

The new year of 1854 found slavery excluded from more than half the States by State Constitutions, and from most of the national territory by Congressional prohibition.

Four days later, commenced the struggle, which ended in repealing that Congressional prohibition.

This opened all the national territory to slavery; and was the first point gained.

But, so far, *Congress* only, had acted; and an *indorsement* by the people, *real* or apparent, was indispensable, to *save* the point already gained, and give chance for more.

This necessity had not been overlooked; but had been provided for, as well as might be, in the notable argument of *"squatter sovereignty,"* otherwise called *"sacred right of self government,"* which latter phrase, though expressive of the only rightful basis of any government, was so perverted in this attempted use of it as to amount to just this: That if any *one* man, choose to enslave *another*, no *third* man shall be allowed to object.

That argument was incorporated into the Nebraska bill itself, in the language which follows: *"It being the true intent and meaning of this act not to legislate slavery into any Territory or state, not exclude it therefrom; but to leave the people thereof perfectly free to form and regulate their domestic institutions in their own way, subject only to the Constitution of the United States."*

Then opened the roar of loose declamation in favor of "Squatter Sovereignty," and "Sacred right of self government."

"But," said opposition members, "let us be more *specific*—let us *amend* the bill so as to expressly declare that the people of the territory *may* exclude slavery." "Not we," said the friends of the measure; and down they voted the amendment.

While the Nebraska bill was passing through congress, a *law case*, involving the question of a negroe's freedom, by reason of his owner having voluntarily taken him first into a free state and then a territory covered by the congressional prohibition, and held him as a slave, for a long time in each, was passing through the U.S. Circuit Court for the District of Missouri; and both Nebraska bill and law suit were brought to a decision in the same month of May, 1854. The negroe's name was "Dred Scott," which name now designates the decision finally made in the case.

Before the *then* next Presidential election, the law case came to, and was argued *in* the Supreme Court of the United States; but the *decision* of it was deferred until *after* the election. Still, *before* the election, Senator Trumbull, on the floor of the Senate, requests the leading advocate of the Nebraska bill to state *his opinion* whether the people of a territory can constitutionally exclude slavery from their limits; and the latter answers, "That is a question for the Supreme Court."

The election came. Mr. Buchanan was elected, and the *indorsement*, such as it was, secured. That was the *second* point gained. The indorsement, however, fell short of a clear popular majority by nearly four hundred thousand votes, and so, perhaps, was not overwhelmingly reliable and satisfactory.

The *outgoing* President, in his last annual message, as impressively as possible *echoed back* upon the people the *weight* and *authority* of the indorsement.

The Supreme Court met again; *did not* announce their decision, but ordered a re-argument.

The Presidential inauguration came, and still no decision of the court; but the *incoming* President, in his inaugural address, fervently exhorted the people to abide by the forthcoming decision, *whatever it might be.*

Then, in a few days, came the decision.

The reputed author of the Nebraska bill finds an early occasion to make a speech at this capitol indorsing the Dred Scott Decision, and vehemently denouncing all opposition to it.

The new President, too, seizes the early occasion of the Silliman letter to *indorse* and strongly *construe* that decision, and to express his *astonishment* that any different view had ever been entertained.

At length a squabble springs up between the President and the author of the Nebraska bill, on the *mere* question of *fact*, whether the Lecompton constitution was or was not, in any just sense, made by the people of Kansas; and in that squabble the latter declares that all he wants is a fair vote for the people, and that he *cares* not whether slavery be voted *down* or voted *up*. I do not understand his declaration that he cares not whether slavery be voted down or voted up, to be intended by him other than as an *apt definition* of the *policy* he would impress upon the public mind—the *principle* for which he declares he has suffered much, and is ready to suffer to the end.

And well may he cling to that principle. If he has any parental feeling, well may he cling to it. That principle, is the only *shred* left of his original Nebraska doctrine. Under the Dred Scott decision, "squatter sovereignty" squatted out of existence, tumbled down like temporary scaffolding—like the mould at the foundry served through one blast and fell back into loose sand—helped to carry an election, and then was kicked to the winds. His late *joint* struggle with the Republicans, against the Lecompton Constitution, involves nothing of the original Nebraska doctrine. That struggle was made on a point, the right of a people to make their own constitution, upon which he and the Republicans have never differed.

The several points of the Dred Scott decision, in connection with Senator Douglas' "care not" policy, constitute the piece of machinery, in its *present* state of advancement. This was the third point gained.

The *working* points of that machinery are:

First, that no negro slave, imported as such from Africa, and no descendant of such slave can ever be a *citizen* of any State, in the sense of that term as used in the Constitution of the United States.

This point is made in order to deprive the negro, in every possible event, of the benefit of this provision of the United States Constitution, which declares that—

"The citizens of each State shall be entitled to all privileges and immunities of citizens in the several States."

Secondly, that "subject to the Constitution of the United States," neither *Congress* nor a *Territorial Legislature* can exclude slavery from any United States territory.

This point is made in order that individual men may *fill up* the territories with slaves, without danger of losing them as property, and thus to enhance the chances of *permanency* to the institution through all the future.

Thirdly, that whether the holding a negro in actual slavery in a free State, makes him free, as against the holder, the United States courts will not decide, but will leave to be decided by the courts of any slave State the negro may be forced into by the master.

This point is made, not to be pressed *immediately;* but, if acquiesced in for a while, and apparently *indorsed* by the people at an election, *then* to sustain the logical conclusion that what Dred Scott's master might lawfully do with Dred Scott, in the free State of Illinois, every other master may lawfully do with any other *one*, or one *thousand* slaves, in Illinois, or in any other free State.

Auxiliary to all this, and working hand in hand with it, the Nebraska doctrine, or what is left of it, is to *educate* and *mould* public opinion, at least *Northern* public opinion, to not *care* whether slavery is voted *down* or voted *up*.

This shows exactly where we now *are;* and *partially* also, whither we are tending.

It will throw additional light on the latter, to go back, and run the mind over the string of historical facts already stated. Several things will *now* appear less *dark* and *mysterious* than they did *when* they were transpiring. The people were to be left "perfectly free" "subject only to the Constitution." What the *Constitution* had to do with it, outsiders could not *then* see. Plainly enough *now*, it was an exactly fitted *niche*, for the Dred Scott decision to afterwards come in, and declare the *perfect freedom* of the people, to be just no freedom at all.

Why was the amendment, expressly declaring the right of the people to exclude slavery, voted down? Plainly enough *now*, the adoption of it, would have spoiled the niche for the Dred Scott decision.

Why was the court decision held up? Why, even a Senator's individual opinion withheld, till *after* the Presidential election? Plainly enough *now*, the speaking out *then* would have damaged the *"perfectly free"* argument upon which the election was to be carried.

Why the *outgoing* President's felicitation on the indorsement? Why the delay of a reargument? Why the incoming President's *advance* exhortation in favor of the decision?

These things *look* like the cautious *patting* and *petting* a spirited horse, preparatory to mounting him, when it is dreaded that he may give the rider a fall.

And why the hasty after indorsements of the decision by the President and others?

We can not absolutely *know* that all these exact adaptations are the result of preconcert. But when we see a lot of framed timbers, different portions of which we know have been gotten out at different times and places and by different workmen—Stephen, Franklin, Roger and James,* for instance—and when we see these timbers joined together, and see they exactly make the frame of a house or a mill, all the tenons and mortices exactly fitting, and all the lengths and proportions of the different pieces exactly adapted to their respective places, and not a piece too many or too few—not omitting even scaffolding—or, if a single piece be lacking, we can see the place in the frame exactly fitted and prepared to yet bring such piece in—in *such* a case, we find it impossible to not *believe* that Stephen and Franklin and Roger and James all understood one another from the beginning, and all worked upon a common *plan* or *draft* drawn up before the first lick was struck.

It should not be overlooked that, by the Nebraska bill, the people of a *State* as well as *Territory*, were to be left *"perfectly free"* *"subject only to the Constitution."*

Why mention a *State*? They were legislating for *territories*, and not *for* or *about* States. Certainly the people of a States *are* and *ought to be* subject to the Constitution of the United States; but why is mention of this *lugged* into this merely *territorial* law? Why are the people of a *territory* and the people of a *state* therein *lumped* together, and their relation to the Constitution therein treated as being *precisely* the same?

While the opinion of *the Court*, by Chief Justice Taney, in the Dred

---

*Stephen A. Douglas, Franklin Pierce, Roger Taney, and James Buchanan.

Scott case, and the separate opinions of all the concurring Judges, expressly declare that the Constitution of the United States neither permits Congress nor a Territorial legislature to exclude slavery from any United States territory, they all *omit* to declare whether or not the same Constitution permits a *state*, or the people of a State, to exclude it.

Possibly, this was a mere *omission*; but who can be *quite* sure, if McLean or Curtis* had sought to get into the opinion a declaration of unlimited power in the people of a *state* to exclude slavery from their limits, just as Chase and Macy sought to get such declaration, in behalf of the people of a territory, into the Nebraska bill—I ask, who can be quite *sure* that it would not have been voted down, in the one case, as it had been in the other.

The nearest approach to the point of declaring the power of a State over slavery, is made by Judge Nelson. He approaches it more than once, using the precise idea, and *almost* the language too, of the Nebraska act. On one occasion his exact language is, "except in cases where the power is restrained by the Constitution of the United States, the law of the State is supreme over the subject of slavery within its jurisdiction."

In what *cases* the power of the *states is* so restrained by the U.S. Constitution, is left an *open* question, precisely as the same question, as to the restraint on the power of the *territories* was left open in the Nebraska act. Put *that* and *that* together, and we have another nice little niche, which we may, ere long, see filled with another Supreme Court decision, declaring that the Constitution of the United States does not permit a *state* to exclude slavery from its limits.

And this may especially be expected if the doctrine of "care not whether slavery be voted *down* or voted *up*," shall gain upon the public mind sufficiently to give promise that such a decision can be maintained when made.

Such a decision is all that slavery now lacks of being alike lawful in all the States.

Welcome or unwelcome, such decision is probably coming, and will soon be upon us, unless the power of the present political dynasty shall be met and overthrown.

---

*Associate Justices John McLean and Benjamin R. Curtis dissented from the Court's decision.

We shall *lie down* pleasantly dreaming that the people of *Missouri* are on the verge of making their State *free*; and we shall *awake* to the *reality*, instead, that the *Supreme* Court has made *Illinois* a *slave* State.

To meet and overthrow the power of that dynasty, is the work now before all those who would prevent that consummation.

That is *what* we have to do.

But *how* can we best do it?

There are those who denounce us *openly* to their *own* friends, and yet whisper *us softly*, that *Senator Douglas* is the *aptest* instrument there is, with which to effect that object. *They* do *not* tell us, nor has *he* told us, that he *wishes* any such object to be effected. They wish us to *infer* all, from the facts, that he now has a little quarrel with the present head of the dynasty; and that he has regularly voted with us, on a single point, upon which, he and we, have never differed.

They remind us that *he* is a very *great man*, and that the largest of *us* are very small ones. Let this be granted. But *"a living dog* is better than a *dead lion."* Judge Douglas, if not a *dead* lion *for this work*, is at least a *caged* and *toothless* one. How can he oppose the advances of slavery? He don't *care* anything about it. His avowed *mission is impressing* the "public heart" to *care* nothing about it.

A leading Douglas Democratic newspaper thinks Douglas' superior talent will be needed to resist the revival of the African slave trade.

Does Douglas believe an effort to revive that trade is approaching? He has not said so. Does he *really* think so? But if it is, how can he resist it? For years he has labored to prove it a *sacred right* of white men to take negro slaves into the new territories. Can he possibly show that it is *less* a sacred right to *buy* them where they can be bought cheapest? And, unquestionably they can be bought *cheaper in Africa* than in *Virginia*.

He has done all in his power to reduce the whole question of slavery to one of a mere *right of property*; and as such, how can *he* oppose the foreign slave trade—how can he refuse that trade in that "property" shall be "perfectly free"—unless he does it as a *protection* to the home production? And as the home *producers* will probably not *ask* the protection, he will be wholly without a ground of opposition.

Senator Douglas holds, we know, that a man may rightfully be *wiser to-day* than he was *yesterday*—that he may rightfully *change* when he finds himself wrong.

But, can we for that reason, run ahead, and *infer* that he *will* make any particular change, of which he, himself, has given no intimation? Can we *safely* base *our* action upon any such *vague* inference?

Now, as ever, I wish to not *misrepresent* Judge Douglas' *position,* question his *motives,* or do ought that can be personally offensive to him.

Whenever, *if ever,* he and we can come together on *principle* so that *our great cause* may have assistance from *his great ability,* I hope to have interposed no adventitious obstacle.

But clearly, he is not *now* with us—he does not *pretend* to be—he does not *promise* to *ever* be.

Our cause, then, must be intrusted to, and conducted by its own undoubted friends—those whose hands are free, whose hearts are in the work—who *do care* for the result.

Two years ago the Republicans of the nation mustered over thirteen hundred thousand strong.

We did this under the single impulse of resistance to a common danger, with every external circumstance against us.

Of *strange, discordant,* and even, *hostile* elements, we gathered from the four winds, and *formed* and fought the battle through, under the constant hot fire of a disciplined, proud, and pampered enemy.

Did we brave all *then,* to *falter* now?—*now*—when that same enemy is *wavering,* dissevered and belligerent?

The result is not doubtful. We shall not fail—if we stand firm, we shall not fail.

Wise councils may *accelerate* or *mistakes delay* it, but, sooner or later the victory is *sure* to come.

"Construed so differently from any thing intended by me"

Letter to John L. Scripps, June 23, 1858

In this letter to John L. Scripps, who was the editor of a Republican newspaper in Chicago, Lincoln responded to the Democratic accusation that his call for the ultimate end of slavery implied any power to interfere with the institution in the southern states. On the defensive because of the House Divided speech, Lincoln throughout the campaign tried to give a conservative meaning to the phrase "ultimate extinction." It was precisely because of such lofty language that Republican leaders had questioned the wisdom of the speech.

Jno. L. Scripps, Esq   Springfield

My dear Sir

Your kind note of yesterday is duly received. I am much flattered by the estimate you place on my late speech; and yet I am much mortified that any part of it should be construed so differently from any thing intended by me. The language, "place it where the public mind shall rest in the belief that it is in course of ultimate extinction," I used deliberately, not dreaming then, nor believing now, that it asserts, or intimates, any power or purpose, to interfere with slavery in the States where it exists. But, to not cavil about language, I declare that whether the clause used by me, will bear such construction or not, I never so intended it. I have declared a thousand times, and now repeat that, in my opinion, neither the General Government, nor any other power outside of the slave states, can constitutionally or rightfully interfere with slaves or slavery where it already exists. I believe that whenever the effort to spread slavery into the new teritories, by whatever means, and into the free states themselves, by Supreme court decisions, shall be fairly headed off, the institution will then be in course of ultimate extinction; and by the language used I meant only this.

I do not intend this for publication; but still you may show it to any one you think fit. I think I shall, as you suggest, take some early occasion to publicly repeat the declaration I have already so often made as before stated. Yours very truly

"Public sentiment is every thing"

Notes for speeches, August 1858

When Lincoln challenged Douglas to debate him in the 1858 campaign, Douglas finally agreed to seven debates in various congressional districts throughout the state (the two had already spoken together in Springfield and Chicago). Lincoln wrote out some notes in preparation for his first debate with Douglas at Ottawa on August 21, and he used some of this

material in several subsequent campaign speeches. Lincoln laid particu-
lar stress on the importance of the battle being waged between Douglas
and himself to shape public sentiment.

Allow me now, in my own way, to state with what aims and objects I did enter upon this campaign. I claim no extraordinary exemption from personal ambition. That I like preferment as well as the average of men may be admitted. But I protest I have not entered upon this hard contest solely, or even chiefly, for a mere personal object. I clearly see, as I think, a powerful plot to make slavery universal and perpetual in this nation. The effort to carry that plot through will be persistent and long contin- ued, extending far beyond the senatorial term for which Judge Douglas and I are just now struggling. I enter upon the contest to contribute my humble and temporary mite in opposition to that effort.

At the Republican State convention at Springfield I made a speech. That speech has been considered the opening of the canvass on my part. In it I arrange a string of incontestable facts which, I think, prove the existence of a conspiracy to nationalize slavery. The evidence was circumstantial only; but nevertheless it seemed inconsistent with every hypothesis, save that of the existence of such conspiracy. I believe the facts can be explained to-day on no other hypothesis. Judge Douglas can so explain them if any one can. From warp to woof his handiwork is everywhere woven in. . . .

Judge Douglas's present course by no means lessens my belief in the existence of a purpose to make slavery alike lawful in all the States. This can be done by a Supreme Court decision holding that the United States Constitution forbids a State to exclude slavery; and probably it can be done in no other way. The idea of forcing slavery into a free State, or out of a slave State, at the point of the bayonet, is alike nonsensical. Slavery can only become extinct by being restricted to its present limits, and dwindling out. It can only become national by a Supreme Court decision. To such a decision, when it comes, Judge Douglas is fully com- mitted. Such a decision acquiesced in by the people effects the whole object. . . .

. . . In this age, and this country, public sentiment is every thing. *With* it, nothing can fail; *against* it, nothing can succeed. Whoever moulds public sentiment, goes deeper than he who enacts statutes, or pronounces judicial decisions. He makes possible the inforcement of these, else impossible.

Judge Douglas is a man of large influence. His bare opinion goes far to fix the opinion of others. Besides this, thousands hang their hopes upon forcing their opinions to agree with his. It is a party necessity with them to *say* they agree with him; and there is danger they will repeat the saying till they really come to believe it. Others dread, and shrink from his denunciations, his sarcasms, and his ingenious misrepresentations. The susceptible young hear lessons from him, such as their fathers never heared when they were young.

If, by all these means, he shall succeed in moulding public sentiment to a perfect accordance with his own—in bringing all men to indorse all court decisions, without caring to know whether they are right or wrong—in bringing all tongues to as perfect a silence as his own, as to there being any wrong in slavery—in bringing all to declare, with him, that they care not whether slavery be voted down or voted up—that if any people want slaves they have a right to have them—that negroes are not men—have no part in the declaration of Independence—that there is no moral question about slavery—that liberty and slavery are perfectly consistent—indeed, necessary accompaniaments—that for a strong man to declare himself the *superior* of a weak one, and thereupon enslave the weak one, is the very *essence* of liberty—the most sacred right of self-government—when, I say, public sentiment shall be brought to all this, in the name of heaven, what barrier will be left against slavery being made lawful every where? Can you find *one* word of his, opposed to it? Can you *not* find many strongly favoring it? If for his life—for his eternal salvation—he was solely striving for that end, could he find any means so well adapted to reach the end?

If our Presidential election, by a mere plurality, and of doubtful significance, brought one Supreme Court decision, that no power can exclude slavery from a Teritory; how much more shall a public sentiment, in exact accordance with the sentiments of Judge Douglas bring another that no power can exclude it from a State?

And then, the negro being doomed, and damned, and forgotten, to everlasting bondage, is the white man quite certain that the tyrant demon will not turn upon him too?

"Blowing out the moral lights around us"

First debate, at Ottawa, August 21, 1858

The first debate between Lincoln and Douglas was held in late August in Ottawa, Illinois, in the northern part of the state where antislavery sentiment was strongest. The crowd substantially exceeded the population of the town, evidence of the great popular interest in the contest and in the confrontation between these two party leaders. When the debate began, Douglas immediately went on the attack and portrayed Lincoln as an abolitionist, a proponent of sectional warfare, and an advocate of racial equality. Lincoln was rather defensive in his reply, yet he struck a new tone at the end of his speech when he invoked the Declaration of Independence and discussed the moral issue of slavery. In these and subsequent excerpts from the debates, the interjections of the audience have been omitted.

What is Popular Sovereignty? Is it the right of the people to have Slavery or not have it, as they see fit, in the territories? I will state—and I have an able man to watch me—my understanding is that Popular Sovereignty, as now applied to the question of Slavery, does allow the people of a Territory to have Slavery if they want to, but does not allow them *not* to have it if they *do not* want it. I do not mean that if this vast concourse of people were in a Territory of the United States, any one of them would be obliged to have a slave if he did not want one; but I do say that, as I understand the Dred Scott decision, if any one man wants slaves, all the rest have no way of keeping that one man from holding them.

When I made my speech at Springfield,* of which the Judge complains, and from which he quotes, I really was not thinking of the things which he ascribes to me at all. I had no thought in the world that I was doing anything to bring about a war between the free and slave States. I had no thought in the world that I was doing anything to bring about a political and social equality of the black and white races. It never occurred to me that I was doing anything or favoring anything to reduce to a dead uniformity all the local institutions of the various States. But I must say, in all fairness to him, if he thinks I am doing

---

*The House Divided speech.

something which leads to these bad results, it is none the better that I did not mean it. It is just as fatal to the country, if I have any influence in producing it, whether I intend it or not. But can it be true, that placing this institution upon the original basis—the basis upon which our fathers placed it—can have any tendency to set the Northern and the Southern States at war with one another? . . .

. . . Henry Clay, my beau ideal of a statesman, the man for whom I fought all my humble life—Henry Clay once said of a class of men who would repress all tendencies to liberty and ultimate emancipation, that they must, if they would do this, go back to the era of our Independence, and muzzle the cannon which thunders its annual joyous return; they must blow out the moral lights around us; they must penetrate the human soul, and eradicate there the love of liberty; and then and not till then, could they perpetuate slavery in this country! To my thinking, Judge Douglas is, by his example and vast influence, doing that very thing in this community, when he says that the negro has nothing in the Declaration of Independence. Henry Clay plainly understood the contrary. Judge Douglas is going back to the era of our Revolution, and to the extent of his ability, muzzling the cannon which thunders its annual joyous return. When he invites any people willing to have slavery, to establish it, he is blowing out the moral lights around us. When he says he "cares not whether slavery is voted down or voted up,"—that it is a sacred right of self government—he is in my judgment penetrating the human soul and eradicating the light of reason and the love of liberty in this American people. And now I will only say that when, by all these means and appliances, Judge Douglas shall succeed in bringing public sentiment to an exact accordance with his own views—when these vast assemblages shall echo back all these sentiments—when they shall come to repeat his views and to avow his principles, and to say all that he says on these mighty questions—then it needs only the formality of the second Dred Scott decision, which he endorses in advance, to make Slavery alike lawful in all the States—old as well as new, North as well as South.

"The social and political equality
of the . . . races"

Fourth debate, at Charleston, September 18, 1858

In their fourth debate, Lincoln and Douglas met in Charleston, in south-
ern Illinois. Lincoln chose this occasion to respond to Douglas's persist-
ent charge that he favored social and political equality for black people.
Lincoln's remarks at Charleston were the most explicit and extensive
comment he made during the campaign on the issue of race. Such views
were popular in Democratic southern Illinois but, contrary to Douglas's
charges, Lincoln said much the same thing in the northern part of the
state, where antislavery sentiment was much stronger. Lincoln's views
on race and black rights, while disappointing to the modern reader, were
in advance of popular sentiment in much of Illinois at the time.

While I was at the hotel to-day an elderly gentleman called upon me to
know whether I was really in favor of producing a perfect equality
between the negroes and white people. While I had not proposed to
myself on this occasion to say much on that subject, yet as the question
was asked me I thought I would occupy perhaps five minutes in saying
something in regard to it. I will say then that I am not, nor ever have
been in favor of bringing about in any way the social and political
equality of the white and black races,—that I am not nor ever have been
in favor of making voters or jurors of negroes, nor of qualifying them
to hold office, nor to intermarry with white people; and I will say in
addition to this that there is a physical difference between the white and
black races which I believe will for ever forbid the two races living
together on terms of social and political equality. And inasmuch as they
cannot so live, while they do remain together there must be the position
of superior and inferior, and I as much as any other man am in favor of
having the superior position assigned to the white race. I say upon this
occasion I do not perceive that because the white man is to have the
superior position the negro should be denied everything. I do not
understand that because I do not want a negro woman for a slave I must
necessarily want her for a wife. My understanding is that I can just let
her alone. . . .

"A moral, a social and a political wrong"

Sixth debate, at Quincy, October 13, 1858

By the time the candidates met in the sixth debate, at Quincy, on October 13, Lincoln had honed his arguments to a keen edge. Focusing on what he called "the real difference" between Douglas and himself, he hammered away at the idea that slavery was a moral evil and accused Douglas of being indifferent to the moral issue of slavery and of seeking to make it a permanent institution. Yet his words were always intended to portray himself as a moderate.

We have in this nation this element of domestic slavery. It is a matter of absolute certainty that it is a disturbing element. It is the opinion of all the great men who have expressed an opinion upon it, that it is a dangerous element. We keep up a controversy in regard to it. That controversy necessarily springs from difference of opinion, and if we can learn exactly—can reduce to the lowest elements—what that difference of opinion is, we perhaps shall be better prepared for discussing the different systems of policy that we would propose in regard to that disturbing element. I suggest that the difference of opinion, reduced to its lowest terms, is no other than the difference between the men who think slavery a wrong and those who do not think it wrong. The Republican party think it wrong—we think it is a moral, a social and a political wrong. We think it is a wrong not confining itself merely to the persons or the States where it exists, but that it is a wrong in its tendency, to say the least, that extends itself to the existence of the whole nation. Because we think it wrong, we propose a course of policy that shall deal with it as a wrong. We deal with it as with any other wrong, in so far as we can prevent its growing any larger, and so deal with it that in the run of time there may be some promise of an end to it. We have a due regard to the actual presence of it amongst us and the difficulties of getting rid of it in any satisfactory way, and all the constitutional obligations thrown about it. I suppose that in reference both to its actual existence in the nation, and to our constitutional obligations, we have no right at all to disturb it in the States where it exists, and we profess that we have no more inclination to disturb it than we have the right to do it. We go further than that; we don't propose to disturb it where, in one instance, we think the Constitution would permit us. We think the Constitution would permit us to disturb it in the District of Columbia. Still we do not propose to do that, unless it should be in terms which I don't suppose the nation is very likely soon to agree to—the terms of making the emancipation gradual and compensating the unwilling owners. Where we suppose we have the constitutional right, we restrain ourselves in reference to the actual existence of the institution and the difficulties thrown about it. We also oppose it as an evil so far as it seeks to spread itself. We insist on the policy that shall restrict it to its present limits. We don't suppose that in doing this we violate anything due to the actual presence of the institution, or anything due to the constitutional guarantees thrown around it.

We oppose the Dred Scott decision in a certain way, upon which I ought perhaps to address you a few words. We do not propose that when Dred Scott has been decided to be a slave by the court, we, as a mob, will decide him to be free. We do not propose that, when any other one, or one thousand, shall be decided by that court to be slaves, we will in any violent way disturb the rights of property thus settled; but we nevertheless do oppose that decision as a political rule which shall be binding on the voter, to vote for nobody who thinks it wrong, which shall be binding on the members of Congress or the President to favor no measure that does not actually concur with the principles of that decision. We do not propose to be bound by it as a political rule in that way, because we think it lays the foundation not merely of enlarging and spreading out what we consider an evil, but it lays the foundation for spreading that evil into the States themselves. We propose so resisting it as to have it reversed if we can, and a new judicial rule established upon this subject. . . .

I wish to return Judge Douglas my profound thanks for his public annunciation here to-day, to be put on record, that his system of policy in regard to the institution of slavery *contemplates that it shall last forever*. We are getting a little nearer the true issue of this controversy, and I am profoundly grateful for this one sentence. Judge Douglas asks you "why cannot the institution of slavery, or rather, why cannot the nation, part slave and part free, continue as our fathers made it *forever?*" In the first place, I insist that our fathers *did not* make this nation half slave and half free, or part slave and part free. I insist that they found the institution of slavery existing here. They did not make it so, but they left it so because they knew of no way to get rid of it at that time. When Judge Douglas undertakes to say that as a matter of choice the fathers of the government made this nation part slave and part free, *he assumes what is historically a falsehood*. More than that; when the fathers of the government cut off the source of slavery by the abolition of the slave trade, and adopted a system of restricting it from the new Territories where it had not existed, I maintain that they placed it where they understood, and all sensible men understood, it was in the course of ultimate extinction, and when Judge Douglas asks me why it cannot continue as our fathers made it, I ask him why he and his friends could not let it remain as our fathers made it? . . .

"The eternal struggle between . . . right and wrong"

Seventh debate, at Alton, October 15, 1858

The last debate was held at Alton three weeks before the election. By now, the two candidates had made all of their points in the previous debates, and the crowd was smaller than at their earlier encounters. In the passages below, Lincoln discussed the policies of the founding generation toward slavery and again took up the issue of the right and wrong of slavery, which had become the keynote of his campaign.

At Galesburg the other day, I said in answer to Judge Douglas, that three years ago there never had been a man, so far as I knew or believed, in the whole world, who had said that the Declaration of Independence did not include negroes in the term "all men." I re-assert it to-day. I assert that Judge Douglas and all his friends may search the whole records of the country, and it will be a matter of great astonishment to me if they shall be able to find that one human being three years ago had ever uttered the astounding sentiment that the term "all men" in the Declaration did not include the negro. Do not let me be misunderstood. I know that more than three years ago there were men who, finding this assertion constantly in the way of their schemes to bring about the ascendancy and perpetuation of slavery, *denied the truth of it*. . . . But I say, with a perfect knowledge of all this hawking at the Declaration without directly attacking it, that three years ago there never had lived a man who had ventured to assail it in the sneaking way of pretending to believe it and then asserting it did not include the negro. . . .

And when this new principle—this new proposition that no human being ever thought of three years ago,—is brought forward, *I combat it* as having an evil tendency, if not an evil design; I combat it as having a tendency to dehumanize the negro—to take away from him the right of ever striving to be a man. I combat it as being one of the thousand things constantly done in these days to prepare the public mind to make property, and nothing but property of the *negro in all the States of this Union.* . . .

There was a collateral object in the introduction of that Nebraska policy which was to clothe the people of the Territories with a superior degree of self-government, beyond what they had ever had before. The first object and the main one of conferring upon the people a higher degree of "self government," is a question of fact to be determined by you in answer to a single question. Have you ever heard or known of a people any where on earth who had as little to do, as, in the first instance of its use, the people of Kansas had with this same right of "self-government"? In its main policy, and in its collateral object, *it has been nothing but a living, creeping lie from the time of its introduction, till to-day.*

I have intimated that I thought the agitation would not cease until a crisis should have been reached and passed. I have stated in what way I thought it would be reached and passed. I have said that it might go one way or the other. We might, by arresting the further spread of it and placing it where the fathers originally placed it, put it where the public mind should rest in the belief that it was in the course of ultimate extinction. Thus the agitation may cease. It may be pushed forward until it shall become alike lawful in all the States, old as well as new, North as well as South. I have said, and I repeat, my wish is that the further spread of it may be arrested, and that it may be placed where the public mind shall rest in the belief that it is in the course of ultimate extinction. I have expressed that as my wish. I entertain the opinion upon evidence sufficient to my mind, that the fathers of this Government placed that institution where the public mind *did* rest in the belief that it was in the course of ultimate extinction. Let me ask why they made provision that the source of slavery—the African slave trade—should be cut off at the end of twenty years? Why did they make provision that in all the new territory we owned at that time slavery should be forever inhibited? Why stop its spread in one direction and cut off its source in another, if they did not look to its being placed in the course of ultimate extinction?

Again; the institution of slavery is only mentioned in the Constitution of the United States two or three times, and in neither of these cases does the word "slavery" or "negro race" occur; but covert language is used each time, and for a purpose full of significance. What is the language in regard to the prohibition of the African slave trade? It runs in about this way: "The migration or importation of such persons as any of the States now existing shall think proper to admit, shall not be prohibited by the Congress prior to the year one thousand eight hundred and eight."

The next allusion in the Constitution to the question of slavery and the black race, is on the subject of the basis of representation, and there the language used is, "Representatives and direct taxes shall be apportioned among the several States which may be included within this Union, according to their respective numbers, which shall be determined by adding to the whole number of free persons; including those bound to service for a term of years, and excluding Indians not taxed—three-fifths of all other persons."

It says "persons," not slaves, not negroes; but this "three-fifths" can be applied to no other class among us than the negroes.

Lastly, in the provision for the reclamation of fugitive slaves it is said: "No person held to service or labor in one State under the laws thereof escaping into another, shall in consequence of any law or regulation therein, be discharged from such service or labor, but shall be delivered up, on claim of the party to whom such service or labor may be due." There again there is no mention of the word "negro" or of slavery. In all three of these places, being the only allusions to slavery in the instrument, covert language is used. Language is used not suggesting that slavery existed or that the black race were among us. And I understand the contemporaneous history of those times to be that covert language was used with a purpose, and that purpose was that in our Constitution, which it was hoped and is still hoped will endure forever—when it should be read by intelligent and patriotic men, after the institution of slavery had passed from among us—there should be nothing on the face of the great charter of liberty suggesting that such a thing as negro slavery had ever existed among us. This is part of the evidence that the fathers of the Government expected and intended the institution of slavery to come to an end. They expected and intended that it should be in the course of ultimate extinction. And when I say that I desire to see the further spread of it arrested I only say I desire to see that done which the fathers have first done. When I say I desire to see it placed where the public mind will rest in the belief that it is in the course of ultimate extinction, I only say I desire to see it placed where they placed it. It is not true that our fathers, as Judge Douglas assumes, made this government part slave and part free. Understand the sense in which he puts it. He assumes that slavery is a rightful thing within itself,—was introduced by the framers of the Constitution. The exact truth is, that they found the institution existing among us, and they left it as they found it. But in making the government they left this institution with many clear marks of disapprobation upon it. They found slavery among them and they left it among them because of the difficulty—the absolute impossibility of its immediate removal. And when Judge Douglas asks me why we cannot let it remain part slave and part free as the fathers of the government made, he asks a question based upon an assumption which is itself a falsehood; and I turn upon him and ask him the question, when the policy that the fathers of the government had adopted in relation to this element among us was the best policy in the world—the only wise policy—the only policy that we can ever safely continue upon—that will ever give us peace unless this dangerous element masters us all and becomes a national institution—*I turn upon him and ask him why he could not let it alone?* I turn and ask him why he was driven to the necessity of introducing a *new policy* in regard to it? He has himself said he introduced a new policy. He said so in his speech on the 22nd of March of the present year, 1858. I ask him why he could not let it remain where our fathers placed it? I ask too of Judge Douglas and his friends why we shall not again place this institution upon the basis on which the fathers left it? I ask you when he infers that I am in favor of setting the free and slave States at war, when the institution was placed in that attitude by those who made the constitution, *did they make any war?* If we had no war out of it when thus placed, wherein is the ground of belief that we shall have war out of it if we return to that policy? Have we had any peace upon this matter springing from any other basis? I maintain that we have not. I have proposed nothing more than a return to the policy of the fathers. . . .

I have stated upon former occasions, and I may as well state again, what I understand to be the real issue in this controversy between Judge Douglas and myself. On the point of my wanting to make war between the free and the slave States, there has been no issue between us. So, too, when he assumes that I am in favor of introducing a perfect social and political equality between the white and black races. These are false issues, upon which Judge Douglas has tried to force the controversy. There is no foundation in truth for the charge that I maintain either of these propositions. The real issue in this controversy—the one pressing upon every mind—is the sentiment on the part of one class that looks upon the institution of slavery *as a wrong*, and of another class that *does not* look upon it as a wrong. The sentiment that contemplates the institution of slavery in this country as a wrong is the sentiment of the Republican party. It is the sentiment around which all their actions—all their arguments circle—from which all their propositions radiate. They look upon it as being a moral, social and political wrong; and while they contemplate it as such, they nevertheless have due regard for its actual existence among us, and the difficulties of getting rid of it in any satisfactory way and to all the constitutional obligations thrown about it. Yet having a due regard for these, they desire a policy in regard to it that looks to its not creating any more danger. They insist that it should as far as may be, *be treated* as a wrong, and one of the methods of treating it as a wrong is to *make provision that it shall grow no larger*. They also desire a policy that looks to a peaceful end of slavery at sometime, as being wrong. These are the views they entertain in regard to it as I understand them; and all their sentiments—all their arguments and propositions are brought within this range. I have said and I repeat it here, that if there be a man amongst us who does not think that the institution of slavery is wrong in any one of the aspects of which I have spoken, he is misplaced and ought not to be with us. And if there be a man amongst us who is so impatient of it as a wrong as to disregard its actual presence among us and the difficulty of getting rid of it suddenly in a satisfactory way, and to disregard the constitutional obligations thrown about it, that man is misplaced if he is on our platform. We disclaim sympathy with him in practical action. He is not placed properly with us.

On this subject of treating it as a wrong, and limiting its spread, let me say a word. Has any thing ever threatened the existence of this Union save and except this very institution of Slavery? What is it that we hold most dear amongst us? Our own liberty and prosperity. What has ever threatened our liberty and prosperity save and except this institution of Slavery? If this is true, how do you propose to improve the condition of things by enlarging Slavery—by spreading it out and making it bigger? You may have a wen or a cancer upon your person and not be able to cut it out lest you bleed to death; but surely it is no way to cure it, to engraft it and spread it over your whole body. That is no proper way of treating what you regard a wrong. You see this peaceful way of dealing with it as a wrong—restricting the spread of it, and not allowing it to go into new countries where it has not already existed. That is the peaceful way, the old-fashioned way, the way in which the fathers themselves set us the example.

On the other hand, I have said there is a sentiment which treats it as *not* being wrong. That is the Democratic sentiment of this day. I do not mean to say that every man who stands within that range positively asserts that it is right. That class will include all who positively assert that it is right, and all who like Judge Douglas treat it as indifferent and do not say it is either right or wrong. These two classes of men fall within the general class of those who do not look upon it as a wrong. . . . Even here to-day you heard Judge Douglas quarrel with me because I uttered a wish that it might sometime come to an end. Although Henry Clay could say he wished every slave in the United States was in the country of his ancestors, I am denounced by those pretending to respect Henry Clay for uttering a wish that it might sometime, in some peaceful way, come to an end. The Democratic policy in regard to that institution will not tolerate the merest breath, the slightest hint, of the least degree of wrong about it. Try it by some of Judge Douglas' arguments. He says he "don't care whether it is voted up or voted down" in the Territories. I do not care myself in dealing with that expression, whether it is intended to be expressive of his individual sentiments on the subject, or only of the national policy he desires to have established. It is alike valuable for my purpose. Any man can say that who does not see anything wrong in slavery, but no man can logically say it who does see a wrong in it; because no man can logically say he don't care whether a wrong is voted up or voted down. He may say he don't care whether an indifferent thing is voted up or down, but he must logically have a choice between a right thing and a wrong thing. He contends that whatever community wants slaves has a right to have them. So they have if it is not a wrong. But if it is a wrong, he cannot say people have a right to do wrong. He says that upon the score of equality, slaves should be allowed to go in a new Territory, like other property. This is strictly logical if there is no difference between it and other property. If it and other property are equal, his argument is entirely logical. But if you insist that one is wrong and the other right, there is no use to institute a comparison between right and wrong. You may turn over everything in the Democratic policy from beginning to end, whether in the shape it takes on the statute book, in the shape it takes in the Dred Scott decision, in the shape it takes in conversation or the shape it takes in short maxim-like arguments—it everywhere carefully excludes the idea that there is anything wrong in it.

That is the real issue. That is the issue that will continue in this country when these poor tongues of Judge Douglas and myself shall be silent. It is the eternal struggle between these two principles—right and wrong—throughout the world. They are the two principles that have stood face to face from the beginning of time; and will ever continue to struggle. The one is the common right of humanity and the other the divine right of kings. It is the same principle in whatever shape it develops itself. It is the same spirit that says, "You work and toil and earn bread, and I'll eat it." No matter in what shape it comes, whether from the mouth of a king who seeks to bestride the people of his own nation and live by the fruit of their labor, or from one race of men as an apology for enslaving another race, it is the same tyrannical principle. I was glad to express my gratitude at Quincy, and I re-express it here to Judge Douglas—*that he looks to no end of the institution of slavery.* That will help the people to see where the struggle really is. It will hereafter place with us all men who really do wish the wrong may have an end. And whenever we can get rid of the fog which obscures the real question—when we can get Judge Douglas and his friends to avow a policy looking to its perpetuation—we can get out from among them that class of men and bring them to the side of those who treat it as a wrong. Then there will soon be an end of it, and that end will be its "ultimate extinction." Whenever the issue can be distinctly made, and all extraneous matter thrown out so that men can fairly see the real difference between the parties, this controversy will soon be settled, and it will be done peaceably too. There will be no war, no violence. It will be placed again where the wisest and best men of the world, placed it. Brooks of South Carolina once declared that when this Constitution was framed, its framers did not look to the institution existing until this day. When he said this, I think he stated a fact that is fully borne out by the history of the times. But he also said they were better and wiser men than the men of these days; yet the men of these days had experience which they had not, and by the invention of the cotton gin it became a necessity in this country that slavery should be perpetual. I now say that willingly or unwillingly, purposely or without purpose, Judge Douglas has been the most prominent instrument in changing the position of the institution of slavery which the fathers of the government expected to come to an end ere this—*and putting it upon Brooks' cotton gin basis,*—placing it where he openly confesses he has no desire there shall ever be an end of it.

"*For,* and not *against* the Union"

Last speech of the campaign, October 30, 1858

Lincoln ended his 1858 senatorial campaign with a speech in his hometown of Springfield. No text of the entire address survives, only the following fragment, which probably was the conclusion of the speech. The fact that Lincoln wrote it out indicates the importance he attached to these particular remarks. In defending his position, Lincoln voiced pain over the criticism of former associates in the Whig party who now opposed him.

My friends, to-day closes the discussions of this canvass. The planting and the culture are over; and there remains but the preparation, and the harvest.

I stand here surrounded by friends—some *political,* all *personal* friends, I trust. May I be indulged, in this closing scene, to say a few words of myself. I have borne a laborious, and, in some respects to myself, a painful part in the contest. Through all, I have neither assailed, nor wrestled with any part of the constitution. The legal right of the Southern people to reclaim their fugitives I have constantly admitted. The legal right of Congress to interfere with their institution in the states, I have constantly denied. In resisting the spread of slavery to new teritory, and with that, what appears to me to be a tendency to subvert the first principle of free government itself my whole effort has consisted. To the best of my judgment I have labored *for*, and not *against* the Union. As I have not felt, so I have not expressed any harsh sentiment towards our Southern bretheren. I have constantly declared, as I really believed, the only difference between them and us, is the difference of circumstances.

I have meant to assail the motives of no party, or individual; and if I have, in any instance (of which I am not conscious) departed from my purpose, I regret it.

I have said that in some respects the contest has been painful to me. Myself, and those with whom I act have been constantly accused of a purpose to destroy the union; and bespattered with every imaginable odious epithet; and some who were friends, as it were but yesterday have made themselves most active in this. I have cultivated patience, and made no attempt at a retort.

Ambition has been ascribed to me. God knows how sincerely I prayed from the first that this field of ambition might not be opened. I claim no insensibility to political honors; but today could the Missouri restriction be restored, and the whole slavery question replaced on the old ground of "toleration["] by *necessity* where it exists, with unyielding hostility to the spread of it, on principle, I would, in consideration, gladly agree, that Judge Douglas should never be *out*, and I never *in*, an office, so long as we both or either, live.

"Opens the way for all"

Address before the Wisconsin State Agricultural Society, September 30, 1859

Lincoln succinctly stated his ideas on political economy in an address to the Wisconsin State Agricultural Society in 1859. Influenced by his own humble beginnings, he viewed the promise of American life in terms of the right of self-advancement. This idea shaped much of Lincoln's political and social thought.

The world is agreed that *labor* is the source from which human wants are mainly supplied. There is no dispute upon this point. From this point, however, men immediately diverge. Much disputation is maintained as to the best way of applying and controlling the labor element. By some it is assumed that labor is available only in connection with capital—that nobody labors, unless somebody else, owning capital, somehow, by the use of that capital, induces him to do it. Having assumed this, they proceed to consider whether it is best that capital shall *hire* laborers, and thus induce them to work by their own consent; or *buy* them, and drive them to it without their consent. Having proceeded so far they naturally conclude that all laborers are necessarily either *hired* laborers, or *slaves*. They further assume that whoever is once a *hired* laborer, is fatally fixed in that condition for life; and thence again that his condition is as bad as, or worse than that of a slave. This is the *"mud-sill"* theory.

But another class of reasoners hold the opinion that there is no *such* relation between capital and labor, as assumed; and that there is no such thing as a freeman being fatally fixed for life, in the condition of a hired laborer, that both these assumptions are false, and all inferences from them groundless. They hold that labor is prior to, and independent of, capital; that, in fact, capital is the fruit of labor, and could never have existed if labor had not *first* existed—that labor can exist without capital, but that capital could never have existed without labor. Hence they hold that labor is the superior—greatly the superior—of capital.

They do not deny that there is, and probably always will be, *a* relation between labor and capital. The error, as they hold, is in assuming that the *whole* labor of the world exists within that relation. A few men own capital; and that few avoid labor themselves, and with their capital, hire, or buy, another few to labor for them. A large majority belong to neither class—neither work for others, nor have others working for them. Even in all our slave States, except South Carolina, a majority of the whole people of all colors, are neither slaves nor masters. In these Free States, a large majority are neither *hirers* nor *hired*. Men, with their families—wives, sons and daughters—work for themselves, on their farms, in their houses and in their shops, taking the whole product to themselves, and asking no favors of capital on the one hand, nor of hirelings or slaves on the other. . . .

The prudent, penniless beginner in the world, labors for wages awhile, saves a surplus with which to buy tools or land, for himself; then labors on his own account another while, and at length hires another new beginner to help him. This, say its advocates, is *free* labor—the just and generous, and prosperous system, which opens the way for all—gives hope to all, and energy, and progress, and improvement of condition to all. If any continue through life in the condition of the hired laborer, it is not the fault of the system, but because of either a dependent nature which prefers it, or improvidence, folly, or singular misfortune. I have said this much about the elements of labor generally, as introductory to the consideration of a new phase which that element is in process of assuming. The old general rule was that *educated* people did not perform manual labor. They managed to eat their bread, leaving the toil of producing it to the uneducated. This was not an insupportable evil to the working bees, so long as the class of drones remained very small. But *now*, especially in these free States, nearly all are educated—quite too nearly all, to leave the labor of the uneducated, in any wise adequate to the support of the whole. It follows from this that henceforth educated people must labor. Otherwise, education itself would become a positive and intolerable evil. No country can sustain, in idleness, more than a small per centage of its numbers. The great majority must labor at something productive. From these premises the problem springs, "How can *labor* and *education* be the most satisfactorily combined?"

By the *"mud-sill"* theory it is assumed that labor and education are incompatible; and any practical combination of them impossible. According to that theory, a blind horse upon a tread-mill, is a perfect illustration of what a laborer should be—all the better for being blind, that he could not tread out of place, or kick understandingly. According to that theory, the education of laborers, is not only useless, but pernicious, and dangerous. In fact, it is, in some sort, deemed a misfortune that laborers should have heads at all. Those same heads are regarded as explosive materials, only to be safely kept in damp places, as far as possible from that peculiar sort of fire which ignites them. A Yankee who could invent a strong *handed* man without a head would receive the everlasting gratitude of the "mud-sill" advocates.

But Free Labor says "no!" Free Labor argues that, as the Author of man makes every individual with one head and one pair of hands, it was probably intended that heads and hands should cooperate as friends; and that that particular head, should direct and control that particular pair of hands. As each man has one mouth to be fed, and one pair of hands to furnish food, it was probably intended that that particular pair of hands should feed that particular mouth—that each head is the natural guardian, director, and protector of the hands and mouth inseparably connected with it; and that being so, every head should be cultivated, and improved, by whatever will add to its capacity for performing its charge. In one word Free Labor insists on universal education.

"Right makes might"

Speech at the Cooper Union, February 27, 1860

Early in 1860 Lincoln traveled to New York City to deliver a political speech. Recognizing the importance of this address, which would introduce him to eastern audiences, Lincoln spent hours doing research in the state library and worked very hard on his text. Outfitted in a new suit he purchased for the occasion, he spoke at the Cooper Union on February 27 to an overflow crowd. In the first part of his speech, he carefully examined the Founding Fathers' attitudes toward slavery to show that they expected the institution to end. In the last section, printed below, he undertook to demonstrate that the Republican party was a conservative organization that simply sought to return to the antislavery ideals of the founding generation. The popular reception to this speech, which was widely reprinted, helped propel Lincoln toward the Republican presidential nomination.

And now, if they would listen—as I suppose they will not—I would address a few words to the Southern people.

I would say to them:—You consider yourselves a reasonable and a just people; and I consider that in the general qualities of reason and justice you are not inferior to any other people. Still, when you speak of us Republicans, you do so only to denounce us as reptiles, or, at the best, as no better than outlaws. You will grant a hearing to pirates or murderers, but nothing like it to "Black Republicans." In all your contentions with one another, each of you deems an unconditional condemnation of "Black Republicanism" as the first thing to be attended to. Indeed, such condemnation of us seems to be an indispensable prerequisite—license, so to speak—among you to be admitted or permitted to speak at all. Now, can you, or not, be prevailed upon to pause and to consider whether this is quite just to us, or even to yourselves? Bring forward your charges and specifications, and then be patient long enough to hear us deny or justify.

You say we are sectional. We deny it. That makes an issue; and the burden of proof is upon you. You produce your proof; and what is it? Why, that our party has no existence in your section—gets no votes in your section. The fact is substantially true; but does it prove the issue? If it does, then in case we should, without change of principle, begin to get votes in your section, we should thereby cease to be sectional. You cannot escape this conclusion; and yet, are you willing to abide by it? If you are, you will probably soon find that we have ceased to be sectional, for we shall get votes in your section this very year. You will then begin to discover, as the truth plainly is, that your proof does not touch the issue. The fact that we get no votes in your section, is a fact of your making, and not of ours. And if there be fault in that fact, that fault is primarily yours, and remains so until you show that we repel you by some wrong principle or practice. If we do repel you by any wrong principle or practice, the fault is ours; but this brings you to where you ought to have started—to a discussion of the right or wrong of our principle. If our principle, put in practice, would wrong your section for the benefit of ours, or for any other object, then our principle, and we with it, are sectional, and are justly opposed and denounced as such. Meet us, then, on the question of whether our principle, put in practice, would wrong your section; and so meet us as if it were possible that something may be said on our side. Do you accept the challenge? No! Then you really believe that the principle which "our fathers who framed the Government under which we live" thought so clearly right as to adopt it, and indorse it again and again, upon their official oaths, is in fact so clearly wrong as to demand your condemnation without a moment's consideration.

Some of you delight to flaunt in our faces the warning against sectional parties given by Washington in his Farewell Address. Less than eight years before Washington gave that warning, he had, as President of the United States, approved and signed an act of Congress, enforcing the prohibition of slavery in the Northwestern Territory, which act embodied the policy of the Government upon that subject up to and at the very moment he penned that warning; and about one year after he penned it, he wrote La Fayette that he considered that prohibition a wise measure, expressing in the same connection his hope that we should at some time have a confederacy of free States.

Bearing this in mind, and seeing that sectionalism has since arisen upon this same subject, is that warning a weapon in your hands against us, or in our hands against you? Could Washington himself speak, would he cast the blame of that sectionalism upon us, who sustain his policy, or upon you who repudiate it? We respect that warning of Washington, and we commend it to you, together with his example pointing to the right application of it.

But you say you are conservative—eminently conservative—while we are revolutionary, destructive, or something of the sort. What is conservatism? Is it not adherence to the old and tried, against the new and untried? We stick to, contend for, the identical old policy on the point in controversy which was adopted by "our fathers who framed the Government under which we live;" while you with one accord reject, and scout, and spit upon that old policy, and insist upon substituting something new. True, you disagree among yourselves as to what that substitute shall be. You are divided on new propositions and plans, but you are unanimous in rejecting and denouncing the old policy of the fathers. Some of you are for reviving the foreign slave trade; some for a Congressional Slave-Code for the Territories; some for Congress forbidding the Territories to prohibit Slavery within their limits; some for maintaining Slavery in the Territories through the judiciary; some for the "gur-reat pur-rinciple" that "if one man would enslave another, no third man should object," fantastically called "Popular Sovereignty;" but never a man among you in favor of federal prohibition of slavery in federal territories, according to the practice of "our fathers who framed the Government under which we live." Not one of all your various plans can show a precedent or an advocate in the century within which our Government originated. Consider, then, whether your claim of conservatism for yourselves, and your charge of destructiveness against us, are based on the most clear and stable foundations.

Again, you say we have made the slavery question more prominent than it formerly was. We deny it. We admit that it is more prominent, but we deny that we made it so. It was not we, but you, who discarded the old policy of the fathers. We resisted, and still resist, your innovation; and thence comes the greater prominence of the question. Would you have that question reduced to its former proportions? Go back to that old policy. What has been will be again, under the same conditions. If you would have the peace of the old times, readopt the precepts and policy of the old times.

You charge that we stir up insurrections among your slaves. We deny it; and what is your proof? Harper's Ferry! John Brown!! John Brown was no Republican; and you have failed to implicate a single Republican in his Harper's Ferry enterprise. If any member of our party is guilty in that matter, you know it or you do not know it. If you do know it, you are inexcusable for not designating the man and proving the fact. If you do not know it, you are inexcusable for asserting it, and especially for persisting in the assertion after you have tried and failed to make the proof. You need not be told that persisting in a charge which one does not know to be true, is simply malicious slander.

Some of you admit that no Republican designedly aided or encouraged the Harper's Ferry affair; but still insist that our doctrines and declarations necessarily lead to such results. We do not believe it. We know we hold to no doctrine, and make no declaration, which were not held to and made by "our fathers who framed the Government under which we live." You never dealt fairly by us in relation to this affair. When it occurred, some important State elections were near at hand, and you were in evident glee with the belief that, by charging the blame upon us, you could get an advantage of us in those elections. The elections came, and your expectations were not quite fulfilled. Every Republican man knew that, as to himself at least, your charge was a slander, and he was not much inclined by it to cast his vote in your favor. Republican doctrines and declarations are accompanied with a continual protest against any interference whatever with your slaves, or with you about your slaves. Surely, this does not encourage them to revolt. True, we do, in common with "our fathers, who framed the Government under which we live," declare our belief that slavery is wrong; but the slaves do not hear us declare even this. For anything we say or do, the slaves would scarcely know there is a Republican party. I believe they would not, in fact, generally know it but for your misrepresentations of us, in their hearing. In your political contests among yourselves, each faction charges the other with sympathy with Black Republicanism; and then, to give point to the charge, defines Black Republicanism to simply be insurrection, blood and thunder among the slaves.

Slave insurrections are no more common now than they were before the Republican party was organized. What induced the Southampton insurrection, twenty-eight years ago, in which, at least, three times as many lives were lost as at Harper's Ferry? You can scarcely stretch your very elastic fancy to the conclusion that Southampton was "got up by Black Republicanism." In the present state of things in the United States, I do not think a general, or even a very extensive slave insurrection, is possible. The indispensable concert of action cannot be attained. The slaves have no means of rapid communication; nor can incendiary freemen, black or white, supply it. The explosive materials are everywhere in parcels; but there neither are, nor can be supplied, the indispensable connecting trains.

Much is said by Southern people about the affection of slaves for their masters and mistresses; and a part of it, at least, is true. A plot for an uprising could scarcely be devised and communicated to twenty individuals before some one of them, to save the life of a favorite master or mistress, would divulge it. This is the rule; and the slave revolution in Hayti was not an exception to it, but a case occurring under peculiar circumstances. The gunpowder plot of British history, though not connected with slaves, was more in point. In that case, only about twenty were admitted to the secret; and yet one of them, in his anxiety to save a friend, betrayed the plot to that friend, and, by consequence, averted the calamity. Occasional poisonings from the kitchen, and open or stealthy assassinations in the field, and local revolts extending to a score or so, will continue to occur as the natural results of slavery; but no general insurrection of slaves, as I think, can happen in this country for a long time. Whoever much fears, or much hopes for such an event, will be alike disappointed.

In the language of Mr. Jefferson, uttered many years ago, "It is still in our power to direct the process of emancipation, and deportation, peaceably, and in such slow degrees, as that the evil will wear off insensibly; and their places be, *pari passu*, filled up by free white laborers. If, on the contrary, it is left to force itself on, human nature must shudder at the prospect held up."

Mr. Jefferson did not mean to say, nor do I, that the power of emancipation is in the Federal Government. He spoke of Virginia; and, as to the power of emancipation, I speak of the slaveholding States only. The Federal Government, however, as we insist, has the power of restraining the extension of the institution—the power to insure that a slave insurrection shall never occur on any American soil which is now free from slavery.

John Brown's effort was peculiar. It was not a slave insurrection. It was an attempt by white men to get up a revolt among slaves, in which the slaves refused to participate. In fact, it was so absurd that the slaves, with all their ignorance, saw plainly enough it could not succeed. That affair, in its philosophy, corresponds with the many attempts, related in history, at the assassination of kings and emperors. An enthusiast broods over the oppression of a people till he fancies himself commissioned by Heaven to liberate them. He ventures the attempt, which ends in little else than his own execution. Orsini's attempt on Louis Napoleon, and John Brown's attempt at Harper's Ferry were, in their philosophy, precisely the same. The eagerness to cast blame on old England in the one case, and on New England in the other, does not disprove the sameness of the two things.

And how much would it avail you, if you could, by the use of John Brown, Helper's Book, and the like, break up the Republican organization? Human action can be modified to some extent, but human nature cannot be changed. There is a judgment and a feeling against slavery in this nation, which cast at least a million and a half of votes. You cannot destroy that judgment and feeling—that sentiment—by breaking up the political organization which rallies around it. You can scarcely scatter and disperse an army which has been formed into order in the face of your heaviest fire; but if you could, how much would you gain by forcing the sentiment which created it out of the peaceful channel of the ballot-box, into some other channel? What would that other channel probably be? Would the number of John Browns be lessened or enlarged by the operation?

But you will break up the Union rather than submit to a denial of your Constitutional rights.

That has a somewhat reckless sound; but it would be palliated, if not fully justified, were we proposing, by the mere force of numbers, to deprive you of some right, plainly written down in the Constitution. But we are proposing no such thing.

When you make these declarations, you have a specific and well-understood allusion to an assumed Constitutional right of yours, to take slaves into the federal territories, and to hold them there as property. But no such right is specifically written in the Constitution. That instrument is literally silent about any such right. We, on the contrary, deny that such a right has any existence in the Constitution, even by implication.

Your purpose, then, plainly stated, is, that you will destroy the Government, unless you be allowed to construe and enforce the Constitution as you please, on all points in dispute between you and us. You will rule or ruin in all events.

This, plainly stated, is your language. Perhaps you will say the Supreme Court has decided the disputed Constitutional question in your favor. Not quite so. But waiving the lawyer's distinction between dictum and decision, the Court have decided the question for you in a sort of way. The Court have substantially said, it is your Constitutional right to take slaves into the federal territories, and to hold them there as property. When I say the decision was made in a sort of way, I mean it was made in a divided Court, by a bare majority of the Judges, and they not quite agreeing with one another in the reasons for making it, that it is so made as that its avowed supporters disagree with one another about its meaning, and that it was mainly based upon a mistaken statement of fact—the statement in the opinion that "the right of property in a slave is distinctly and expressly affirmed in the Constitution."

An inspection of the Constitution will show that the right of property in a slave is not "*distinctly* and *expressly* affirmed" in it. Bear in mind, the Judges do not pledge their judicial opinion that such right is *impliedly* affirmed in the Constitution; but they pledge their veracity that it is "*distinctly* and *expressly*" affirmed there—"distinctly," that is, not mingled with anything else—"expressly," that is, in words meaning just that, without the aid of any inference, and susceptible of no other meaning.

If they had only pledged their judicial opinion that such right is affirmed in the instrument by implication, it would be open to others to show that neither the word "slave" nor "slavery" is to be found in the Constitution, nor the word "property" even, in any connection with language alluding to the things slave, or slavery, and that wherever in that instrument the slave is alluded to, he is called a "person;"—and wherever his master's legal right in relation to him is alluded to, it is spoken of as "service or labor which may be due,"—as a debt payable in service or labor. Also, it would be open to show, by contemporaneous history, that this mode of alluding to slaves and slavery, instead of speaking of them, was employed on purpose to exclude from the Constitution the idea that there could be property in man.

To show all this, is easy and certain.

When this obvious mistake of the Judges shall be brought to their notice, is it not reasonable to expect that they will withdraw the mistaken statement, and reconsider the conclusion based upon it?

And then it is to be remembered that "our fathers, who framed the Government under which we live"—the men who made the Constitution—decided this same Constitutional question in our favor, long ago —decided it without division among themselves, when making the decision; without division among themselves about the meaning of it after it was made, and, so far as any evidence is left, without basing it upon any mistaken statement of facts.

Under all these circumstances, do you really feel yourselves justified to break up this Government, unless such a court decision as yours is, shall be at once submitted to as a conclusive and final rule of political action? But you will not abide the election of a Republican President! In that supposed event, you say, you will destroy the Union; and then, you say, the great crime of having destroyed it will be upon us! That is cool. A highwayman holds a pistol to my ear, and mutters through his teeth, "Stand and deliver, or I shall kill you, and then you will be a murderer!"

To be sure, what the robber demanded of me—my money—was my own; and I had a clear right to keep it; but it was no more my own than my vote is my own; and the threat of death to me, to extort my money, and the threat of destruction to the Union, to extort my vote, can scarcely be distinguished in principle.

A few words now to Republicans. *It is exceedingly desirable that all parts of this great Confederacy shall be at peace, and in harmony, one with another. Let us Republicans do our part to have it so. Even though much provoked, let us do nothing through passion and ill temper. Even though the southern people will not so much as listen to us, let us calmly consider their demands, and yield to them if, in our deliberate view of our duty, we possibly can.* Judging by all they say and do, and by the subject and nature of their controversy with us, let us determine, if we can, what will satisfy them.

Will they be satisfied if the Territories be unconditionally surrendered to them? We know they will not. In all their present complaints against us, the Territories are scarcely mentioned. Invasions and insurrections are the rage now. Will it satisfy them, if, in the future, we have nothing to do with invasions and insurrections? We know it will not. We so know, because we know we never had anything to do with invasions and insurrections; and yet this total abstaining does not exempt us from the charge and the denunciation.

The question recurs, what will satisfy them? Simply this: We must not only let them alone, but we must, somehow, convince them that we do let them alone. This, we know by experience, is no easy task. We have been so trying to convince them from the very beginning of our organization, but with no success. In all our platforms and speeches we have constantly protested our purpose to let them alone; but this has had no tendency to convince them. Alike unavailing to convince them, is the fact that they have never detected a man of us in any attempt to disturb them.

These natural, and apparently adequate means all failing, what will convince them? This, and this only: cease to call slavery *wrong*, and join them in calling it *right*. And this must be done thoroughly—done in *acts* as well as in *words*. Silence will not be tolerated—we must place ourselves avowedly with them. Senator Douglas's new sedition law must be enacted and enforced, suppressing all declarations that slavery is wrong, whether made in politics, in presses, in pulpits, or in private. We must arrest and return their fugitive slaves with greedy pleasure. We must pull down our Free State constitutions. The whole atmosphere must be disinfected from all taint of opposition to slavery, before they will cease to believe that all their troubles proceed from us.

I am quite aware they do not state their case precisely in this way. Most of them would probably say to us, "Let us alone, *do* nothing to us, and *say* what you please about slavery." But we do let them alone— have never disturbed them—so that, after all, it is what we say, which dissatisfies them. They will continue to accuse us of doing, until we cease saying.

I am also aware they have not, as yet, in terms, demanded the overthrow of our Free-State Constitutions. Yet those Constitutions declare

the wrong of slavery, with more solemn emphasis, than do all other sayings against it; and when all these other sayings shall have been silenced,
the overthrow of these Constitutions will be demanded, and nothing be
left to resist the demand. It is nothing to the contrary, that they do not
demand the whole of this just now. Demanding what they do, and for
the reason they do, they can voluntarily stop nowhere short of this consummation. Holding, as they do, that slavery is morally right, and
socially elevating, they cannot cease to demand a full national recognition of it, as a legal right, and a social blessing.

Nor can we justifiably withhold this, on any ground save our conviction that slavery is wrong. If slavery is right, all words, acts, laws, and
constitutions against it, are themselves wrong, and should be silenced,
and swept away. If it is right, we cannot justly object to its nationality—
its universality; if it is wrong, they cannot justly insist upon its extension
—its enlargement. All they ask, we could readily grant, if we thought
slavery right; all we ask, they could as readily grant, if they thought it
wrong. Their thinking it right, and our thinking it wrong, is the precise
fact upon which depends the whole controversy. Thinking it right, as
they do, they are not to blame for desiring its full recognition, as being
right; but, thinking it wrong, as we do, can we yield to them? Can we
cast our votes with their view, and against our own? In view of our
moral, social, and political responsibilities, can we do this?

Wrong as we think slavery is, we can yet afford to let it alone where
it is, because that much is due to the necessity arising from its actual
presence in the nation; but can we, while our votes will prevent it, allow
it to spread into the National Territories, and to overrun us here in
these Free States? If our sense of duty forbids this, then let us stand by
our duty, fearlessly and effectively. Let us be diverted by none of those
sophistical contrivances wherewith we are so industriously plied and
belabored—contrivances such as groping for some middle ground
between the right and the wrong, vain as the search for a man who
should be neither a living man nor a dead man—such as a policy of
"don't care" on a question about which all true men do care—such as
Union appeals beseeching true Union men to yield to Disunionists,
reversing the divine rule, and calling, not the sinners, but the righteous
to repentance—such as invocations to Washington, imploring men to
unsay what Washington said, and undo what Washington did.

Neither let us be slandered from our duty by false accusations against us, nor frightened from it by menaces of destruction to the Government nor of dungeons to ourselves. LET US HAVE FAITH THAT RIGHT MAKES MIGHT, AND IN THAT FAITH, LET US, TO THE END, DARE TO DO OUR DUTY AS WE UNDERSTAND IT.

"I am not the *first* choice of . . . many"

Letter to Samuel Galloway, March 24, 1860

By the time he returned from New York, Lincoln had decided to seek the Republican presidential nomination. In this letter to an Ohio Republican leader and personal supporter, he outlined his basic strategy to win the nomination. His main advantage was that he was acceptable to all factions of the party, and at the Chicago convention, his campaign managers argued that he was the most electable of all the possible nominees and sought commitments from delegates to switch to Lincoln if their first choice could not be nominated, a strategy that in the end was successful.

Hon. Samuel Galloway   Chicago

My dear Sir: I am here attending a trial in court. Before leaving home I received your kind letter of the 15th. Of course I am gratified to know I have friends in Ohio who are disposed to give me the highest evidence of their friendship and confidence. Mr Parrott of the Legislature, had written me to the same effect. If I have any chance, it consists mainly in the fact that the *whole* opposition would vote for me if nominated. (I dont mean to include the pro-slavery opposition of the South, of course.) My name is new in the field; and I suppose I am not the *first* choice of a very great many. Our policy, then, is to give no offence to others—leave them in a mood to come to us, if they shall be compelled to give up their first love. This, too, is dealing justly with all, and leaving us in a mood to support heartily whoever shall be nominated. I believe I have once before told you that I especially wish to do no ungenerous thing towards Governor Chase, because he gave us his sympathy in 1858, when scarcely any other distinguished man did. Whatever you may do for me, consistently with these suggestions, will be appreciated, and gratefully remembered.

Please write me again. Yours very truly

"The taste *is* in my mouth"

Letter to Lyman Trumbull, April 29, 1860

In the antebellum period, it was considered improper to actively seek a presidential nomination, and therefore Lincoln was wary about acknowledging his desire to be nominated. In this confidential letter to Republican Senator Lyman Trumbull, who had defeated Lincoln for the senatorship in 1855, however, Lincoln frankly admitted he wanted to be nominated and subtly apprised Trumbull that he had better board the Lincoln bandwagon. Lincoln's emphasis on the importance of carrying the legislature was a further nudge for Trumbull to commit himself, since the next legislature would elect Trumbull's successor in the Senate.

Hon: L. Trumbull: ⠀⠀⠀⠀⠀⠀⠀⠀⠀⠀⠀⠀⠀⠀⠀⠀⠀⠀⠀⠀⠀⠀⠀⠀⠀⠀⠀Springfield

My dear Sir:

Yours of the 24th. was duly received; and I have postponed answering it, hoping by the result at Charleston, to know who is to lead our adversaries, before writing. But Charleston hangs fire, and I wait no longer.*

As you request, I will be entirely frank. The taste *is* in my mouth a little; and this, no doubt, disqualifies me, to some extent, to form correct opinions. You may confidently rely, however, that by no advice or consent of mine, shall my pretentions be pressed to the point of endangering our common cause.

Now, as to my opinions about the chances of others in Illinois. I think neither Seward nor Bates can carry Illinois if Douglas shall be on the track; and that either of them can, if he shall not be. I rather think McLean could carry it with D. on or off—in other words, I think McLean is stronger in Illinois, taking all sections of it, than either S. or B; and I think S. the weakest of the three. I hear no objection to McLean, except his age; but that objection seems to occur to every one; and it is possible it might leave him no stronger than the others. By the way, if we should nominate him, how would we save to ourselves the chance of filling his vacancy in the Court? Have him hold on up to the moment of his inauguration? Would that course be no draw-back upon us in the canvass?

---

*The Democratic national convention at Charleston failed to make a nomination.

Recurring to Illinois, we want something here quite as much as, and which is harder to get than, the electoral vote—the Legislature. And it is exactly in this point that Seward's nomination would be hard upon us. Suppose he should gain us a thousand votes in Winnebago, it would not compensate for the loss of fifty in Edgar.

A word now for your own special benefit. You better write no letters which can possibly be distorted into opposition, or quasi opposition to me. There are men on the constant watch for such things out of which to prejudice my peculiar friends against you. While I have no more suspicion of you than I have of my best friend living, I am kept in a constant struggle against suggestions of this sort. I have hesitated some to write this paragraph, lest you should suspect I do it for my own benefit, and not for yours; but on reflection I conclude you will not suspect me.

Let no eye but your own see this—not that there is anything wrong, or even ungenerous, in it; but it would be misconstrued.

Your friend as ever

"I accept the nomination"

Letter to George Ashmun, May 23, 1860

In accepting the Republican presidential nomination, Lincoln included the traditional endorsement of the party's platform, but his letter was notable primarily for its lack of specifics. As the front runner, Lincoln had nothing to gain by outlining his principles and future policies, and in fact the Republicans downplayed issues during the campaign in favor of their candidate's personality and image as a self-made man.

Hon: George Ashmun: Springfield, Ills.
President of the Republican National Convention.

Sir: I accept the nomination tendered me by the Convention over which you presided, and of which I am formally apprized in the letter of yourself and others, acting as a committee of the convention, for that purpose.

The declaration of principles and sentiments, which accompanies your letter, meets my approval; and it shall be my care not to violate, or disregard it, in any part.

Imploring the assistance of Divine Providence, and with due regard to the views and feelings of all who were represented in the convention; to the rights of all the states, and territories, and people of the nation; to the inviolability of the constitution, and the perpetual union, harmony, and prosperity of all, I am most happy to co-operate for the practical success of the principles declared by the convention. Your obliged friend, and fellow citizen

"A piece of silly affection"

Letter to Grace Bedell, October 19, 1860

During the 1860 campaign, eleven-year-old Grace Bedell of Westfield, New York, suggested to Lincoln that he grow a beard. "You would look a good deal better for your face is so thin," she wrote, and besides, "all the ladies like whiskers." Lincoln's response was noncommittal, but shortly thereafter, he began to let his whiskers grow. Lincoln met his young admirer when the train taking him to Washington stopped in her hometown in February 1861.

PRIVATE

Miss. Grace Bedell   Springfield, Ills.

My dear little Miss.

Your very agreeable letter of the 15th. is received.

I regret the necessity of saying I have no daughters. I have three sons —one seventeen, one nine, and one seven, years of age. They, with their mother, constitute my whole family.

As to the whiskers, having never worn any, do you not think people would call it a piece of silly affection if I were to begin it now? Your very sincere well-wisher

III

"THE PERPETUITY OF POPULAR GOVERNMENT," 1860–1861

"The tug has to come"

Letter to Lyman Trumbull, December 10, 1860

Lincoln's election set the wheels of the secession movement in motion in the South. After Congress assembled in December, a number of compromise proposals were introduced to resolve the crisis, but in the end Congress was unable to agree on any compromise solution. One important reason for this outcome was Lincoln's strong opposition to compromise. While the president-elect said nothing publicly, privately he urged Republican leaders in Congress to reject any compromise, especially on the question of the extension of slavery.

PRIVATE, & CONFIDENTIAL

Hon. L. Trumbull.   Springfield, Ills.

My dear Sir: Let there be no compromise on the question of *extending* slavery. If there be, all our labor is lost, and, ere long, must be done again. The dangerous ground—that into which some of our friends have a hankering to run—is Pop. Sov. Have none of it. Stand firm. The tug has to come, & better now, than any time hereafter. Yours as ever

"There is no cause for such fears"

Letter to Alexander H. Stephens, December 22, 1860

Following his election, Lincoln was slow to recognize the gravity of the secession crisis. Immediately after South Carolina seceded, however, he wrote to Alexander H. Stephens, a prominent southern political leader he knew from their service together in Congress in the 1840s. Lincoln insisted that the South had nothing to fear from his election, yet he did not discuss the sectional conflict in any detail and refrained from outlining his policies. Moreover, by marking the letter as confidential, he severely lessened its value in reassuring southern Unionists. Stephens would subsequently serve as vice president of the Confederacy.

FOR YOUR OWN EYE ONLY.

Hon. A. H. Stephens—   Springfield, Ills.

My dear Sir

Your obliging answer to my short note is just received, and for which please accept my thanks. I fully appreciate the present peril the country is in, and the weight of responsibility on me.

Do the people of the South really entertain fears that a Republican administration would, *directly*, or *indirectly*, interfere with their slaves, or with them, about their slaves? If they do, I wish to assure you, as once a friend, and still, I hope, not an enemy, that there is no cause for such fears.

The South would be in no more danger in this respect, than it was in the days of Washington. I suppose, however, this does not meet the case. You think slavery is *right* and ought to be extended; while we think it is *wrong* and ought to be restricted. That I suppose is the rub. It certainly is the only substantial difference between us. Yours very truly

"It is the end of us"

Letter to James T. Hale, January 11, 1861

When a Pennsylvania Republican congressman wrote suggesting a possible compromise, Lincoln condemned what he considered southern blackmail to extort concessions from the North by the use of threats.

Implicit in his reply was his belief that the minority could not dictate to the majority, an idea Lincoln would develop more fully in his first inaugural address.

CONFIDENTIAL.

Hon. J. T. Hale   Springfield, Ill.

My dear Sir—Yours of the 6th is received. I answer it only because I fear you would misconstrue my silence. What is our present condition? We have just carried an election on principles fairly stated to the people. Now we are told in advance, the government shall be broken up, unless we surrender to those we have beaten, before we take the offices. In this they are either attempting to play upon us, or they are in dead earnest. Either way, if we surrender; it is the end of us, and of the government. They will repeat the experiment upon us *ad libitum*. A year will not pass, till we shall have to take Cuba as a condition upon which they will stay in the Union. They now have the Constitution, under which we have lived over seventy years, and acts of Congress of their own framing, with no prospect of their being changed; and they can never have a more shallow pretext for breaking up the government, or extorting a compromise, than now. There is, in my judgment, but one compromise which would really settle the slavery question, and that would be a prohibition against acquiring any more territory. Yours very truly,

"An affectionate farewell"

Farewell Address at Springfield, February 11, 1861

After he boarded the train that would take him to Washington for his inauguration, Lincoln said a few impromptu words of farewell to the townsfolk and friends who had gathered at the station to see him off. Lincoln was usually outwardly undemonstrative, but his emotions welled up on this occasion. Impressed by the power of his words, reporters requested a transcript, and his little speech was widely printed throughout the North.

My friends—No one, not in my situation, can appreciate my feeling of sadness at this parting. To this place, and the kindness of these people, I owe every thing. Here I have lived a quarter of a century, and have passed from a young to an old man. Here my children have been born, and one is buried. I now leave, not knowing when, or whether ever, I may return, with a task before me greater than that which rested upon Washington. Without the assistance of that Divine Being, who ever attended him, I cannot succeed. With that assistance I cannot fail. Trusting in Him, who can go with me, and remain with you and be every where for good, let us confidently hope that all will yet be well. To His care commending you, as I hope in your prayers you will commend me, I bid you an affectionate farewell

"The Union . . . is perpetual"

First Inaugural Address, March 4, 1861

Lincoln wrote a draft of his inaugural address before he left Springfield. He showed it to several advisers in Washington and then revised it; most of the revisions softened his language at key points without abandoning the underlying principles. In his speech, he tried to reassure Southerners about his policies, especially with regard to slavery, while at the same time firmly denying that any state had the right to secede. While the address made clear Lincoln's determination to maintain the Union, it was purposely vague about how he intended to do this. The closing words were based on a draft by Seward, which Lincoln rephrased in his unique style.

Fellow citizens of the United States:

In compliance with a custom as old as the government itself, I appear before you to address you briefly, and to take, in your presence, the oath prescribed by the Constitution of the United States, to be taken by the President "before he enters on the execution of his office."

I do not consider it necessary, at present, for me to discuss those matters of administration about which there is no special anxiety, or excitement.

Apprehension seems to exist among the people of the Southern States, that by the accession of a Republican Administration, their property, and their peace, and personal security, are to be endangered. There has never been any reasonable cause for such apprehension. Indeed, the most ample evidence to the contrary has all the while existed, and been open to their inspection. It is found in nearly all the published speeches of him who now addresses you. I do but quote from one of those speeches when I declare that "I have no purpose, directly or indirectly, to interfere with the institution of slavery in the States where it exists. I believe I have no lawful right to do so, and I have no inclination to do so." Those who nominated and elected me did so with full knowledge that I had made this, and many similar declarations, and had never recanted them. And more than this, they placed in the platform, for my acceptance, and as a law to themselves, and to me, the clear and emphatic resolution which I now read:

"*Resolved*, That the maintenance inviolate of the rights of the States, and especially the right of each State to order and control its own domestic institutions according to its own judgment exclusively, is essential to that balance of power on which the perfection and endurance of our political fabric depend; and we denounce the lawless and invasion by armed force of the soil of any State or Territory, no matter under what pretext, as among the gravest of crimes."

I now reiterate these sentiments: and in doing so, I only press upon the public attention the most conclusive evidence of which the case is susceptible, that the property, peace and security of no section are to be in anywise endangered by the now incoming Administration. I add too, that all the protection which, consistently with the Constitution and the laws, can be given, will be cheerfully given to all the States when lawfully demanded, for whatever cause—as cheerfully to one section, as to another.

There is much controversy about the delivering up of fugitives from service or labor. The clause I now read is as plainly written in the Constitution as any other of its provisions:

"No person held to service or labor in one State, under the laws thereof, escaping into another, shall, in consequence of any law or regulation therein, be discharged from such service or labor, but shall be delivered up on claim of the party to whom such service or labor may be due."

It is scarcely questioned that this provision was intended by those who made it, for the reclaiming of what we call fugitive slaves; and the intention of the law-giver is the law. All members of Congress swear their support to the whole Constitution—to this provision as much as to any other. To the proposition, then, that slaves whose cases come within the terms of this clause, "shall be delivered up," their oaths are unanimous. Now, if they would make the effort in good temper, could they not, with nearly equal unanimity, frame and pass a law, by means of which to keep good that unanimous oath?

There is some difference of opinion whether this clause should be enforced by national or by state authority; but surely that difference is not a very material one. If the slave is to be surrendered, it can be of but little consequence to him, or to others, by which authority it is done. And should any one, in any case, be content that his oath shall go unkept, on a merely unsubstantial controversy as to *how* it shall be kept?

Again, in any law upon this subject, ought not all the safeguards of liberty known in civilized and humane jurisprudence to be introduced, so that a free man be not, in any case, surrendered as a slave? And might it not be well, at the same time, to provide by law for the enforcement of that clause in the Constitution which guarranties that "The citizens of each State shall be entitled to all previleges and immunities of citizens in the several States?"

I take the official oath to-day, with no mental reservations, and with no purpose to construe the Constitution or laws, by any hypercritical rules. And while I do not choose now to specify particular acts of Congress as proper to be enforced, I do suggest, that it will be much safer for all, both in official and private stations, to conform to, and abide by, all those acts which stand unrepealed, than to violate any of them, trusting to find impunity in having them held to be unconstitutional.

It is seventy-two years since the first inauguration of a President under our national Constitution. During that period fifteen different and greatly distinguished citizens, have, in succession, administered the executive branch of the government. They have conducted it through many perils; and, generally, with great success. Yet, with all this scope for precedent, I now enter upon the same task for the brief constitutional term of four years, under great and peculiar difficulty. A disruption of the Federal Union heretofore only menaced, is now formidably attempted.

I hold, that in contemplation of universal law, and of the Constitution, the Union of these States is perpetual. Perpetuity is implied, if not expressed, in the fundamental law of all national governments. It is safe to assert that no government proper, ever had a provision in its organic law for its own termination. Continue to execute all the express provisions of our national Constitution, and the Union will endure forever— it being impossible to destroy it, except by some action not provided for in the instrument itself.

Again, if the United States be not a government proper, but an association of States in the nature of contract merely, can it, as a contract, be peaceably unmade, by less than all the parties who made it? One party to a contract may violate it—break it, so to speak; but does it not require all to lawfully rescind it?

Descending from these general principles, we find the proposition that, in legal contemplation, the Union is perpetual, confirmed by the history of the Union itself. The Union is much older than the Constitution. It was formed in fact, by the Articles of Association in 1774. It was matured and continued by the Declaration of Independence in 1776. It was further matured and the faith of all the then thirteen States expressly plighted and engaged that it should be perpetual, by the Articles of Confederation in 1778. And finally, in 1787, one of the declared objects for ordaining and establishing the Constitution, was *"to form a more perfect union."*

But if destruction of the Union, by one, or by a part only, of the States, be lawfully possible, the Union is *less* perfect than before the Constitution, having lost the vital element of perpetuity.

It follows from these views that no State, upon its own mere motion, can lawfully get out of the Union,—that *resolves* and *ordinances* to that effect are legally void; and that acts of violence, within any State or States, against the authority of the United States, are insurrectionary or revolutionary, according to circumstances.

I therefore consider that, in view of the Constitution and the laws, the Union is unbroken; and, to the extent of my ability, I shall take care, as the Constitution itself expressly enjoins upon me, that the laws of the Union be faithfully executed in all the States. Doing this I deem to be only a simple duty on my part; and I shall perform it, so far as practicable, unless my rightful masters, the American people, shall withhold the requisite means, or, in some authoritative manner, direct the contrary. I trust this will not be regarded as a menace, but only as the declared purpose of the Union that it *will* constitutionally defend, and maintain itself.

In doing this there needs to be no bloodshed or violence; and there shall be none, unless it be forced upon the national authority. The power confided to me, will be used to hold, occupy, and possess the property, and places belonging to the government, and to collect the duties and imposts; but beyond what may be necessary for these objects, there will be no invasion—no using of force against, or among the people anywhere. Where hostility to the United States, in any interior locality, shall be so great and so universal, as to prevent competent resident citizens from holding the Federal offices, there will be no attempt to force obnoxious strangers among the people for that object. While the strict legal right may exist in the government to enforce the exercise of these offices, the attempt to do so would be so irritating, and so nearly impracticable with all, that I deem it better to forego, for the time, the uses of such offices.

The mails, unless repelled, will continue to be furnished in all parts of the Union. So far as possible, the people everywhere shall have that sense of perfect security which is most favorable to calm thought and reflection. The course here indicated will be followed, unless current events, and experience, shall show a modification, or change, to be proper; and in every case and exigency, my best discretion will be exercised, according to circumstances actually existing, and with a view and a hope of a peaceful solution of the national troubles, and the restoration of fraternal sympathies and affections.

That there are persons in one section, or another who seek to destroy the Union at all events, and are glad of any pretext to do it, I will neither affirm or deny; but if there be such, I need address no word to them. To those, however, who really love the Union, may I not speak?

Before entering upon so grave a matter as the destruction of our national fabric, with all its benefits, its memories, and its hopes, would it not be wise to ascertain precisely why we do it? Will you hazard so desperate a step, while there is any possibility that any portion of the ills you fly from, have no real existence? Will you, while the certain ills you fly to, are greater than all the real ones you fly from? Will you risk the commission of so fearful a mistake?

All profess to be content in the Union, if all constitutional rights can be maintained. Is it true, then, that any right, plainly written in the Constitution, has been denied? I think not. Happily the human mind is so constituted, that no party can reach to the audacity of doing this. Think, if you can, of a single instance in which a plainly written provision of the Constitution has ever been denied. If, by the mere force of numbers, a majority should deprive a minority of any clearly written constitutional right, it might, in a moral point of view, justify revolution—certainly would, if such right were a vital one. But such is not our case. All the vital rights of minorities, and of individuals, are so plainly assured to them, by affirmations and negations, guarranties and prohibitions, in the Constitution, that controversies never arise concerning them. But no organic law can ever be framed with a provision specifically applicable to every question which may occur in practical administration. No foresight can anticipate, nor any document of reasonable length contain express provisions for all possible questions. Shall fugitives from labor be surrendered by national or by State authority? The Constitution does not expressly say. *May* Congress prohibit slavery in the territories? The Constitution does not expressly say. *Must* Congress protect slavery in the territories? The Constitution does not expressly say.

From questions of this class spring all our constitutional controversies, and we divide upon them into majorities and minorities. If the minority will not acquiesce, the majority must, or the government must cease. There is no other alternative; for continuing the government, is acquiescence on one side or the other. If a minority, in such case, will secede rather than acquiesce, they make a precedent which, in turn, will divide and ruin them; for a minority of their own will secede from them, whenever a majority refuses to be controlled by such minority. For instance, why may not any portion of a new confederacy, a year or two hence, arbitrarily secede again, precisely as portions of the present Union now claim to secede from it. All who cherish disunion sentiments, are now being educated to the exact temper of doing this. Is there such perfect identity of interests among the States to compose a new Union, as to produce harmony only, and prevent renewed secession?

Plainly, the central idea of secession, is the essence of anarchy. A majority, held in restraint by constitutional checks, and limitations, and always changing easily, with deliberate changes of popular opinions and sentiments, is the only true sovereign of a free people. Whoever rejects it, does, of necessity, fly to anarchy or to despotism. Unanimity is impossible; the rule of a minority, as a permanent arrangement, is wholly inadmissable; so that, rejecting the majority principle, anarchy, or despotism in some form, is all that is left.

I do not forget the position assumed by some, that constitutional questions are to be decided by the Supreme Court; nor do I deny that such decisions must be binding in any case, upon the parties to a suit, as to the object of that suit, while they are also entitled to very high respect and consideration, in all paralel cases, by all other departments of the government. And while it is obviously possible that such decision may be erroneous in any given case, still the evil effect following it, being limited to that particular case, with the chance that it may be over-ruled, and never become a precedent for other cases, can better be borne than could the evils of a different practice. At the same time the candid citizen must confess that if the policy of the government, upon vital questions, affect-ing the whole people, is to be irrevocably fixed by decisions of the Supreme Court, the instant they are made, in ordinary litigation between parties, in personal actions, the people will have ceased, to be their own rulers, having, to that extent, practically resigned their government, into the hands of that eminent tribunal. Nor is there, in this view, any assault upon the court, or the judges. It is a duty, from which they may not shrink, to decide cases properly brought before them; and it is no fault of theirs, if others seek to turn their decisions to political purposes.

One section of our country believes slavery is *right*, and ought to be extended, while the other believes it is *wrong*, and ought not to be extended. This is the only substantial dispute. The fugitive slave clause of the Constitution, and the law for the suppression of the foreign slave trade, are each as well enforced, perhaps, as any law can ever be in a community where the moral sense of the people imperfectly supports the law itself. The great body of the people abide by the dry legal obli-gation in both cases, and a few break over in each. This, I think, cannot be perfectly cured; and it would be worse in both cases *after* the separa-tion of the sections, than before. The foreign slave trade, now imper-fectly suppressed, would be ultimately revived without restriction, in one section; while fugitive slaves, now only partially surrendered, would not be surrendered at all, by the other.

Physically speaking, we cannot separate. We cannot remove our respective sections from each other, nor build an impassable wall between them. A husband and wife may be divorced, and go out of the presence, and beyond the reach of each other; but the different parts of our country cannot do this. They cannot but remain face to face; and intercourse, either amicable or hostile, must continue between them. Is it possible then to make that intercourse more advantageous, or more satisfactory, *after* separation than *before*? Can aliens make treaties easier than friends can make laws? Can treaties be more faithfully enforced between aliens, than laws can among friends? Suppose you go to war, you cannot fight always; and when, after much loss on both sides, and no gain on either, you cease fighting, the identical old questions, as to terms of intercourse, are again upon you.

This country, with its institutions, belongs to the people who inhabit it. Whenever they shall grow weary of the existing government, they can exercise their *constitutional* right of amending it, or their *revolutionary* right to dismember, or overthrow it. I can not be ignorant of the fact that many worthy, and patriotic citizens are desirous of having the national constitution amended. While I make no recommendation of amendments, I fully recognize the rightful authority of the people over the whole subject, to be exercised in either of the modes prescribed in the instrument itself; and I should, under existing circumstances, favor, rather than oppose, a fair oppertunity being afforded the people to act upon it.

I will venture to add that, to me, the convention mode seems preferable, in that it allows amendments to originate with the people themselves, instead of only permitting them to take, or reject, propositions, originated by others, not especially chosen for the purpose, and which might not be precisely such, as they would wish to either accept or refuse. I understand a proposed amendment to the Constitution—which amendment, however, I have not seen, has passed Congress, to the effect that the federal government, shall never interfere with the domestic institutions of the States, including that of persons held to service. To avoid misconstruction of what I have said, I depart from my purpose not to speak of particular amendments, so far as to say that, holding such a provision to now be implied constitutional law, I have no objection to its being made express, and irrevocable.

The Chief Magistrate derives all his authority from the people, and they have conferred none upon him to fix terms for the separation of the States. The people themselves can do this also if they choose; but the executive, as such, has nothing to do with it. His duty is to administer the present government, as it came to his hands, and to transmit it, unimpaired by him, to his successor.

Why should there not be a patient confidence in the ultimate justice of the people? Is there any better, or equal hope, in the world? In our present differences, is either party without faith of being in the right? If the Almighty Ruler of nations, with his eternal truth and justice, be on your side of the North, or on yours of the South, that truth, and that justice, will surely prevail, by the judgment of this great tribunal, the American people.

By the frame of the government under which we live, this same people have wisely given their public servants but little power for mischief; and have, with equal wisdom, provided for the return of that little to their own hands at very short intervals.

While the people retain their virtue, and vigilence, no administration, by any extreme of wickedness or folly, can very seriously injure the government, in the short space of four years.

My countrymen, one and all, think calmly and *well*, upon this whole subject. Nothing valuable can be lost by taking time. If there be an object to *hurry* any of you, in hot haste, to a step which you would never take *deliberately*, that object will be frustrated by taking time; but no good object can be frustrated by it. Such of you as are now dissatisfied, still have the old Constitution unimpaired, and, on the sensitive point, the laws of your own framing under it; while the new administration will have no immediate power, if it would, to change either. If it were admitted that you who are dissatisfied, hold the right side in the dispute, there still is no single good reason for precipitate action. Intelligence, patriotism, Christianity, and a firm reliance on Him, who has never yet forsaken this favored land, are still competent to adjust, in the best way, all our present difficulty.

In *your* hands, my dissatisfied fellow countrymen, and not in *mine*, is the momentous issue of civil war. The government will not assail *you*. You can have no conflict, without being yourselves the aggressors. *You* have no oath registered in Heaven to destroy the government, while *I* shall have the most solemn one to "preserve, protect and defend" it.

I am loth to close. We are not enemies, but friends. We must not be enemies. Though passion may have strained, it must not break our bonds of affection. The mystic chords of memory, streching from every battle-field, and patriot grave, to every heart and hearthstone, all over this broad land, will yet swell the chorus of the Union, when again touched, as surely they will be, by the better angels of our nature.

"To suppress said combinations"

Proclamation calling the militia, April 15, 1861

Consistently maintaining that the war was a domestic rebellion, the United States never formally declared war on the Confederacy. Instead, following the attack on Fort Sumter Lincoln called on the states to provide troops to put down what he designated as "combinations" in the South that were resisting federal authority. Underestimating the magnitude of the military challenge the Union confronted, Lincoln summoned only 75,000 troops to serve for three months. Like northern public opinion at the beginning of the war, Lincoln did not foresee how long and difficult the conflict would be. Four days later, he proclaimed a blockade of the southern coast.

Whereas the laws of the United States have been for some time past, and now are opposed, and the execution thereof obstructed, in the States of South Carolina, Georgia, Alabama, Florida, Mississippi, Louisiana and Texas, by combinations too powerful to be suppressed by the ordinary course of judicial proceedings, or by the powers vested in the Marshals by law,

Now therefore, I, Abraham Lincoln, President of the United States, in virtue of the power in me vested by the Constitution, and the laws, have thought fit to call forth, and hereby do call forth, the militia of the several States of the Union, to the aggregate number of seventy-five thousand, in order to suppress said combinations, and to cause the laws to be duly executed. The details, for this object, will be immediately communicated to the State authorities through the War Department.

I appeal to all loyal citizens to favor, facilitate and aid this effort to maintain the honor, the integrity, and the existence of our National

Union, and the perpetuity of popular government; and to redress wrongs already long enough endured.

I deem it proper to say that the first service assigned to the forces hereby called forth will probably be to re-possess the forts, places, and property which have been seized from the Union; and in every event, the utmost care will be observed, consistently with the objects aforesaid, to avoid any devastation, any destruction of, or interference with, property, or any disturbance of peaceful citizens in any part of the country.

And I hereby command the persons composing the combinations aforesaid to disperse, and retire peaceably to their respective abodes within twenty days from this date.

Deeming that the present condition of public affairs presents an extraordinary occasion, I do hereby, in virtue of the power in me vested by the Constitution, convene both Houses of Congress. Senators and Representatives are therefore summoned to assemble at their respective chambers, at 12 o'clock, noon, on Thursday, the fourth day of July, next, then and there to consider and determine, such measures, as, in their wisdom, the public safety, and interest may seem to demand.

"The most prompt, and efficient means"

Letter to Winfield Scott, April 25, 1861

As soon as the war began, Lincoln indicated that he intended to do whatever was necessary to preserve the Union, including exceeding his constitutional authority. In this letter, Lincoln authorized Winfield Scott, the commanding general of the Union army, to take vigorous action if Maryland tried to secede. Yet Lincoln's political sagacity was apparent in his instructions to do so only in response to acts, not threats and rumors. Contrary to Lincoln's fears, the legislature did not seriously consider secession. Still, the actions of Maryland citizens who sympathized with the Confederacy prompted Lincoln two days later to suspend the writ of habeas corpus in parts of the state.

Lieutenant General Scott   Washington

My dear Sir: The Maryland Legislature assembles to-morrow at Anapolis; and, not improbably, will take action to arm the people of that State against the United States. The question has been submitted to, and considered by me, whether it would not be justifiable, upon the ground of necessary defence, for you, as commander in Chief of the United States Army, to arrest, or disperse the members of that body. I think it would *not* be justifiable; nor, efficient for the desired object.

First, they have a clearly legal right to assemble; and, we can not know in advance, that their action will not be lawful, and peaceful. And if we wait until they shall *have* acted, their arrest, or dispersion, will not lessen the effect of their action.

Secondly, we *can* not permanently prevent their action. If we arrest them, we can not long hold them as prisoners; and when liberated, they will immediately re-assemble, and take their action. And, precisely the same if we simply disperse them. They will immediately re-assemble in some other place.

I therefore conclude that it is only left to the commanding General to watch, and await their action, which, if it shall be to arm their people against the United States, he is to adopt the most prompt, and efficient means to counteract, even, if necessary, to the bombardment of their cities—and in the extremest necessity, the suspension of the writ of habeas corpus. Your Obedient Servant

"A People's contest"

Message to Congress, July 4, 1861

Lincoln called Congress to meet in special session on July 4. In his message to Congress, he sought to rally northern public opinion to the war effort by placing the struggle in a larger ideological context. As he would repeatedly do throughout the conflict, he portrayed the war as a struggle to preserve democracy, not just in this country, but throughout the world. He justified the controversial steps he had taken since the war began as necessary to meet the crisis, secure in the knowledge that Congress had no choice but to ratify them.

And this issue embraces more than the fate of these United States. It presents to the whole family of man, the question, whether a constitutional republic, or a democracy—a government of the people, by the same people—can, or cannot, maintain its territorial integrity, against its own domestic foes. It presents the question, whether discontented individuals, too few in numbers to control administration, according to organic law, in any case, can always, upon the pretences made in this case, or on any other pretences, or arbitrarily, without any pretence, break up their Government, and thus practically put an end to free government upon the earth. It forces us to ask: "Is there, in all republics, this inherent, and fatal weakness?" "Must a government, of necessity, be too *strong* for the liberties of its own people, or too *weak* to maintain its own existence?"

So viewing the issue, no choice was left but to call out the war power of the Government; and so to resist force, employed for its destruction, by force, for its preservation. . . .

Other calls were made for volunteers, to serve three years, unless sooner discharged; and also for large additions to the regular Army and Navy. These measures, whether strictly legal or not, were ventured upon, under what appeared to be a popular demand, and a public necessity; trusting, then as now, that Congress would readily ratify them. It is believed that nothing has been done beyond the constitutional competency of Congress.

Soon after the first call for militia, it was considered a duty to authorize the Commanding General, in proper cases, according to his discretion, to suspend the privilege of the writ of habeas corpus; or, in other words, to arrest, and detain, without resort to the ordinary processes and forms of law, such individuals as he might deem dangerous to the public safety. This authority has purposely been exercised but very sparingly. Nevertheless, the legality and propriety of what has been done under it, are questioned; and the attention of the country has been called to the proposition that one who is sworn to "take care that the laws be faithfully executed," should not himself violate them. Of course some consideration was given to the questions of power, and propriety, before this matter was acted upon. The whole of the laws which were required to be faithfully executed, were being resisted, and failing of execution, in nearly one-third of the States. Must they be allowed to finally fail of execution, even had it been perfectly clear, that by the use of the means necessary to their execution, some single law, made in such extreme tenderness of the citizen's liberty, that practically, it relieves more of the guilty, than of the innocent, should, to a very limited extent, be violated? To state the question more directly, are all the laws, *but one*, to go unexecuted, and the government itself go to pieces, lest that one be violated? Even in such a case, would not the official oath be broken, if the government should be overthrown, when it was believed that disregarding the single law, would tend to preserve it? But it was not believed that this question was presented. It was not believed that any law was violated. The provision of the Constitution that "The privilege of the writ of habeas corpus, shall not be suspended unless when, in cases of rebellion or invasion, the public safety may require it," is equivalent to a provision—is a provision—that such privilege may be suspended when, in cases of rebellion, or invasion, the public safety *does* require it. It was decided that we have a case of rebellion, and that the public safety does require the qualified suspension of the privilege of the writ which was authorized to be made. Now it is insisted that Congress, and not the Executive, is vested with this power. But the Constitution itself, is silent as to which, or who, is to exercise the power; and as the provision was plainly made for a dangerous emergency, it cannot be believed the framers of the instrument intended, that in every case, the danger should run its course, until Congress could be called together; the very assembling of which might be prevented, as was intended in this case, by the rebellion. . . .

It might seem, at first thought, to be of little difference whether the present movement at the South be called "secession" or "rebellion." The movers, however, well understand the difference. At the beginning, they knew they could never raise their treason to any respectable magnitude, by any name which implies *violation* of law. They knew their people possessed as much of moral sense, as much of devotion to law and order, and as much pride in, and reverence for, the history, and government, of their common country, as any other civilized, and patriotic people. They knew they could make no advancement directly in the teeth of these strong and noble sentiments. Accordingly they commenced by an insidious debauching of the public mind. They invented an ingenious sophism, which, if conceded, was followed by perfectly logical steps, through all the incidents, to the complete destruction of the Union. The sophism itself is, that any state of the Union may, *consistently* with the national Constitution, and therefore *lawfully*, and *peacefully*, withdraw from the Union, without the consent of the Union, or of any other state. The little disguise that the supposed right is to be exercised only for just cause, themselves to be the sole judge of its justice, is too thin to merit any notice.

With rebellion thus sugar-coated, they have been drugging the public mind of their section for more than thirty years; and, until at length, they have brought many good men to a willingness to take up arms against the government the day *after* some assemblage of men have enacted the farcical pretence of taking their State out of the Union, who could have been brought to no such thing the day *before*.

This sophism derives much—perhaps the whole—of its currency, from the assumption, that there is some omnipotent, and sacred supremacy, pertaining to a *State*—to each State of our Federal Union. Our States have neither more, nor less power, than that reserved to them, in the Union, by the Constitution—no one of them ever having been a State *out* of the Union. The original ones passed into the Union even *before* they cast off their British colonial dependence; and the new ones each came into the Union directly from a condition of dependence, excepting Texas. And even Texas, in its temporary independence, was never designated a State. The new ones only took the designation of States, on coming into the Union, while that name was first adopted for the old ones, in, and by, the Declaration of Independence. Therein the "United Colonies" were declared to be "Free and Independent States"; but, even then, the object plainly was not to declare their independence of *one another*, or of the *Union*; but directly the contrary, as their mutual pledge, and their mutual action, before, at the time, and afterwards, abundantly show. The express plighting of faith, by each and all of the original thirteen, in the Articles of Confederation, two years later, that the Union shall be perpetual, is most conclusive. Having never been States, either in substance, or in name, *outside* of the Union, whence this magical omnipotence of "State rights," asserting a claim of power to lawfully destroy the Union itself? Much is said about the "sovereignty" of the States; but the word, even, is not in the national Constitution; nor, as is believed, in any of the State constitutions. What is a "sovereignty," in the political sense of the term? Would it be far wrong to define it "A political community, without a political superior"? Tested by this, no one of our States, except Texas, ever was a sovereignty. And even Texas gave up the character on coming into the Union; by which act, she acknowledged the Constitution of the United States, and the laws and treaties of the United States made in pursuance of the Constitution, to be, for her, the supreme law of the land. The States have their *status* IN the Union, and they have no other *legal status*. If they break from this, they can only do so against law, and by revolution. The Union, and not themselves separately, procured their independence, and their liberty. By conquest, or purchase, the Union gave each of them, whatever of independence, and liberty, it has. The Union is older than any of the States; and, in fact, it created them as States. Originally, some dependent colonies made the Union; and, in turn, the Union threw off their old dependence, for them, and made them States, such as they are. Not one of them ever had a State constitution, independent of the Union. Of course, it is not forgotten that all the new States framed their constitutions, before they entered the Union; nevertheless, dependent upon, and preparatory to, coming into the Union.

Unquestionably the States have the powers, and rights, reserved to them in, and by the National Constitution; but among these, surely, are not included all conceivable powers, however mischievous, or destructive; but, at most, such only, as were known in the world, at the time, as governmental powers; and certainly, a power to destroy the government itself, had never been known as a governmental—as a merely administrative power. This relative matter of National power, and State rights, as a principle, is no other than the principle of *generality*, and *locality*. Whatever concerns the whole, should be confided to the whole—to the general government; while, whatever concerns *only* the State, should be left exclusively, to the State. This is all there is of original principle about it. Whether the National Constitution, in defining boundaries between the two, has applied the principle with exact accuracy, is not to be questioned. We are all bound by that defining, without question.

What is now combatted, is the position that secession is *consistent* with the Constitution—is *lawful*, and *peaceful*. It is not contended that there is any express law for it; and nothing should ever be implied as law, which leads to unjust, or absurd consequences. The nation purchased, with money, the countries out of which several of these States were formed. Is it just that they shall go off without leave, and without refunding? The nation paid very large sums, (in the aggregate, I believe, nearly a hundred millions) to relieve Florida of the aboriginal tribes. Is it just that she shall now be off without consent, or without making any return? The nation is now in debt for money applied to the benefit of these so-called seceding States, in common with the rest. Is it just, either that creditors shall go unpaid, or the remaining States pay the whole? A part of the present national debt was contracted to pay the old debts of Texas. Is it just that she shall leave, and pay no part of this herself?

Again, if one State may secede, so may another; and when all shall have seceded, none is left to pay the debts. Is this quite just to creditors? Did we notify them of this sage view of ours, when we borrowed their money? If we now recognize this doctrine, by allowing the seceders to go in peace, it is difficult to see what we can do, if others choose to go, or to extort terms upon which they will promise to remain.

The seceders insist that our Constitution admits of secession. They have assumed to make a National Constitution of their own, in which, of necessity, they have either *discarded*, or *retained*, the right of secession, as they insist, it exists in ours. If they have discarded it, they thereby admit that, on principle, it ought not to be in ours. If they have retained it, by their own construction of ours they show that to be consistent they must secede from one another, whenever they shall find it the easiest way of settling their debts, or effecting any other selfish, or unjust object. The principle itself is one of disintegration, and upon which no government can possibly endure.

If all the States, save one, should assert the power to *drive* that one out of the Union, it is presumed the whole class of seceder politicians would at once deny the power, and denounce the act as the greatest outrage upon State rights. But suppose that precisely the same act, instead of being called "driving the one out," should be called "the seceding of the others from that one," it would be exactly what the seceders claim to do; unless, indeed, they make the point, that the one, because it is a minority, may rightfully do, what the others, because they are a majority, may not rightfully do. These politicians are subtle, and profound, on the rights of minorities. They are not partial to that power which made the Constitution, and speaks from the preamble, calling itself "We, the People."

It may well be questioned whether there is, to-day, a majority of the legally qualified voters of any State, except perhaps South Carolina, in favor of disunion. There is much reason to believe that the Union men are the majority in many, if not in every other one, of the so-called seceded States. The contrary has not been demonstrated in any one of them. It is ventured to affirm this, even of Virginia and Tennessee; for the result of an election, held in military camps, where the bayonets are all on one side of the question voted upon, can scarcely be considered as demonstrating popular sentiment. At such an election, all that large class who are, at once, *for* the Union, and *against* coercion, would be coerced to vote against the Union. . . .

This is essentially a People's contest. On the side of the Union, it is a struggle for maintaining in the world, that form, and substance of government, whose leading object is, to elevate the condition of men—to lift artificial weights from all shoulders—to clear the paths of laudable pursuit for all—to afford all, an unfettered start, and a fair chance, in the race of life. Yielding to partial, and temporary departures, from necessity, this is the leading object of the government for whose existence we contend.

I am most happy to believe that the plain people understand, and appreciate this. It is worthy of note, that while in this, the government's hour of trial, large numbers of those in the Army and Navy, who have been favored with the offices, have resigned, and proved false to the hand which had pampered them, not one common soldier, or common sailor is is known to have deserted his flag.

Great honor is due to those officers who remain true, despite the example of their treacherous associates; but the greatest honor, and most important fact of all, is the unanimous firmness of the common soldiers, and common sailors. To the last man, so far as known, they have successfully resisted the traitorous efforts of those, whose commands, but an hour before, they obeyed as absolute law. This is the patriotic instinct of the plain people. They understand, without an argument, that destroying the government, which was made by Washington, means no good to them.

Our popular government has often been called an experiment. Two points in it, our people have already settled—the successful *establishing*, and the successful *administering* of it. One still remains—its successful *maintenance* against a formidable internal attempt to overthrow it. It is now for them to demonstrate to the world, that those who can fairly carry an election, can also suppress a rebellion—that ballots are the rightful, and peaceful, successors of bullets; and that when ballots have fairly, and constitutionally, decided, there can be no successful appeal, back to bullets; that there can be no successful appeal, except to ballots themselves, at succeeding elections. Such will be a great lesson of peace; teaching men that what they cannot take by an election, neither can they take it by a war—teaching all, the folly of being the beginners of a war.

Lest there be some uneasiness in the minds of candid men, as to what is to be the course of the government, towards the Southern States, *after* the rebellion shall have been suppressed, the Executive deems it proper to say, it will be his purpose then, as ever, to be guided by the Constitution, and the laws; and that he probably will have no different understanding of the powers, and duties of the Federal government, relatively to the rights of the States, and the people, under the Constitution, than that expressed in the inaugural address.

He desires to preserve the government, that it may be administered for all, as it was administered by the men who made it. Loyal citizens everywhere, have the right to claim this of their government; and the government has no right to withhold, or neglect it. It is not perceived that, in giving it, there is any coercion, any conquest, or any subjugation, in any just sense of those terms.

The Constitution provides, and all the States have accepted the provision, that "The United States shall guarantee to every State in this Union a republican form of government." But, if a State may lawfully go out of the Union, having done so, it may also discard the republican form of government; so that to prevent its going out, is an indispensable *means*, to the *end*, of maintaining the guaranty mentioned; and when an end is lawful and obligatory, the indispensable means to it, are also lawful, and obligatory.

It was with the deepest regret that the Executive found the duty of employing the war-power, in defence of the government, forced upon him. He could but perform this duty, or surrender the existence of the government. No compromise, by public servants, could, in this case, be a cure; not that compromises are not often proper, but that no popular government can long survive a marked precedent, that those who carry an election, can only save the government from immediate destruction, by giving up the main point, upon which the people gave the election. The people themselves, and not their servants, can safely reverse their own deliberate decisions. As a private citizen, the Executive could not have consented that these institutions shall perish; much less could he, in betrayal of so vast, and so sacred a trust, as these free people had confided to him. He felt that he had no moral right to shrink; nor even to count the chances of his own life, in what might follow. In full view of his great responsibility, he has, so far, done what he has deemed his duty. You will now, according to your own judgment, perform yours. He sincerely hopes that your views, and your action, may so accord with his, as to assure all faithful citizens, who have been disturbed in their rights, of a certain, and speedy restoration to them, under the Constitution, and the laws.

And having thus chosen our course, without guile, and with pure purpose, let us renew our trust in God, and go forward without fear, and with manly hearts.

"Constantly drilled, disciplined, and instructed"

Memoranda of military policy suggested by the Bull Run defeat, July 23, 27, 1861

In the aftermath of the Union disaster at Bull Run, for which he bore significant responsibility, Lincoln drafted these memoranda outlining a series of steps Union military forces were to take. This document manifested Lincoln's new appreciation of the importance of raising and properly training a much larger army of long-term volunteers. His attention to western movements demonstrated the growing sophistication of his military thought even this early in the war.

1. Let the plan for making the Blockade effective be pushed forward with all possible despatch.

2. Let the volunteer forces at Fort-Monroe & vicinity—under Genl. Butler—be constantly drilled, disciplined, and instructed without more for the present.

3. Let Baltimore be held, as now, with a gentle, but firm, and certain hand.

4. Let the force now under Patterson, or Banks, be strengthened, and made secure in it's possition.

5. Let the forces in Western Virginia act, till further orders, according to instructions, or orders from Gen. McClellan.

6. [Let] Gen. Fremont push forward his organization, and operations in the West as rapidly as possible, giving rather special attention to Missouri.

7. Let the forces late before Manassas, except the three months men, be reorganized as rapidly as possible, in their camps here and about Arlington.

8. Let the three months forces, who decline to enter the longer service, be discharged as rapidly as circumstances will permit.

9. Let the new volunteer forces be brought forward as fast as possible; and especially into the camps on the two sides of the river here.

July 27, 1861

When the foregoing shall have been substantially attended to—

1. Let Manassas junction, (or some point on one or other of the railroads near it;); and Strasburg, be seized, and permanently held, with an open line from Washington to Manassas; and open line from Harper's Ferry to Strasburg—the military men to find the way of doing these.

2. This done, a joint movement from Cairo on Memphis; and from Cincinnati on East Tennessee.

"To conform to . . . the act of Congress"

Letter to John C. Frémont, September 2, 1861

Lincoln placed John C. Frémont, the Republican party's presidential nominee in 1856, in command of the Union forces in Missouri. Frémont was soon overwhelmed by the political and military problems he faced, and finally in an effort to restore control of the state, he issued a proclamation emancipating the slaves of disloyal residents and threatening to execute Confederate guerrillas. Lincoln asked the general to modify his proclamation to agree with the recently passed confiscation act, which freed only slaves who had been used by the Confederacy for military purposes, and when he refused, Lincoln revoked the emancipation edict on his own authority as commander-in-chief. Frémont was soon removed from command (in spite of what Lincoln says in the document following this one), but antislavery radicals strongly endorsed his policy, and in 1864 they nominated him for president as an independent Republican candidate, thereby threatening Lincoln's reelection.

Major General Fremont: Washington D.C.

My dear Sir: Two points in your proclamation of August 30th give me some anxiety. First, should you shoot a man, according to the proclamation, the Confederates would very certainly shoot our best man in their hands in retaliation; and so, man for man, indefinitely. It is therefore my order that you allow no man to be shot, under the proclamation, without first having my approbation or consent.

Secondly, I think there is great danger that the closing paragraph, in relation to the confiscation of property, and the liberating slaves of traiterous owners, will alarm our Southern Union friends, and turn them against us—perhaps ruin our rather fair prospect for Kentucky. Allow me therefore to ask, that you will as of your own motion, modify that paragraph so as to conform to the *first* and *fourth* sections of the act of Congress, entitled, "An act to confiscate property used for insurrectionary purposes," approved August, 6th, 1861, and a copy of which act I herewith send you. This letter is written in a spirit of caution and not of censure.

I send it by a special messenger, in order that it may certainly and speedily reach you. Yours very truly

"I cannot assume this reckless position"

Letter to Orville H. Browning, September 22, 1861

Lincoln's revocation of Frémont's emancipation order produced a flurry of protest in the North. Among those who strongly criticized the president was Senator Orville H. Browning of Illinois, a longtime political associate. Browning was rather conservative among Republicans, and as Lincoln's reply indicated, the president was taken aback by his criticism. In justifying his policy, Lincoln resorted to both constitutional and political arguments. Ironically, a year later Browning vigorously opposed Lincoln's decision to issue the Emancipation Proclamation.

Hon. O. H. Browning   Executive Mansion, Washington

My dear Sir

Yours of the 17th is just received; and coming from you, I confess it astonishes me. That you should object to my adhering to a law, which you had assisted in making, and presenting to me, less than a month before, is odd enough. But this is a very small part. Genl. Fremont's proclamation, as to confiscation of property, and the liberation of slaves, is *purely political*, and not within the range of *military* law, or necessity. If a commanding General finds a necessity to seize the farm of a private owner, for a pasture, an encampment, or a fortification, he has the right to do so, and to so hold it, as long as the necessity lasts; and this is within military law, because within military necessity. But to say the farm shall no longer belong to the owner, or his heirs forever; and this as well when the farm is not needed for military purposes as when it is, is purely political, without the savor of military law about it. And the same is true of slaves. If the General needs them, he can seize them, and use them; but when the need is past, it is not for him to fix their permanent future condition. That must be settled according to laws made by law-makers, and not by military proclamations. The proclamation in the point in question, is simply "dictatorship." It assumes that the general may do *anything* he pleases—confiscate the lands and free the slaves of *loyal* people, as well as of disloyal ones. And going the whole figure I have no doubt would be more popular with some thoughtless people, then that which has been done! But I cannot assume this reckless position; nor allow others to assume it on my responsibility. You speak of it as being the only means of *saving* the government. On the contrary it is itself the surrender of the government. Can it be pretended that it is any longer the government of the U.S.— any government of Constitution and laws,—wherein a General, or a President, may make permanent rules of property by proclamation?

I do not say Congress might not with propriety pass a law, on the point, just such as General Fremont proclaimed. I do not say I might not, as a member of Congress, vote for it. What I object to, is, that I as President, shall expressly or impliedly seize and exercise the permanent legislative functions of the government.

So much as to principle. Now as to policy. No doubt the thing was popular in some quarters, and would have been more so if it had been a general declaration of emancipation. The Kentucky Legislature would not budge till that proclamation was modified; and Gen. Anderson telegraphed me that on the news of Gen. Fremont having actually issued deeds of manumission, a whole company of our Volunteers threw down their arms and disbanded. I was so assured, as to think it probable, that the very arms we had furnished Kentucky would be turned against us. I think to lose Kentucky is nearly the same as to lose the whole game. Kentucky gone, we can not hold Missouri, nor, as I think, Maryland. These all against us, and the job on our hands is too large for us. We would as well consent to separation at once, including the surrender of this capitol. On the contrary, if you will give up your restlessness for new positions, and back me manfully on the grounds upon which you and other kind friends gave me the election, and have approved in my public documents, we shall go through triumphantly.

You must not understand I took my course on the proclamation *because* of Kentucky. I took the same ground in a private letter to General Fremont before I heard from Kentucky.

You think I am inconsistent because I did not also forbid Gen. Fremont to shoot men under the proclamation. I understand that part to be within military law; but I also think, and so privately wrote Gen. Fremont, that it is impolitic in this, that our adversaries have the power, and will certainly exercise it, to shoot as many of our men as we shoot of theirs. I did not say this in the public letter, because it is a subject I prefer not to discuss in the hearing of our enemies.

There has been no thought of removing Gen. Fremont on any ground connected with his proclamation; and if there has been any wish for his removal on any ground, our mutual friend Sam. Glover can probably tell you what it was. I hope no real necessity for it exists on any ground.

. . . Your friend as ever

"For a vast future also"

Message to Congress, December 3, 1861

In his message to Congress in December 1861 Lincoln reviewed his poli-
cies since the war began and used the occasion to set forth some basic
economic and political ideals before once again voicing the idea that the

war was a struggle, not just for the present, but for future generations as well. Lincoln's caution and conservatism were especially apparent in his expressed fear of the war becoming a revolution.

The war continues. In considering the policy to be adopted for suppressing the insurrection, I have been anxious and careful that the inevitable conflict for this purpose shall not degenerate into a violent and remorseless revolutionary struggle. I have, therefore, in every case, thought it proper to keep the integrity of the Union prominent as the primary object of the contest on our part, leaving all questions which are not of vital military importance to the more deliberate action of the legislature.

In the exercise of my best discretion I have adhered to the blockade of the ports held by the insurgents, instead of putting in force, by proclamation, the law of Congress enacted at the late session, for closing those ports.

So, also, obeying the dictates of prudence, as well as the obligations of law, instead of transcending, I have adhered to the act of Congress to confiscate property used for insurrectionary purposes. If a new law upon the same subject shall be proposed, its propriety will be duly considered.

The Union must be preserved, and hence, all indispensable means must be employed. We should not be in haste to determine that radical and extreme measures, which may reach the loyal as well as the disloyal, are indispensable.

The inaugural address at the beginning of the Administration, and the message to Congress at the late special session, were both mainly devoted to the domestic controversy out of which the insurrection and consequent war have sprung. Nothing now occurs to add or subtract, to or from, the principles or general purposes stated and expressed in those documents. . . .

It has been said that one bad general is better than two good ones; and the saying is true, if taken to mean no more than that an army is better directed by a single mind, though inferior, than by two superior ones, at variance, and cross-purposes with each other.

And the same is true, in all joint operations wherein those engaged, *can* have none but a common end in view, and *can* differ only as to the choice of means. In a storm at sea, no one on board *can* wish the ship to sink; and yet, not unfrequently, all go down together, because too many will direct, and no single mind can be allowed to control.

It continues to develop that the insurrection is largely, if not exclusively, a war upon the first principle of popular government—the rights of the people. Conclusive evidence of this is found in the most grave and maturely considered public documents, as well as in the general tone of the insurgents. In those documents we find the abridgement of the existing right of suffrage and the denial to the people of all right to participate in the selection of public officers, except the legislative boldly advocated, with labored arguments to prove that large control of the people in government, is the source of all political evil. Monarchy itself is sometimes hinted at as a possible refuge from the power of the people.

In my present position, I could scarcely be justified were I to omit raising a warning voice against this approach of returning despotism.

It is not needed, nor fitting here, that a general argument should be made in favor of popular institutions; but there is one point, with its connexions, not so hackneyed as most others, to which I ask a brief attention. It is the effort to place *capital* on an equal footing with, if not above *labor*, in the structure of government. It is assumed that labor is available only in connexion with capital; that nobody labors unless somebody else, owning capital, somehow by the use of it, induces him to labor. This assumed, it is next considered whether it is best that capital shall *hire* laborers, and thus induce them to work by their own consent, or *buy* them, and drive them to it without their consent. Having proceeded so far, it is naturally concluded that all laborers are either *hired* laborers, or what we call slaves. And further it is assumed that whoever is once a hired laborer, is fixed in that condition for life.

Now, there is no such relation between capital and labor as assumed; nor is there any such thing as a free man being fixed for life in the condition of a hired laborer. Both these assumptions are false, and all inferences from them are groundless.

Labor is prior to, and independent of, capital. Capital is only the fruit of labor, and could never have existed if labor had not first existed. Labor is the superior of capital, and deserves much the higher consideration. Capital has its rights, which are as worthy of protection as any other rights. Nor is it denied that there is, and probably always will be, a relation between labor and capital, producing mutual benefits. The error is in assuming that the whole labor of community exists within that relation. A few men own capital, and that few avoid labor themselves, and, with their capital, hire or buy another few to labor for them. A large majority belong to neither class—neither work for others, nor have others working for them. In most of the southern States, a majority of the whole people of all colors are neither slaves nor masters; while in the northern a large majority are neither hirers nor hired. Men with their families—wives, sons, and daughters—work for themselves, on their farms, in their houses, and in their shops, taking the whole product to themselves, and asking no favors of capital on the one hand, nor of hired laborers or slaves on the other. It is not forgotten that a considerable number of persons mingle their own labor with capital— that is, they labor with their own hands, and also buy or hire others to labor for them; but this is only a mixed, and not a distinct class. No principle stated is disturbed by the existence of this mixed class.

Again: as has already been said, there is not, of necessity, any such thing as the free hired laborer being fixed to that condition for life. Many independent men everywhere in these States, a few years back in their lives, were hired laborers. The prudent, penniless beginner in the world, labors for wages awhile, saves a surplus with which to buy tools or land for himself; then labors on his own account another while, and at length hires another new beginner to help him. This is the just, and generous, and prosperous system, which opens the way to all—gives hope to all, and consequent energy, and progress, and improvement of condition to all. No men living are more worthy to be trusted than those who toil up from poverty—none less inclined to take, or touch, aught which they have not honestly earned. Let them beware of surrendering a political power which they already possess, and which, if surrendered, will surely be used to close the door of advancement against such as they, and to fix new disabilities and burdens upon them, till all of liberty shall be lost.

From the first taking of our national census to the last are seventy years; and we find our population at the end of the period eight times as great as it was at the beginning. The increase of those other things which men deem desirable has been even greater. We thus have at one view, what the popular principle applied to government, through the machinery of the States and the Union, has produced in a given time;

and also what, if firmly maintained, it promises for the future. There are already among us those, who, if the Union be preserved, will live to see it contain two hundred and fifty millions. The struggle of today, is not altogether for today—it is for a vast future also. With a reliance on Providence, all the more firm and earnest, let us proceed in the great task which events have devolved upon us.

"Grumbling despatches and letters"

Letter to David Hunter, December 31, 1861

One of the constant aggravations Lincoln confronted as commander-in-chief was to deal with the complaints and petty jealousies of his generals. A good example was General David Hunter, who bombarded the president with letters expressing his unhappiness about his situation. Appealing to reason and the common good, Lincoln tried to soothe Hunter's wounded feelings, while at the same time making his displeasure clear.

Major General Hunter.   Executive Mansion, Washington

Dear Sir: Yours of the 23rd. is received; and I am constrained to say it is difficult to answer so ugly a letter in good temper. I am, as you intimate, losing much of the great confidence I placed in you, not from any act or omission of yours touching the public service, up to the time you were sent to Leavenworth, but from the flood of grumbling despatches and letters I have seen from you since. I knew you were being ordered to Leavenworth at the time it was done; and I aver that with as tender a regard for your honor and your sensibilities as I had for my own, it never occurred to me that you were being "humiliated, insulted and disgraced"; nor have I, up to this day, heard an intimation that you have been wronged, coming from any one but yourself. No one has blamed you for the retrograde movement from Springfield, nor for the information you gave Gen. Cameron; and this you could readily understand, if it were not for your unwarranted assumption that the ordering you to Leavenworth must necessarily have been done as a *punishment* for some *fault.* I thought then, and think yet, the position assigned to you is as respo[n]sible, and as honorable, as that assigned to Buell. I know that

Gen. McClellan expected more important results from it. My impression is that at the time you were assigned to the new Western Department, it had not been determined to re-place Gen. Sherman in Kentucky; but of this I am not certain, because the idea that a command in Kentucky was very desireable, and one in the farther West, very undesireable, had never occurred to me. You constantly speak of being placed in command of only 3000. Now tell me, is not this mere impatience? Have you not known all the while that you are to command four or five times that many?

I have been, and am sincerely your friend; and if, as such, I dare to make a suggestion, I would say you are adopting the best possible way to ruin yourself. "Act well your part, there all the honor lies." He who does *something* at the head of one Regiment, will eclipse him who does *nothing* at the head of a hundred. Your friend as ever,

IV

"*WE* CANNOT ESCAPE HISTORY"

1862

"Making *our* advantage an over-match for *his*"

Letter to Don Carlos Buell, January 13, 1862

This letter, written in early 1862 to Don Carlos Buell, who commanded a Union army in Tennessee, demonstrated how much Lincoln's ideas on military strategy had matured since the war started. He correctly noted that the Union had to find a way to bring its superior numbers to bear in the contest. His solution—a coordinated advance over a long front—was the essence of Grant's strategy in 1864. Lincoln's desire to liberate unionist East Tennessee from Confederate control would continue to be one of his major objectives in the western theater.

Brig. Genl. Buell. Executive Mansion, Washington

My dear Sir:

Your despatch of yesterday is received, in which you say "I have received your letter and Gen. McClellan's; and will, at once devote all my efforts to your views, and his." In the midst of my many cares, I have not seen, or asked to see, Gen. McClellan's letter to you. For my own views, I have not offered, and do not now offer them as orders; and while I am glad to have them respectfully considered, I would blame you to follow them contrary to your own clear judgment—unless I should put them in the form of orders. As to Gen. McClellan's views, you understand your duty in regard to them better than I do. With this preliminary, I state my general idea of this war to be that we have the *greater* numbers, and the enemy has the *greater* facility of concentrating forces upon points of collision; that we must fail, unless we can find some way of making *our* advantage an over-match for *his*; and that this can only be done by menacing him with superior forces at *different* points, at the *same* time; so that we can safely attack, one, or both, if he makes no change; and if he *weakens* one to *strengthen* the other, forbear to attack the strengthened one, but seize, and hold the weakened one, gaining so much. To illustrate, suppose last summer, when Winchester ran away to re-inforce Mannassas, we had forborne to attack Mannassas, but had seized and held Winchester. I mention this to illustrate, and not to criticise. I did not lose confidence in McDowell, and I think less harshly of Patterson than some others seem to. In application of the general rule I am suggesting, every particular case will have its modifying circumstances, among which the most constantly present, and most difficult to meet, will be the want of perfect knowledge of the enemies' movements. This had it's part in the Bull-Run case; but worse, in that case, was the expiration of the terms of the three months men. Applying the principle to your case, my idea is that Halleck shall menace Columbus, and "down river" generally; while you menace Bowling-Green, and East Tennessee. If the enemy shall concentrate at Bowling-Green, do not retire from his front; yet do not fight him there, either, but seize Columbus and East Tennessee, one or both, left exposed by the concentration at Bowling Green. It is matter of no small anxiety to me and one which I am sure you will not over-look, that the East Tennessee line, is so long, and over so bad a road. Yours very truly

"Gradual . . . emancipation, is better for all"

Message to Congress, March 6, 1862

In his annual message in December 1861, Lincoln had asked Congress to offer federal funds to any state that adopted a program of gradual emancipation. When Congress failed to act on this suggestion, he sent a special message urging approval of this proposal. In his message, he again avowed his preference for gradual, compensated emancipation by the states. In response Congress passed a joint resolution offering financial assistance to any state that adopted emancipation.

Fellow-citizens of the Senate, and House of Representatives,

I recommend the adoption of a Joint Resolution by your honorable bodies which shall be substantially as follows:

"Resolved that the United States ought to co-operate with any state which may adopt gradual abolishment of slavery, giving to such state pecuniary aid, to be used by such state in it's discretion, to compensate for the inconveniences public and private, produced by such change of system."

If the proposition contained in the resolution does not meet the approval of Congress and the country, there is the end; but if it does command such approval, I deem it of importance that the states and people immediately interested, should be at once distinctly notified of the fact, so that they may begin to consider whether to accept or reject it. The federal government would find it's highest interest in such a measure, as one of the most efficient means of self-preservation. The leaders of the existing insurrection entertain the hope that this government will ultimately be forced to acknowledge the independence of some part of the disaffected region, and that all the slave states North of such part will then say "the Union, for which we have struggled, being already gone, we now choose to go with the Southern section." To deprive them of this hope, substantially ends the rebellion; and the initiation of emancipation completely deprives them of it, as to all the states initiating it. The point is not that *all* the states tolerating slavery would very soon, if at all, initiate emancipation; but that, while the offer is equally made to all, the more Northern shall, by such initiation, make it certain to the more Southern, that in no event, will the former ever join the latter, in their proposed confederacy. I say "initiation" because, in my judgment, gradual, and not sudden emancipation, is better for all. In the mere financial, or pecuniary view, any member of Congress, with the census-tables and Treasury-reports before him, can readily see for himself how very soon the current expenditures of this war would purchase, at fair valuation, all the slaves in any named State. Such a proposition, on the part of the general government, sets up no claim of a right, by federal authority, to interfere with slavery within state limits, referring, as it does, the absolute control of the subject, in each case, to the state and it's people, immediately interested. It is proposed as a matter of perfectly free choice with them.

In the annual message last December, I thought fit to say "The Union must be preserved; and hence all indispensable means must be employed." I said this, not hastily, but deliberately. War has been made, and continues to be, an indispensable means to this end. A practical re-acknowledgement of the national authority would render the war unnecessary, and it would at once cease. If, however, resistance contin-ues, the war must also continue; and it is impossible to foresee all the incidents, which may attend and all the ruin which may follow it. Such as may seem indispensable, or may obviously promise great efficiency towards ending the struggle, must and will come.

The proposition now made, though an offer only, I hope it may be esteemed no offence to ask whether the pecuniary consideration ten-dered would not be of more value to the States and private persons concerned, than are the institution, and property in it, in the present aspect of affairs.

While it is true that the adoption of the proposed resolution would be merely initiatory, and not within itself a practical measure, it is rec-ommended in the hope that it would soon lead to important practical results. In full view of my great responsibility to my God, and to my country, I earnestly beg the attention of Congress and the people to the subject.

"But you must act"

Letter to George McClellan, April 9, 1862

Lincoln favored a direct movement against the Confederate army at Manassas, but McClellan proposed instead to transport his army by sea to the York peninsula and operate against Richmond from the east. In reluctantly acquiescing in McClellan's plan, the president stipulated that a sufficient force be left to protect Washington. When McClellan ignored this order, Lincoln held back part of the Army of the Potomac to make the capital secure. Once he arrived on the peninsula, McClellan's manifold shortcomings as a commander quickly became apparent. His pace was agonizingly slow, thereby allowing the Confederates to re-deploy their forces, and rather than attack the enemy, he constantly demanded reinforcements. Lincoln tried to impress upon McClellan that public opinion could not be ignored and that more vigorous action was necessary. This was a lesson that the obtuse McClellan never learned, which contributed to his eventual downfall.

Major General McClellan.   Washington

My dear Sir.

Your despatches complaining that you are not properly sustained, while they do not offend me, do pain me very much.

Blencker's Division was withdrawn from you before you left here; and you knew the pressure under which I did it, and, as I thought, acquiesced in it—certainly not without reluctance.

After you left, I ascertained that less than twenty thousand unorganized men, without a single field battery, were all you designed to be left for the defence of Washington, and Manassas Junction; and part of this even, was to go to Gen. Hooker's old position. Gen. Banks' corps, once designed for Manassas Junction, was diverted, and tied up on the line of Winchester and Strausburg, and could not leave it without again exposing the upper Potomac, and the Baltimore and Ohio Railroad. This presented, (or would present, when McDowell and Summer should be gone) a great temptation to the enemy to turn back from the Rappahanock, and sack Washington. My explicit order that Washington should, by the judgment of *all* the commanders of Army corps, be left entirely secure, had been neglected. It was precisely this that drove me to detain McDowell.

I do not forget that I was satisfied with your arrangement to leave Banks at Mannassas Junction; but when that arrangement was broken up, and *nothing* was substituted for it, of course I was not satisfied. I was constrained to substitute something for it myself. And now allow me to ask "Do you really think I should permit the line from Richmond, *via* Mannassas Junction, to this city to be entirely open, except what resistance could be presented by less than twenty thousand unorganized troops?" This is a question which the country will not allow me to evade.

There is a curious mystery about the *number* of the troops now with you. When I telegraphed you on the 6th. saying you had over a hundred thousand with you, I had just obtained from the Secretary of War, a statement, taken as he said, from your own returns, making 108,000 then with you, and *en route* to you. You now say you will have but

85,000, when all *en route* to you shall have reached you. How can the discrepancy of 23,000 be accounted for?

As to Gen. Wool's command, I understand it is doing for you precisely what a like number of your own would have to do, if that command was away.

I suppose the whole force which has gone forward for you, is with you by this time; and if so, I think it is the precise time for you to strike a blow. By delay the enemy will relatively gain upon you—that is, he will gain faster, by *fortifications* and *re-inforcements,* than you can by reinforcements alone.

And, once more let me tell you, it is indispensable to *you* that you strike a blow. *I* am powerless to help this. You will do me the justice to remember I always insisted, that going down the Bay in search of a field, instead of fighting at or near Mannassas, was only shifting, and not surmounting, a difficulty—that we would find the same enemy, and the same, or equal, intrenchments, at either place. The country will not fail to note—is now noting—that the present hesitation to move upon an intrenched enemy, is but the story of Manassas repeated.

I beg to assure you that I have never written you, or spoken to you, in greater kindness of feeling than now, nor with a fuller purpose to sustain you, so far as in my most anxious judgment, I consistently can. *But you must act.* Yours very truly

"Questions . . . I reserve to myself"

Proclamation revoking General Hunter's order of emancipation, May 19, 1862

In May 1862, General David Hunter issued a proclamation freeing the slaves in the military district of South Carolina, Georgia, and Florida (he actually controlled only very limited areas of these three states). As he had done earlier when General John C. Frémont had issued an emancipation edict, Lincoln intervened and overturned Hunter's order. In rescinding Hunter's decree, Lincoln made it clear that he would not allow his generals to determine political questions related to the prosecution of the war, which was his responsibility. Nevertheless, he hinted that the policy of emancipation might prove indispensable to subduing the rebellion and used the occasion to press the border states to end slavery.

I, Abraham Lincoln, president of the United States, proclaim and declare, that the government of the United States, had no knowledge, information, or belief, of an intention on the part of General Hunter to issue such a proclamation; nor has it yet, any authentic information that the document is genuine. And further, that neither General Hunter, nor any other commander, or person, has been authorized by the Government of the United States, to make proclamations declaring the slaves of any State free; and that the supposed proclamation, now in question, whether genuine or false, is altogether void, so far as respects such declaration.

I further make known that whether it be competent for me, as Commander-in-Chief of the Army and Navy, to declare the Slaves of any state or states, free, and whether at any time, in any case, it shall have become a necessity indispensable to the maintainance of the government, to exercise such supposed power, are questions which, under my responsibility, I reserve to myself, and which I can not feel justified in leaving to the decision of commanders in the field. These are totally different questions from those of police regulations in armies and camps.

On the sixth day of March last, by a special message, I recommended to Congress the adoption of a joint resolution to be substantially as follows:

Resolved, That the United States ought to co-operate with any State which may adopt a gradual abolishment of slavery, giving to such State pecuniary aid, to be used by such State in its discretion to compensate for the inconveniences, public and private, produced by such change of system.

The resolution, in the language above quoted, was adopted by large majorities in both branches of Congress, and now stands an authentic, definite, and solemn proposal of the nation to the States and people most immediately interested in the subject matter. To the people of those states I now earnestly appeal. I do not argue. I beseech you to make the arguments for yourselves. You can not if you would, be blind to the signs of the times. I beg of you a calm and enlarged consideration of them, ranging, if it may be, far above personal and partizan politics. This proposal makes common cause for a common object, casting no reproaches upon any. It acts not the pharisee. The change it contemplates would come gently as the dews of heaven, not rending or wrecking anything. Will you not embrace it? So much good has not been done, by one effort, in all past time, as, in the providence of God, it is now your high previlege to do. May the vast future not have to lament that you have neglected it.

"I expect to maintain this contest"

Letter to William H. Seward, June 28, 1862

As the Seven Days battles raged in Virginia, McClellan sent increasingly alarmist reports, yet Lincoln offered the following level-headed evaluation of the military situation. In it Lincoln made two critical points: first, because of the need to protect Washington, more troops were required before operations could resume in Virginia; and, second, the Union had a better opportunity to advance in the western theater. Already Lincoln grasped the crucial importance of opening the Mississippi and occupying east Tennessee, two goals that would continue to dominate his military thinking for more than a year. Seward used this letter to induce a conference of Union governors to publicly endorse the need for more troops. On July 1, Lincoln issued a call for 300,000 additional men.

Hon. W. H. Seward   Executive Mansion

My dear Sir

My view of the present condition of the War is about as follows:

The evacuation of Corinth, and our delay by the flood in the Chicahominy, has enabled the enemy to concentrate too much force in Richmond for McClellan to successfully attack. In fact there soon will be no substantial rebel force any where else. But if we send all the force from here to McClellan, the enemy will, before we can know of it, send a force from Richmond and take Washington. Or, if a large part of the Western Army be brought here to McClellan, they will let us have Richmond, and retake Tennessee, Kentucky, Missouri &c. What should be done is to hold what we have in the West, open the Mississippi, and, take Chatanooga & East Tennessee, without more—a reasonable force should, in every event, be kept about Washington for it's protection. Then let the country give us a hundred thousand new troops in the shortest possible time, which added to McClellan, directly or indirectly, will take Richmond, without endangering any other place which we now hold—and will substantially end the war. I expect to maintain this contest until successful, or till I die, or am conquered, or my term expires, or Congress or the country forsakes me; and I would publicly appeal to the country for this new force, were it not that I fear a general panic and stampede would follow—so hard is it to have a thing understood as it really is. I think the new force should be all, or nearly all infantry, principally because such can be raised most cheaply and quickly. Yours very truly

"The incidents of the war can not be avoided"

Appeal to the border state representatives, July 12, 1862

Lincoln believed that if the border states adopted emancipation, their action would shorten the war by ending Confederate hopes that these states would eventually join the Confederacy. Early in 1862 he met with the border state representatives, but they refused to endorse his program of state-sponsored emancipation. In July, after Congress had agreed to underwrite the cost of emancipation, he summoned these representatives to the White House for another meeting, in which he again appealed to them to endorse his program. Ignoring Lincoln's blunt warnings, the border state leaders rejected his proposal a second time.

Gentlemen. After the adjournment of Congress, now very near, I shall have no opportunity of seeing you for several months. Believing that you of the border-states hold more power for good than any other equal number of members, I feel it a duty which I can not justifiably waive, to make this appeal to you. I intend no reproach or complaint when I assure you that in my opinion, if you all had voted for the resolution in the gradual emancipation message of last March, the war would now be substantially ended. And the plan therein proposed is yet one of the most potent, and swift means of ending it. Let the states which are in rebellion see, definitely and certainly, that, in no event, will the states you represent ever join their proposed Confederacy, and they can not, much longer maintain the contest. But you can not divest them of their hope to ultimately have you with them so long as you show a determination to perpetuate the institution within your own states. Beat them at elections, as you have overwhelmingly done, and, nothing daunted, they still claim you as their own. You and I know what the lever of their power is. Break that lever before their faces, and they can shake you no more forever.

Most of you have treated me with kindness and consideration; and I trust you will not now think I improperly touch what is exclusively your own, when, for the sake of the whole country I ask "Can you, for your states, do better than to take the course I urge?["] Discarding *punctillio*, and maxims adapted to more manageable times, and looking only to the unprecedentedly stern facts of our case, can you do better in any possible event? You prefer that the constitutional relation of the states to the nation shall be practically restored, without disturbance of the institution; and if this were done, my whole duty, in this respect, under the constitution, and my oath of office, would be performed. But it is not done, and we are trying to accomplish it by war. The incidents of the war can not be avoided. If the war continue long, as it must, if the object be not sooner attained, the institution in your states will be extinguished by mere friction and abrasion—by the mere incidents of the war. It will be gone, and you will have nothing valuable in lieu of it. Much of it's value is gone already. How much better for you, and for your people, to take the step which, at once, shortens the war, and secures substantial compensation for that which is sure to be wholly lost in any other event. How much better to thus save the money which else we sink forever in the war. How much better to do it while we can, lest the war ere long render us pecuniarily unable to do it. How much better for you, as seller, and the nation as buyer, to sell out, and buy out, that without which the war could never have been, than to sink both the thing to be sold, and the price of it, in cutting one another's throats.

I do not speak of emancipation *at once*, but of a *decision* at once to emancipate *gradually*. Room in South America for colonization, can be obtained cheaply, and in abundance; and when numbers shall be large enough to be company and encouragement for one another, the freed people will not be so reluctant to go.

I am pressed with a difficulty not yet mentioned—one which threatens division among those who, united are none too strong. An instance of it is known to you. Gen. Hunter is an honest man. He was, and I hope, still is, my friend. I valued him none the less for his agreeing with me in the general wish that all men everywhere, could be free. He pro-

claimed all men free within certain states, and I repudiated the proclamation. He expected more good, and less harm from the measure, than
I could believe would follow. Yet in repudiating it, I gave dissatisfaction,
if not offence, to many whose support the country can not afford to
lose. And this is not the end of it. The pressure, in this direction, is still
upon me, and is increasing. By conceding what I now ask, you can
relieve me, and much more, can relieve the country, in this important
point. Upon these considerations I have again begged your attention to
the message of March last. Before leaving the Capital, consider and discuss it among yourselves. You are patriots and statesmen; and, as such, I
pray you, consider this proposition; and, at the least, commend it to the
consideration of your states and people. As you would perpetuate popular government for the best people in the world, I beseech you that
you do in no wise omit this. Our common country is in great peril,
demanding the loftiest views, and boldest action to bring it speedy
relief. Once relieved, it's form of government is saved to the world; it's
beloved history, and cherished memories, are vindicated; and it's happy
future fully assured, and rendered inconceivably grand. To you, more
than to any others, the previlege is given, to assure that happiness, and
swell that grandeur, and to link your own names therewith forever.

"Leaving any available card unplayed"

Letter to Reverdy Johnson, July 26, 1862

*As the war continued, Lincoln became increasingly impatient with
southern Unionists, who, he complained, demanded that the government not strike at its enemies "lest they be struck by accident." Lincoln
sent Senator Reverdy Johnson of Maryland to New Orleans to report on
the Union occupation of the city. Disagreeing with Johnson's assessment, Lincoln declared that if necessary, he would inflict harder blows.*

PRIVATE

Hon Reverdy Johnson   Executive Mansion, Washington

My Dear Sir. Yours of the 16th. by the hand of Governor Shepley is
received. It seems the Union feeling in Louisiana is being crushed out by
the course of General Phelps. Please pardon me for believing that is a

false pretense. The people of Louisiana—all intelligent people every where—know full well, that I never had a wish to touch the foundations of their society, or any right of theirs. With perfect knowledge of this, they forced a necessity upon me to send armies among them, and it is their own fault, not mine, that they are annoyed by the presence of General Phelps. They also know the remedy—know how to be cured of General Phelps. Remove the necessity of his presence. And might it not be well for them to consider whether they have not already had *time* enough to do this? If they can conceive of anything worse than General Phelps, within my power, would they not better be looking out for it? They very well know the way to avert all this is simply to take their place in the Union upon the old terms. If they will not do this, should they not receive harder blows rather than lighter ones?

You are ready to say I apply to *friends* what is due only to *enemies*. I distrust the *wisdom* if not the *sincerity* of friends, who would hold my hands while my enemies stab me. This appeal of professed friends has paralyzed me more in this struggle than any other one thing. You remember telling me the day after the Baltimore mob in April 1861, that it would crush all Union feeling in Maryland for me to attempt bringing troops over Maryland soil to Washington. I brought the troops notwithstanding, and yet there was Union feeling enough left to elect a Legislature the next autumn which in turn elected a very excellent Union U.S. Senator!

I am a patient man—always willing to forgive on the Christian terms of repentance; and also to give ample *time* for repentance. Still I must save this government if possible. What I *cannot* do, of course I *will* not do; but it may as well be understood, once for all, that I shall not surrender this game leaving any available card unplayed. Yours truly

"A single half-defeat"

Letter to Agénor-Etienne de Gasparin, August 4, 1862

After Robert E. Lee checked McClellan's advance toward Richmond and forced him to retreat to the James River, the Union commander refrained from resuming the offensive, so Lincoln ordered the Peninsula Campaign abandoned. McClellan's failure shocked northern public opinion, which had expected his summer campaign to end the war. In the West, however, Union arms had made significant gains, capturing the upper and lower reaches of the Mississippi and occupying most of Tennessee. Unlike many Northerners, Lincoln grasped the crucial importance of the western theater in the war, shown in this letter to a French liberal politician, author, and reformer who supported the Union.

Executive Mansion, Washington

Dear Sir: Your very acceptable letter dated Orbe Canton de Vaud, Switzerland 18th of July 1862 is received. The moral effect was the worst of the affair before Richmond; and that has run its course downward; we are now at a stand, and shall soon be rising again, as we hope. I believe it is true that in men and material, the enemy suffered more than we, in that series of conflicts; while it is certain he is less able to bear it.

With us every soldier is a man of character and must be treated with more consideration than is customary in Europe. Hence our great army for slighter causes than could have prevailed there has dwindled rapidly, bringing the necessity for a new call, earlier than was anticipated. We shall easily obtain the new levy, however. Be not alarmed if you shall learn that we shall have resorted to a draft for part of this. It seems strange, even to me, but it is true, that the Government is now pressed to this course by a popular demand. Thousands who wish not to personally enter the service are nevertheless anxious to pay and send substitutes, provided they can have assurance that unwilling persons similarly situated will be compelled to do like wise. Besides this, volunteers mostly choose to enter newly forming regiments, while drafted men can be sent to fill up the old ones, wherein, man for man, they are quite doubly as valuable.

You ask "why is it that the North with her great armies, so often is found, with inferiority of numbers, face to face with the armies of the South?" While I painfully know the fact, a military man, which I am not, would better answer the question. The fact I know, has not been overlooked; and I suppose the cause of its continuance lies mainly in the other facts that the enemy holds the interior, and we the exterior lines; and that we operate where the people convey information to the enemy, while he operates where they convey none to us. . . .

You are quite right, as to the importance to us, for its bearing upon Europe, that we should achieve military successes; and the same is true for us at home as well as abroad. Yet it seems unreasonable that a series of successes, extending through half-a-year, and clearing more than a hundred thousand square miles of country, should help us so little, while a single half-defeat should hurt us so much. But let us be patient.

I am very happy to know that my course has not conflicted with your judgement, of propriety and policy.

I can only say that I have acted upon my best convictions without self-ishness or malice, and that by the help of God, I shall continue to do so.

Please be assured of my highest respect and esteem.

"The ban is still upon you"

Address on colonization, August 14, 1862

In the summer of 1862, as he neared an announcement on emancipation, Lincoln met with a group of free black leaders to urge them to promote the idea of colonization. African Americans had little interest in colonization, and the project Lincoln outlined in his remarks failed miserably (he sent the navy to bring back the survivors in 1864). While he had long supported voluntary colonization, the Caribbean experiment was designed to make emancipation more acceptable to northern whites. Lincoln spent only a small portion of the money Congress appropriated for this project, and once he issued the Emancipation Proclamation, he lost interest in colonization.

This afternoon the President of the United States gave audience to a Committee of colored men at the White House. They were introduced by the Rev. J. Mitchell, Commissioner of Emigration. E. M. Thomas, the Chairman, remarked that they were there by invitation to hear what the Executive had to say to them. Having all been seated, the President, after a few preliminary observations, informed them that a sum of money had been appropriated by Congress, and placed at his disposi-tion for the purpose of aiding the colonization in some country of the people, or a portion of them, of African descent, thereby making it his duty, as it had for a long time been his inclination, to favor that cause; and why, he asked, should the people of your race be colonized, and where? Why should they leave this country? This is, perhaps, the first question for proper consideration. You and we are different races. We have between us a broader difference than exists between almost any other two races. Whether it is right or wrong I need not discuss, but this physical difference is a great disadvantage to us both, as I think your race suffer very greatly, many of them by living among us, while ours suffer from your presence. In a word we suffer on each side. If this is admitted, it affords a reason at least why we should be separated. You here are freemen I suppose.

A Voice: Yes, sir.

The President—Perhaps you have long been free, or all your lives. Your race are suffering, in my judgment, the greatest wrong inflicted on any people. But even when you cease to be slaves, you are yet far removed from being placed on an equality with the white race. You are cut off from many of the advantages which the other race enjoy. The aspiration of men is to enjoy equality with the best when free, but on this broad continent, not a single man of your race is made the equal of a single man of ours. Go where you are treated the best, and the ban is still upon you.

I do not propose to discuss this, but to present it as a fact with which we have to deal. I cannot alter it if I would. It is a fact, about which we all think and feel alike, I and you. We look to our condition, owing to the existence of the two races on this continent. I need not recount to you the effects upon white men, growing out of the institution of Slavery. I believe in its general evil effects on the white race. See our present condition—the country engaged in war!—our white men cutting one another's throats, none knowing how far it will extend; and then consider what we know to be the truth. But for your race among us there could not be war, although many men engaged on either side do not care for you one way or the other. Nevertheless, I repeat, without the institution of Slavery and the colored race as a basis, the war could not have an existence.

It is better for us both, therefore, to be separated. I know that there are free men among you, who even if they could better their condition are not as much inclined to go out of the country as those, who being slaves could obtain their freedom on this condition. I suppose one of the principal difficulties in the way of colonization is that the free colored man cannot see that his comfort would be advanced by it. You may believe you can live in Washington or elsewhere in the United States the remainder of your life [as easily], perhaps more so than you can in any foreign country, and hence you may come to the conclusion that you have nothing to do with the idea of going to a foreign country. This is (I speak in no unkind sense) an extremely selfish view of the case.

But you ought to do something to help those who are not so fortunate as yourselves. There is an unwillingness on the part of our people, harsh as it may be, for you free colored people to remain with us. Now, if you could give a start to white people, you would open a wide door for many to be made free. If we deal with those who are not free at the beginning, and whose intellects are clouded by Slavery, we have very poor materials to start with. If intelligent colored men, such as are before me, would move in this matter, much might be accomplished. It is exceedingly important that we have men at the beginning capable of thinking as white men, and not those who have been systematically oppressed.

There is much to encourage you. For the sake of your race you should sacrifice something of your present comfort for the purpose of being as grand in that respect as the white people. It is a cheering thought throughout life that something can be done to ameliorate the condition of those who have been subject to the hard usage of the world. . . .

The colony of Liberia has been in existence a long time. In a certain sense it is a success. The old President of Liberia, Roberts, has just been with me—the first time I ever saw him. He says they have within the bounds of that colony between 300,000 and 400,000 people, or more than in some of our old States, such as Rhode Island or Delaware, or in some of our newer States, and less than in some of our larger ones. They are not all American colonists, or their descendants. Something less than 12,000 have been sent thither from this country. Many of the original settlers have died, yet, like people elsewhere, their offspring outnumber those deceased.

The question is if the colored people are persuaded to go anywhere, why not there? One reason for an unwillingness to do so is that some of you would rather remain within reach of the country of your nativity. I do not know how much attachment you may have toward our race. It does not strike me that you have the greatest reason to love them. But still you are attached to them at all events.

The place I am thinking about having for a colony is in Central America. It is nearer to us than Liberia—not much more than one-fourth as far as Liberia, and within seven days' run by steamers. Unlike

Liberia it is on a great line of travel—it is a highway. The country is a very excellent one for any people, and with great natural resources and advantages, and especially because of the similarity of climate with your native land—thus being suited to your physical condition.

The particular place I have in view is to be a great highway from the Atlantic or Caribbean Sea to the Pacific Ocean, and this particular place has all the advantages for a colony. On both sides there are harbors among the finest in the world. Again, there is evidence of very rich coal mines. A certain amount of coal is valuable in any country, and there may be more than enough for the wants of the country. Why I attach so much importance to coal is, it will afford an opportunity to the inhabitants for immediate employment till they get ready to settle permanently in their homes. . . .

. . . You are intelligent, and know that success does not as much depend on external help as on self-reliance. Much, therefore, depends upon yourselves. As to the coal mines, I think I see the means available for your self-reliance.

I shall, if I get a sufficient number of you engaged, have provisions made that you shall not be wronged. If you will engage in the enterprise I will spend some of the money intrusted to me. I am not sure you will succeed. The Government may lose the money, but we cannot succeed unless we try; but we think, with care, we can succeed.

The political affairs in Central America are not in quite as satisfactory condition as I wish. There are contending factions in that quarter; but it is true all the factions are agreed alike on the subject of colonization, and want it, and are more generous than we are here. To your colored race they have no objection. Besides, I would endeavor to have you made equals, and have the best assurance that you should be the equals of the best.

The practical thing I want to ascertain is whether I can get a number of able-bodied men, with their wives and children, who are willing to go, when I present evidence of encouragement and protection. Could I get a hundred tolerably intelligent men, with their wives and children, to "cut their own fodder," so to speak? Can I have fifty? If I could find twenty-five able-bodied men, with a mixture of women and children, good things in the family relation, I think I could make a successful commencement.

I want you to let me know whether this can be done or not. This is the practical part of my wish to see you. These are subjects of very great importance, worthy of a month's study, [instead] of a speech delivered in an hour. I ask you then to consider seriously not pertaining to yourselves merely, nor for your race, and ours, for the present time, but as one of the things, if successfully managed, for the good of mankind—not confined to the present generation, but as

> "From age to age descends the lay,
>   To millions yet to be,
>   Till far its echoes roll away,
>   Into eternity."

The above is merely given as the substance of the President's remarks.

The Chairman of the delegation briefly replied that "they would hold a consultation and in a short time give an answer." The President said: "Take your full time—no hurry at all."

"I would save the Union"

Letter to Horace Greeley, August 22, 1862

Horace Greeley was a longtime antislavery advocate and editor of the New York Tribune, *perhaps the most influential Republican newspaper in the country. In the summer of 1862, he published an editorial, which he titled "The Prayer of Twenty Millions," calling on Lincoln to attack slavery as part of the war effort. Lincoln replied in a letter that was widely published throughout the North. Although in his letter Lincoln placed paramount importance on the Union, its purpose was to prepare northern public opinion for a change in policy on slavery. Indeed, Lincoln had already circulated in the cabinet a draft of a proposed proclamation of emancipation.*

Hon. Horace Greely: Executive Mansion, Washington

Dear Sir

I have just read yours of the 19th. addressed to myself through the New-York Tribune. If there be in it any statements, or assumptions of fact, which I may know to be erroneous, I do not, now and here, controvert them. If there be in it any inferences which I may believe to be falsely drawn, I do not now and here, argue against them. If there be perceptable in it an impatient and dictatorial tone, I waive it in deference to an old friend, whose heart I have always supposed to be right.

As to the policy I "seem to be pursuing" as you say, I have not meant to leave any one in doubt.

I would save the Union. I would save it the shortest way under the Constitution. The sooner the national authority can be restored; the nearer the Union will be "the Union as it was." If there be those who would not save the Union, unless they could at the same time *save* slavery, I do not agree with them. If there be those who would not save the Union unless they could at the same time *destroy* slavery, I do not agree with them. My paramount object in this struggle *is* to save the Union, and is *not* either to save or to destroy slavery. If I could save the Union without freeing *any* slave I would do it, and if I could save it by freeing *all* the slaves I would do it; and if I could save it by freeing some and leaving others alone I would also do that. What I do about slavery, and the colored race, I do because I believe it helps to save the Union; and what I forbear, I forbear because I do *not* believe it would help to save the Union. I shall do *less* whenever I shall believe what I am doing hurts the cause, and I shall do *more* whenever I shall believe doing more will help the cause. I shall try to correct errors when shown to be errors; and I shall adopt new views so fast as they shall appear to be true views.

I have here stated my purpose according to my view of *official* duty; and I intend no modification of my oft-expressed *personal* wish that all men every where could be free. Yours,

"The will of God prevails"

Meditation on divine will, September 2?, 1862

The war deepened Lincoln's sense of fatalism. Sometime in September 1862, probably following the Union defeat in the Second Battle of Bull Run, he penned the following reflection on divine will and the war. It was at this time that Lincoln's spirits reached their lowest point. Lincoln considered it important that his actions be in accord with God's intentions, but unlike his self-righteous critics, he believed discerning divine will was not easy.

The will of God prevails. In great contests each party claims to act in accordance with the will of God. Both *may* be, and one *must* be wrong. God can not be *for*, and *against* the same thing at the same time. In the present civil war it is quite possible that God's purpose is something different from the purpose of either party—and yet the human instru-mentalities, working just as they do, are of the best adaptation to effect His purpose. I am almost ready to say this is probably true—that God wills this contest, and wills that it shall not end yet. By his mere quiet power, on the minds of the now contestants, He could have either *saved* or *destroyed* the Union without a human contest. Yet the contest began. And having begun He could give the final victory to either side any day. Yet the contest proceeds.

"Shall be . . . thenceforward, and forever free"

Preliminary Emancipation Proclamation, September 22, 1862

Lincoln issued the preliminary Emancipation Proclamation on Septem-ber 22, 1862, following the Union victory at Antietam. The preliminary proclamation gave the seceded states 100 days to return to their loyalty, after which he would issue a proclamation freeing the slaves in those areas still in rebellion. Lincoln's strategy was to give northern opinion time to adjust to this new policy, while placing responsibility for its implementation on the Confederate states. His allusion to colonization was also intended to make emancipation more palatable to Northerners. The preliminary proclamation represented a significant turning point in the Civil War, as well as a major escalation of the Union's war strategy.

I, Abraham Lincoln, President of the United States of America, and Commander-in-chief of the Army and Navy thereof, do hereby proclaim and declare that hereafter, as heretofore, the war will be prossecuted for the object of practically restoring the constitutional relation between the United States, and each of the states, and the people thereof, in which states that relation is, or may be suspended, or disturbed.

That it is my purpose, upon the next meeting of Congress to again recommend the adoption of a practical measure tendering pecuniary aid to the free acceptance or rejection of all slave-states, so called, the people whereof may not then be in rebellion against the United States, and which states, may then have voluntarily adopted, or thereafter may voluntarily adopt, immediate, or gradual abolishment of slavery within their respective limits; and that the effort to colonize persons of African descent, with their consent, upon this continent, or elsewhere, with the previously obtained consent of the Governments existing there, will be continued.

That on the first day of January in the year of our Lord, one thousand eight hundred and sixty-three, all persons held as slaves within any state, or designated part of a state, the people whereof shall then be in rebellion against the United States shall be then, thenceforward, and forever free; and the executive government of the United States, including the military and naval authority thereof, will recognize and maintain the freedom of such persons, and will do no act or acts to repress such persons, or any of them, in any efforts they may make for their actual freedom.

That the executive will, on the first day of January aforesaid, by proclamation, designate the States, and parts of states, if any, in which the people thereof respectively, shall then be in rebellion against the United States; and the fact that any state, or the people thereof shall, on that day be, in good faith represented in the Congress of the United States, by members chosen thereto, at elections wherein a majority of the qualified voters of such state shall have participated, shall, in the absence of strong countervailing testimony, be deemed conclusive evidence that such state and the people thereof, are not then in rebellion against the United States. . . .

And the executive will in due time recommend that all citizens of the United States who shall have remained loyal thereto throughout the rebellion, shall (upon the restoration of the constitutional relation between the United States, and their respective states, and people, if that relation shall have been suspended or disturbed) be compensated for all losses by acts of the United States, including the loss of slaves.

"The Writ of Habeas Corpus is suspended"

Proclamation, September 24, 1862

Shortly after issuing the preliminary Emancipation Proclamation, Lincoln suspended the writ of habeas corpus throughout the North for the

duration of the war. In addition, for the first time he authorized mili-
tary trials of civilians accused of disloyalty practices.

Whereas, it has become necessary to call into service not only volunteers but also portions of the militia of the States by draft in order to
suppress the insurrection existing in the United States, and disloyal persons are not adequately restrained by the ordinary processes of law
from hindering this measure and from giving aid and comfort in various ways to the insurrection;

Now, therefore, be it ordered, first, that during the existing insurrection and as a necessary measure for suppressing the same, all Rebels and
Insurgents, their aiders and abettors within the United States, and all persons discouraging volunteer enlistments, resisting militia drafts, or guilty
of any disloyal practice, affording aid and comfort to Rebels against the
authority of the United States, shall be subject to martial law and liable
to trial and punishment by Courts Martial or Military Commission:

Second. That the Writ of Habeas Corpus is suspended in respect to
all persons arrested, or who are now, or hereafter during the rebellion
shall be, imprisoned in any fort, camp, arsenal, military prison, or other
place of confinement by any military authority or by the sentence of
any Court Martial or Military Commission.

"Breath alone kills no rebels"

Letter to Hannibal Hamlin, September 28, 1862

When Lincoln issued the preliminary Emancipation Proclamation, Vice
President Hannibal Hamlin wrote offering his congratulations for what
he termed a "noble act." Lincoln was worried about the reaction to the
Proclamation, and the initial northern response was mixed. His reply to
Hamlin was rather downcast.

(STRICTLY PRIVATE.)

Executive Mansion, Washington

My Dear Sir: Your kind letter of the 25th is just received. It is known to
some that while I hope something from the proclamation, my expectations are not as sanguine as are those of some friends. The time for its

effect southward has not come; but northward the effect should be instantaneous.

It is six days old, and while commendation in newspapers and by distinguished individuals is all that a vain man could wish, the stocks have declined, and troops come forward more slowly than ever. This, looked soberly in the face, is not very satisfactory. We have fewer troops in the field at the end of six days than we had at the beginning—the attrition among the old outnumbering the addition by the new. The North responds to the proclamation sufficiently in breath; but breath alone kills no rebels.

I wish I could write more cheerfully; nor do I thank you the less for the kindness of your letter. Yours very truly,

"If we never try, we shall never succeed"

Letter to George McClellan, October 13, 1862

After the Battle of Antietam, Lincoln wanted McClellan to vigorously pursue the Army of Northern Virginia, but, as usual, McClellan ignored the urgency of time and moved so slowly Lee escaped. This outcome marked the end of McClellan's tenure as commander, and also Lincoln's concern about capturing Richmond. For the remainder of the war, Lincoln considered the destruction of Lee's army the main objective of the fighting in Virginia. As he became a more skilled strategist, Lincoln increasingly discarded McClellan's concept of a war of maneuver and occupation.

Major General McClellan   Executive Mansion, Washington

My dear Sir

You remember my speaking to you of what I called your over-cautiousness. Are you not over-cautious when you assume that you can not do what the enemy is constantly doing? Should you not claim to be at least his equal in prowess, and act upon the claim?

As I understand, you telegraph Gen. Halleck that you can not subsist your army at Winchester unless the Railroad from Harper's Ferry to that point be put in working order. But the enemy does now subsist his army at Winchester at a distance nearly twice as great from railroad transportation as you would have to do without the railroad last named. He now wagons from Culpepper C.H. which is just about twice as far as you would have to do from Harper's Ferry. He is certainly not more than half as well provided with wagons as you are. I certainly should be pleased for you to have the advantage of the Railroad from Harper's Ferry to Winchester, but it wastes all the remainder of autumn to give it to you; and, in fact ignores the question of *time*, which can not, and must not be ignored.

Again, one of the standard maxims of war, as you know, is "to operate upon the enemy's communications as much as possible without exposing your own." You seem to act as if this applies *against* you, but can not apply in your *favor*. Change positions with the enemy, and think you not he would break your communication with Richmond within the next twentyfour hours? You dread his going into Pennsylvania. But if he does so in full force, he gives up his communications to you absolutely, and you have nothing to do but to follow, and ruin him; if he does so with less than full force, fall upon, and beat what is left behind all the easier.

Exclusive of the water line, you are now nearer Richmond than the enemy is by the route that you *can*, and he *must* take. Why can you not reach there before him, unless you admit that he is more than your equal on a march. His route is the arc of a circle, while yours is the chord. The roads are as good on yours as on his.

You know I desired, but did not order, you to cross the Potomac below, instead of above the Shenandoah and Blue Ridge. My idea was that this would at once menace the enemies' communications, which I would seize if he would permit. If he should move Northward I would follow him closely, holding his communications. If he should prevent our seizing his communications, and move towards Richmond, I would press closely to him, fight him if a favorable opportunity should present, and, at least, try to beat him to Richmond on the inside track. I say "try"; if we never try, we shall never succeed. If he make a stand at Winchester, moving neither North or South, I would fight him there, on the idea that if we can not beat him when he bears the wastage of coming to us, we never can when we bear the wastage of going to him. This proposition is a simple truth, and is too important to be lost sight of for a moment. In coming to us, he tenders us an advantage which we should not waive. We should not so operate as to merely drive him away. As we must beat him somewhere, or fail finally, we can do it, if at all, easier near to us, than far away. If we can not beat the enemy where he now is, we never can, he again being within the entrenchments of Richmond.

Recurring to the idea of going to Richmond on the inside track, the facility of supplying from the side away from the enemy is remarkable —as it were, by the different spokes of a wheel extending from the hub towards the rim—and this whether you move directly by the chord, or on the inside arc, hugging the Blue Ridge more closely. The chord-line, as you see, carries you by Aldie, Hay-Market, and Fredericksburg; and you see how turn-pikes, railroads, and finally, the Potomac by Acquia Creek, meet you at all points from Washington. The same, only the lines lengthened a little, if you press closer to the Blue Ridge part of the way. The gaps through the Blue Ridge I understand to be about the following distances from Harper's Ferry, towit: Vestal's five miles; Gregorie's, thirteen, Snicker's eighteen, Ashby's, twenty-eight, Mannassas, thirty-eight, Chester fortyfive, and Thornton's fifty-three. I should think it preferable to take the route nearest the enemy, disabling him to make an important move without your knowledge, and compelling him to keep his forces together, for dread of you. The gaps would enable you to attack if you should wish. For a great part of the way, you would be practically between the enemy and both Washington and Richmond, enabling us to spare you the greatest number of troops from here. When at length, running for Richmond ahead of him enables him to move this way; if he does so, turn and attack him in rear. But I think he should be engaged long before such point is reached. It is all easy if our troops march as well as the enemy; and it is unmanly to say they can not do it.

This letter is in no sense an order. Yours truly

"I do not see that their superiority of success has been so marked"

Letter to Carl Schurz, November 10, 1862

The Republicans suffered a serious setback in the 1862 state and congressional elections. The German-American leader Carl Schurz blamed this result on Lincoln's policies, particularly that of giving Democrats mili-

tary commands. Lincoln in his reply was unable to completely hide his
exasperation at such criticism. His observation about the relative suc-
cess of Republican and Democratic generals was especially apt, as
Schurz, who owed his appointment entirely to political considerations,
had compiled a rather mediocre record as a Union general.

"PRIVATE & CONFIDENTIAL"

Gen. Schurz.   Executive Mansion, Washington

My dear Sir

Yours of the 8th. was, to-day, read to me by Mrs. S[churz]. We have lost the elections; and it is natural that each of us will believe, and say, it has been because his peculiar views was not made sufficiently prominent. I think I know what it was, but I may be mistaken. Three main causes told the whole story. 1. The democrats were left in a majority by our friends going to the war. 2. The democrats observed this & determined to re-instate themselves in power, and 3. Our newspaper's, by vilifying and disparaging the administration, furnished them all the weapons to do it with. Certainly, the ill-success of the war had much to do with this.

You give a different set of reasons. If you had not made the following statements, I should not have suspected them to be true. "The defeat of the administration is the administrations own fault." (opinion) "It admitted its professed opponents to its counsels" (Asserted as a fact) "It placed the Army, now a great power in this Republic, into the hands of its' enemys" (Asserted as a fact) "In all personal questions, to be hostile to the party of the Government, seemed, to be a title to consideration." (Asserted as a fact) "If to forget the great rule, that if you are true to your friends, your friends will be true to you, and that you make your enemies stronger by placing them upon an equality with your friends." "Is it surprising that the opponents of the administration should have got into their hands the government of the principal states, after they have had for a long time the principal management of the war, the great business of the national government."

I can not dispute about the matter of opinion. On the three matters (stated as facts) I shall be glad to have your evidence upon them when I shall meet you. The plain facts, as they appear to me, are these. The administration came into power, very largely in a minority of the popular vote. Notwithstanding this, it distributed to it's party friends as nearly all the civil patronage as any administration ever did. The war came. The administration could not even start in this, without assistance outside of it's party. It was mere nonsense to suppose a minority could put down a majority in rebellion. Mr. Schurz (now Gen. Schurz) was about here then & I do not recollect that he then considered all who were not republicans, were enemies of the government, and that none of them must be appointed to military positions. He will correct me if I am mistaken. It so happened that very few of our friends had a military education or were of the profession of arms. It would have been a question whether the war should be conducted on military knowledge, or on political affinity, only that our own friends (I think Mr. Schurz included) seemed to think that such a question was inadmissible. Accordingly I have scarcely appointed a democrat to a command, who was not urged by many republicans and opposed by none. It was so as to McClellan. He was first brought forward by the Republican Governor of Ohio, & claimed, and contended for at the same time by the Republican Governor of Pennsylvania. I received recommendations from the republican delegations in congress, and I believe every one of them recommended a majority of democrats. But, after all many Republicans were appointed; and I mean no disparagement to them when I say I do not see that their superiority of success has been so marked as to throw great suspicion on the good faith of those who are not Republicans. Yours truly,

"The last best, hope of earth"

Message to Congress, December 1, 1862

In his December 1862 message to Congress, Lincoln once again took up the question of the larger meaning of the war. Attributing the war to the existence of slavery, Lincoln advocated a program of gradual, compensated, state-sponsored emancipation as the means to shorten the war and assure future domestic harmony. He proposed three constitutional amendments: to provide federal funds to any state that abolished slavery by 1900; to compensate owners for slaves freed by "the chances of war"; and to colonize "free colored persons, with their own consent" outside the United States. In the final paragraph, Lincoln's eloquence burst forth as he called on his fellow Americans to confront the challenges posed by the war and slavery.

A nation may be said to consist of its territory, its people, and its laws. The territory is the only part which is of certain durability. "One generation passeth away, and another generation cometh, but the earth abideth forever." It is of the first importance to duly consider, and estimate, this ever-enduring part. That portion of the earth's surface which is owned and inhabited by the people of the United States, is well adapted to be the home of one national family; and it is not well adapted for two, or more. Its vast extent, and its variety of climate and productions, are of advantage, in this age, for one people, whatever they might have been in former ages. Steam, telegraphs, and intelligence, have brought these, to be an advantageous combination, for one united people.

In the inaugural address I briefly pointed out the total inadequacy of disunion, as a remedy for the differences between the people of the two sections. . . .

There is no line, straight or crooked, suitable for a national boundary, upon which to divide. Trace through, from east to west, upon the line between the free and slave country, and we shall find a little more than one-third of its length are rivers, easy to be crossed, and populated, or soon to be populated, thickly upon both sides; while nearly all its remaining length, are merely surveyor's lines, over which people may walk back and forth without any consciousness of their presence. No part of this line can be made any more difficult to pass, by writing it down on paper, or parchment, as a national boundary. The fact of separation, if it comes, gives up, on the part of the seceding section, the fugitive slave clause, along with all other constitutional obligations upon the section seceded from, while I should expect no treaty stipulation would ever be made to take its place.

But there is another difficulty. The great interior region, bounded east by the Alleghanies, north by the British dominions, west by the Rocky mountains, and south by the line along which the culture of corn and cotton meets, and which includes part of Virginia, part of Tennessee, all of Kentucky, Ohio, Indiana, Michigan, Wisconsin, Illinois, Missouri, Kansas, Iowa, Minnesota and the Territories of Dakota, Nebraska, and part of Colorado, already has above ten millions of people, and will have fifty millions within fifty years, if not prevented by any political folly or mistake. It contains more than one-third of the country owned by the United States—certainly more than one million of square miles. Once half as populous as Massachusetts already is, it would have more than seventy-five millions of people. A glance at the map shows that, territorially speaking, it is the great body of the republic. The other parts are but marginal borders to it, the magnificent region sloping west from the rocky mountains to the Pacific, being the deepest, and also the richest, in undeveloped resources. In the production of provisions, grains, grasses, and all which proceed from them, this great interior region is naturally one of the most important in the world. Ascertain from the statistics the small proportion of the region which has, as yet, been brought into cultivation, and also the large and rapidly increasing amount of its products, and we shall be overwhelmed with the magnitude of the prospect presented. An[d] yet this region has no sea-coast, touches no ocean anywhere. As part of the nation, its people now find, and may forever find, their way to Europe by New York, to South America and Africa by New Orleans, and to Asia by San Francisco. But separate our common country into two nations, as designed by the present rebellion, and every man of this great interior region is thereby cut off from some one or more of these outlets, not, perhaps, by a physical barrier, but by embarrassing and onerous trade regulations.

And this is true, *wherever* a dividing, or boundary line, may be fixed. Place it between the now free and slave country, or place it south of Kentucky, or north of Ohio, and still the truth remains, that none south of it, can trade to any port or place north of it, and none north of it, can trade to any port or place south of it, except upon terms dictated by a government foreign to them. These outlets, east, west, and south, are indispensable to the well-being of the people inhabiting, and to inhabit, this vast interior region. *Which* of the three may be the best, is no proper question. All, are better than either, and all, of right, belong to that people, and to their successors forever. True to themselves, they will not ask *where* a line of separation shall be, but will vow, rather, that there shall be no such line. Nor are the marginal regions less interested in these communications to, and through them, to the great outside world. They too, and each of them, must have access to this Egypt of the West, without paying toll at the crossing of any national boundary.

Our national strife springs not from our permanent part; not from the land we inhabit; not from our national homestead. There is no possible severing of this, but would multiply, and not mitigate, evils among us. In all its adaptations and aptitudes, it demands union, and abhors separation. In fact, it would, ere long, force reunion, however much of blood and treasure the separation might have cost.

Our strife pertains to ourselves—to the passing generations of men; and it can, without convulsion, be hushed forever with the passing of one generation. . . .

. . . Without slavery the rebellion could never have existed; without slavery it could not continue.

Among the friends of the Union there is great diversity, of sentiment, and of policy, in regard of slavery, and the African race amongst us. Some would perpetuate slavery; some would abolish it suddenly, and without compensation; some would abolish it gradually, and with compensation; some would remove the freed people from us, and some would retain them with us; and there are yet other minor diversities. Because of these diversities, we waste much strength in struggles among ourselves. By mutual concession we should harmonize, and act together. This would be compromise; but it would be compromise among the friends, and not with the enemies of the Union. These articles are intended to embody a plan of such mutual concessions. If the plan shall be adopted, it is assumed that emancipation will follow, at least, in several of the States. . . .

The proposed emancipation would shorten the war, perpetuate peace, insure this increase of population, and proportionately the wealth of the country. With these, we should pay all the emancipation would cost, together with our other debt, easier than we should pay our other debt, without it. If we had allowed our old national debt to run at six per cent. per annum, simple interest, from the end of our revolutionary struggle until to day, without paying anything on either principal or interest, each man of us would owe less upon that debt now, than each man owed upon it then; and this because our increase of men, through the whole period, has been greater than six per cent.; has run faster than the interest upon the debt. Thus, time alone relieves a debtor nation, so long as its population increases faster than unpaid interest accumulates on its debt.

This fact would be no excuse for delaying payment of what is justly due; but it shows the great importance of time in this connexion—the great advantage of a policy by which we shall not have to pay until we number a hundred millions, what, by a different policy, we would have to pay now, when we number but thirty one millions. In a word, it shows that a dollar will be much harder to pay for the war, than will be a dollar for emancipation on the proposed plan. And then the latter will cost no blood, no precious life. It will be a saving of both. . . .

I cannot make it better known than it already is, that I strongly favor colonization. And yet I wish to say there is an objection urged against free colored persons remaining in the country, which is largely imaginary, if not sometimes malicious.

It is insisted that their presence would injure, and displace white labor and white laborers. If there ever could be a proper time for mere catch arguments, that time surely is not now. In times like the present, men should utter nothing for which they would not willingly be responsible through time and in eternity. Is it true, then, that colored people can displace any more white labor, by being free, than by remaining slaves? If they stay in their old places, they jostle no white laborers; if they leave their old places, they leave them open to white laborers. Logically, there is neither more nor less of it. Emancipation, even without deportation, would probably enhance the wages of white labor, and, very surely, would not reduce them. Thus, the customary amount of labor would still have to be performed; the freed people would surely not do more than their old proportion of it, and very probably, for a time, would do less, leaving an increased part to white laborers, bringing their labor into greater demand, and, consequently, enhancing the wages of it. With deportation, even to a limited extent, enhanced wages to white labor is mathematically certain. Labor is like any other commodity in the market—increase the demand for it, and you increase the price of it. Reduce the supply of black labor, by colonizing the black laborer out of the country, and, by precisely so much, you increase the demand for, and wages of, white labor.

But it is dreaded that the freed people will swarm forth, and cover the whole land? Are they not already in the land? Will liberation make them any more numerous? Equally distributed among the whites of the whole country, and there would be but one colored to seven whites. Could the one, in any way, greatly disturb the seven? There are many communities now, having more than one free colored person, to seven whites; and this, without any apparent consciousness of evil from it.

The District of Columbia, and the States of Maryland and Delaware, are all in this condition. The District has more than one free colored to six whites; and yet, in its frequent petitions to Congress, I believe it has never presented the presence of free colored persons as one of its grievances. But why should emancipation south, send the free people north? People, of any color, seldom run, unless there be something to run from. *Heretofore* colored people, to some extent, have fled north from bondage; and *now*, perhaps, from both bondage and destitution. But if gradual emancipation and deportation be adopted, they will have neither to flee from. Their old masters will give them wages at least until new laborers can be procured; and the freed men, in turn, will gladly give their labor for the wages, till new homes can be found for them, in congenial climes, and with people of their own blood and race. This proposition can be trusted on the mutual interests involved. And, in any event, cannot the north decide for itself, whether to receive them?

Again, as practice proves more than theory, in any case, has there been any irruption of colored people northward, because of the abolishment of slavery in this District last spring?

What I have said of the proportion of free colored persons to the whites, in the District, is from the census of 1860, having no reference to persons called contrabands, nor to those made free by the act of Congress abolishing slavery here.

The plan consisting of these articles is recommended, not but that a restoration of the national authority would be accepted without its adoption.

Nor will the war, nor proceedings under the proclamation of September 22, 1862, be stayed because of the *recommendation* of this plan. Its timely *adoption*, I doubt not, would bring restoration and thereby stay both.

And, notwithstanding this plan, the recommendation that Congress provide by law for compensating any State which may adopt emancipation, before this plan shall have been acted upon, is hereby earnestly renewed. Such would be only an advance part of the plan, and the same arguments apply to both.

This plan is recommended as a means, not in exclusion of, but additional to, all others for restoring and preserving the national authority throughout the Union. The subject is presented exclusively in its economical aspect. The plan would, I am confident, secure peace more speedily, and maintain it more permanently, than can be done by force alone; while all it would cost, considering amounts, and manner of payment, and times of payment, would be easier paid than will be the additional cost of the war, if we rely solely upon force. It is much—very much—that it would cost no blood at all.

The plan is proposed as permanent constitutional law. It cannot become such without the concurrence of, first, two-thirds of Congress, and, afterwards, three-fourths of the States. The requisite three-fourths of the States will necessarily include seven of the Slave states. Their concurrence, if obtained, will give assurance of their severally adopting emancipation, at no very distant day, upon the new constitutional terms. This assurance would end the struggle now, and save the Union forever.

I do not forget the gravity which should characterize a paper addressed to the Congress of the nation by the Chief Magistrate of the nation. Nor do I forget that some of you are my seniors, nor that many of you have more experience than I, in the conduct of public affairs. Yet I trust that in view of the great responsibility resting upon me, you will perceive no want of respect to yourselves, in any undue earnestness I may seem to display.

Is it doubted, then, that the plan I propose, if adopted, would shorten the war, and thus lessen its expenditure of money and of blood? Is it doubted that it would restore the national authority and national prosperity, and perpetuate both indefinitely? Is it doubted that we here —Congress and Executive—can secure its adoption? Will not the good people respond to a united, and earnest appeal from us? Can we, can they, by any other means, so certainly, or so speedily, assure these vital objects? We can succeed only by concert. It is not "can *any* of us *imagine* better?" but "can we *all* do better?" Object whatsoever is possible, still the question recurs "can we do better?" The dogmas of the quiet past, are inadequate to the stormy present. The occasion is piled high with difficulty, and we must rise with the occasion. As our case is new, so we must think anew, and act anew. We must disenthrall our selves, and then we shall save our country.

Fellow-citizens, *we* cannot escape history. We of this Congress and this administration, will be remembered in spite of ourselves. No personal significance, or insignificance, can spare one or another of us. The fiery trial through which we pass, will light us down, in honor or dishonor, to the latest generation. We *say* we are for the Union. The world will not forget that we say this. We know how to save the Union. The world knows we do know how to save it. We—even *we here*—hold the power, and bear the responsibility. In *giving* freedom to the *slave*, we *assure* freedom to the *free*—honorable alike in what we give, and what we preserve. We shall nobly save, or meanly lose, the last best, hope of earth. Other means may succeed; this could not fail. The way is plain, peaceful, generous, just—a way which, if followed, the world will forever applaud, and God must forever bless.

"In this sad world of ours"

Letter to Fanny McCullough, December 23, 1862

Lincoln wrote this letter of condolence to a young Illinois girl whose father had been killed in the war. Her father, Lieutenant-Colonel William McCullough, had been a circuit court clerk in McLean County before the war and was a good friend of Lincoln's.

Dear Fanny   Executive Mansion, Washington

It is with deep grief that I learn of the death of your kind and brave Father; and, especially, that it is affecting your young heart beyond what is common in such cases. In this sad world of ours, sorrow comes to all; and, to the young, it comes with bitterest agony, because it takes them unawares. The older have learned to ever expect it. I am anxious to afford some alleviation of your present distress. Perfect relief is not possible, except with time. You can not now realize that you will ever feel better. Is not this so? And yet it is a mistake. You are sure to be happy again. To know this, which is certainly true, will make you some less miserable now. I have had experience enough to know what I say; and you need only to believe it, to feel better at once. The memory of your dear Father, instead of an agony, will yet be a sad sweet feeling in your heart, of a purer, and holier sort than you have known before.

Please present my kind regards to your afflicted mother.

Your sincere friend

V

"A NEW BIRTH OF FREEDOM"

1863

"Are, and henceforth shall be free"

Emancipation Proclamation, January 1, 1863

During the traditional New Year's Day reception at the White House, Lincoln went upstairs to his office to sign the Emancipation Proclamation. As he had promised to do, he declared the slaves free in those areas he now designated to be in rebellion. The Proclamation did not apply to all areas of the South, and it contained none of Lincoln's usual appeal to higher ideals, since he believed his action could be justified only on the grounds of military necessity. Lincoln's hand was swollen from having greeted the throng of visitors, and it visibly shook as he signed the document. Nevertheless, he assured those present, "I never, in my life, felt more certain that I was doing right, than I do in signing this paper." The sections quoted from the preliminary Emancipation Proclamation have been omitted.

Whereas, on the twentysecond day of September, in the year of our Lord one thousand eight hundred and sixty two, a proclamation was issued by the President of the United States, containing, among other things, the following, towit: . . .

Now, therefore I, Abraham Lincoln, President of the United States, by virtue of the power in me vested as Commander-in-Chief, of the Army and Navy of the United States in time of actual armed rebellion against authority and government of the United States, and as a fit and necessary war measure for suppressing said rebellion, do, on this first day of January, in the year of our Lord one thousand eight hundred and sixty three, and in accordance with my purpose so to do publicly proclaimed for the full period of one hundred days, from the day first above mentioned, order and designate as the States and parts of States wherein the people thereof respectively, are this day in rebellion against the United States, the following, towit:

Arkansas, Texas, Louisiana, (except the Parishes of St. Bernard, Plaquemines, Jefferson, St. Johns, St. Charles, St. James[,] Ascension, Assumption, Terrebonne, Lafourche, St. Mary, St. Martin, and Orleans, including the City of New-Orleans) Mississippi, Alabama, Florida, Georgia, South-Carolina, North-Carolina, and Virginia, (except the fortyeight counties designated as West Virginia, and also the counties of Berkley, Accomac, Northampton, Elizabeth-City, York, Princess Ann, and Norfolk, including the cities of Norfolk & Portsmouth[)]; and which excepted parts are, for the present, left precisely as if this proclamation were not issued.

And by virtue of the power, and for the purpose aforesaid, I do order and declare that all persons held as slaves within said designated States, and parts of States, are, and henceforward shall be free; and that the Executive government of the United States, including the military and naval authorities thereof, will recognize and maintain the freedom of said persons.

And I hereby enjoin upon the people so declared to be free to abstain from all violence, unless in necessary self-defence; and I recommend to them that, in all cases when allowed, they labor faithfully for reasonable wages.

And I further declare and make known, that such persons of suitable condition, will be received into the armed service of the United States to garrison forts, positions, stations, and other places, and to man vessels of all sorts in said service.

And upon this act, sincerely believed to be an act of justice, warranted by the Constitution, upon military necessity, I invoke the considerate judgment of mankind, and the gracious favor of Almighty God.

"Broken eggs can not be mended"

Letter to John A. McClernand, January 8, 1863

Lincoln defended the Emancipation Proclamation in a letter to John A. McClernand, a former Democratic congressman from Illinois who was now a general in the Union army. He pointed out that he had resisted interfering with slavery for more than a year, but having finally issued the Proclamation, he would not retract it.

Major General McClernand   Executive Mansion, Washington

My dear Sir Your interesting communication by the hand of Major Scates is received. I never did ask more, nor ever was willing to accept less, than for all the States, and the people thereof, to take and hold their places, and their rights, in the Union, under the Constitution of the United States. For this alone have I felt authorized to struggle; and I seek neither more nor less now. Still, to use a coarse, but an expressive figure, broken eggs can not be mended. I have issued the emancipation proclamation, and I can not retract it.

After the commencement of hostilities I struggled nearly a year and a half to get along without touching the "institution"; and when finally I conditionally determined to touch it, I gave a hundred days fair notice of my purpose, to all the States and people, within which time they could have turned it wholly aside, by simply again becoming good citizens of the United States. They chose to disregard it, and I made the peremptory proclamation on what appeared to me to be a military necessity. And being made, it must stand. As to the States not included in it, of course they can have their rights in the Union as of old. Even the people of the states included, if they choose, need not to be hurt by it. Let them adopt systems of apprenticeship for the colored people, conforming substantially to the most approved plans of gradual emancipation; and, with the aid they can have from the general government, they may be nearly as well off, in this respect, as if the present trouble had not occurred, and much better off than they can possibly be if the contest continues persistently.

As to any dread of my having a "purpose to enslave, or exterminate, the whites of the South," I can scarcely believe that such dread exists. It is too absurd. I believe you can be my personal witness that no man is less to be dreaded for undue severity, in any case.

If the friends you mention really wish to have peace upon the old terms, they should act at once. Every day makes the case more difficult. They can so act, with entire safety, so far as I am concerned.

I think you would better not make this letter public; but you may rely confidently on my standing by whatever I have said in it. Please write me if any thing more comes to light. Yours very truly

"I will risk the dictatorship"

Letter to Joseph Hooker, January 26, 1863

When he appointed Joseph Hooker to take command of the Army of the Potomac in early 1863, Lincoln offered the voluble general some sage advice. He presumably handed this letter to Hooker during a personal interview in Washington after the general had assumed command. The letter illustrated Lincoln's unusual ability to criticize associates without alienating them.

Major General Hooker: Executive Mansion, Washington

General.

I have placed you at the head of the Army of the Potomac. Of course I have done this upon what appear to me to be sufficient reasons. And yet I think it best for you to know that there are some things in regard to which, I am not quite satisfied with you. I believe you to be a brave and a skilful soldier, which, of course, I like. I also believe you do not mix politics with your profession, in which you are right. You have confidence in yourself, which is a valuable, if not an indispensable quality. You are ambitious, which, within reasonable bounds, does good rather than harm. But I think that during Gen. Burnside's command of the Army, you have taken counsel of your ambition, and thwarted him as much as you could, in which you did a great wrong to the country, and to a most meritorious and honorable brother officer. I have heard, in such way as to believe it, of your recently saying that both the Army and the Government needed a Dictator. Of course it was not *for* this, but in spite of it, that I have given you the command. Only those generals who gain successes, can set up dictators. What I now ask of you is military success, and I will risk the dictatorship. The government will support you to the utmost of it's ability, which is neither more nor less than it has done and will do for all commanders. I much fear that the spirit which you have aided to infuse into the Army, of criticising their Commander, and withholding confidence from him, will now turn upon you. I shall assist you as far as I can, to put it down. Neither you, nor Napoleon, if he were alive again, could get any good out of an army, while such a spirit prevails in it.

And now, beware of rashness. Beware of rashness, but with energy, and sleepless vigilance, go forward, and give us victories.

Yours very truly

"There is *no* eligible route for us into Richmond"

Memorandum on Joseph Hooker's plan of campaign against
Richmond, ca. April 6–10, 1863

Lincoln probably wrote this undated memorandum during his visit to the Army of the Potomac in early April 1863. In it, Lincoln emphasized the importance of the Union's main eastern army focusing on Lee's army rather than Richmond. The eastern theater had already become a military stalemate, but, as Lincoln noted, pressure there was important to prevent the Confederacy from shifting troops to its hard-pressed armies in the West. Time would show Lincoln overestimated Hooker's ability to use his manpower advantage to pin down Lee.

My opinion is, that just now, with the enemy directly ahead of us, there is *no* eligible route for us into Richmond; and consequently a question of preference between the Rappahannock route, and the James River route is a contest about nothing. Hence our prime object is the enemies' army in front of us, and is not with, or about, Richmond—at all, unless it be incidental to the main object.

What then? The two armies are face to face with a narrow river between them. Our communications are shorter and safer than are those of the enemy. For this reason, we can, with equal powers fret him more than he can us. I do not think that by raids towards Washington he can derange the Army of the Potomac at all. He has no distant opperations which can call any of the Army of the Potomac away; we have such operations which may call him away, at least in part. While he remains in tact, I do not think we should take the disadvantage of attacking him in his entrenchments; but we should continually harrass and menace him, so that he shall have no leisure, nor safety in sending away detachments. If he weakens himself, then pitch into him.

"Constantly denounced and opposed"

Letter to Isaac Arnold, May 26, 1863

Illinois Congressman Isaac Arnold was one of Lincoln's most reliable supporters in Congress, but even he criticized Lincoln's military appointments. In this letter Lincoln irritably responded to the demand that he remove Henry W. Halleck, whom he had appointed commanding general in 1862. The ceaseless political carping directed at Union generals was a major impediment to Lincoln's conduct of the war.

PRIVATE & CONFIDENTIAL

Hon. I. N. Arnold.   Executive Mansion, Washington

My dear Sir:

Your letter advising me to dismiss Gen. Halleck is received. If the public believe, as you say, that he has driven Fremont, Butler, and Sigel from the service, they believe what I know to be false; so that if I were to yield to it, it would only be to be instantly beset by some other demand based on another falsehood equally gross. You know yourself that Fremont was relieved at his own request, before Halleck could have had any thing to do with it—went out near the end of June, while Halleck only came in near the end of July. I know equally well that no wish of Halleck's had any thing to do with the removal of Butler or Sigel. Sigel, like Fremont, was relieved at his own request, pressed upon me almost constantly for six months, and upon complaints that could have been made as justly by almost any corps commander in the army, and more justly by some. So much for the way they got out. Now a word as to their not getting back. In the early Spring, Gen. Fremont sought active service again; and, as it seemed to me, sought it in a very good, and reasonable spirit. But he holds the highest rank in the Army, except McClellan, so that I could not well offer him a subordinate command. Was I to displace Hooker, or Hunter, or Rosecrans, or Grant, or Banks? If not, what was I to do? And similar to this, is the case of both the others. One month after Gen. Butler's return, I offered him a position in which I thought and still think, he could have done himself the highest credit, and the country the greatest service, but he declined it. When Gen. Sigel was relieved, at his own request as I have said, of course I had to put another in command of his corps. Can I instantly thrust that other out to put him in again?

And now my good friend, let me turn your eyes upon another point. Whether Gen. Grant shall or shall not consummate the capture of Vicksburg, his campaign from the beginning of this month up to the twenty second day of it, is one of the most brilliant in the world. His corps commanders, & Division commanders, in part, are McClernand, McPherson, Sherman, Steele, Hovey, Blair, & Logan. And yet taking Gen. Grant & these seven of his generals, and you can scarcely name one of them that has not been constantly denounced and opposed by the same men who are now so anxious to get Halleck out, and Fremont & Butler & Sigel in. I believe no one of them went through the Senate easily, and certainly one failed to get through at all. I am compelled to take a more impartial and unprejudiced view of things. Without claiming to be your superior, which I do not, my position enables me to understand my duty in all these matters better than you possibly can, and I hope you do not yet doubt my integrity. Your friend, as ever

"*Lee's* Army . . . is your true objective point"

Letter to Joseph Hooker, June 10, 1863

When the Army of Northern Virginia began its invasion of Pennsylvania, Hooker proposed that rather than shadowing Lee northward he would advance against Richmond. Lincoln's strategic analysis demonstrated his growing confidence and authority in military matters, and he quickly vetoed this proposal. Lincoln was increasingly convinced that Hooker had no desire to confront Lee in battle again, and he soon removed him from command.

"Cypher"   United States Military Telegraph

Major General Hooker   War Department. Washington DC.

Your long despatch of to-day is just received. If left to me, I would not go South of the Rappahannock, upon Lee's moving North of it. If you had Richmond invested to-day, you would not be able to take it in twenty days; meanwhile, your communications, and with them, your army would be ruined. I think *Lee's* Army, and not *Richmond*, is your true objective point. If he comes towards the Upper Potomac, follow on his flank, and on the inside track, shortening your lines, whilst he lengthens his. Fight him when oppertunity offers. If he stays where he is, fret him, and fret him.

"Indispensable to the public Safety"

Letter to Erastus Corning, June 12, 1863

In May 1863 military officials arrested Clement Vallandigham, a former Democratic congressman from Ohio, for a speech he delivered opposing the war. Under terms of Lincoln's September 1862 order suspending the writ of habeas corpus, Vallandigham was tried by a military court, and, following his conviction, Lincoln banished him to the Confederacy. When a Democratic meeting in Albany protested Vallandigham's arrest, Lincoln responded in a widely circulated public letter defending the suspension of the writ as necessary to preserve the public safety and prevent interference with the war effort. With Lee's army moving northward toward Maryland and Pennsylvania, Lincoln had good reason to fear the consequences of disloyal activities in the North, and his letter was a warning to antiwar elements that the government would respond energetically.

Hon. Erastus Corning & others   Executive Mansion, Washington

Gentlemen Your letter of May 19th. inclosing the resolutions of a public meeting held at Albany, N.Y. on the 16th. of the same month, was received several days ago. . . .

. . . The resolutions promise to support me in every constitutional and lawful measure to suppress the rebellion; and I have not knowingly employed, nor shall knowingly employ, any other. But the meeting, by their resolutions, assert and argue, that certain military arrests and proceedings following them for which I am ultimately responsible, are unconstitutional. I think they are not. The resolutions quote from the constitution, the definition of treason; and also the limiting safe-guards and guarrantees therein provided for the citizen, on trials for treason, and on his being held to answer for capital or otherwise infamous crimes, and, in criminal prosecutions, his right to a speedy and public trial by an impartial jury. They proceed to resolve "That these safe-guards of the rights of the citizen against the pretentions of arbitrary power, were intended more *especially* for his protection in times of civil commotion." And, apparantly, to demonstrate the proposition, the resolutions proceed "They were secured substantially to the English people, *after* years of protracted civil war, and were adopted into our constitution at the *close* of the revolution." Would not the demonstration have been better, if it could have been truly said that these safe-guards had been adopted, and applied *during* the civil wars and *during* our revolution, instead of *after* the one, and at the *close* of the other. I too am devotedly for them *after* civil war, and *before* civil war, and at all times "except when, in cases of Rebellion or Invasion, the public Safety may require" their suspension. The resolutions proceed to tell us that these safe-guards "have stood the test of seventysix years of trial, under our republican system, under circumstances which show that while they constitute the foundation of all free government, they are the elements of the enduring stability of the Republic." No one denies that they have so stood the test up to the beginning of the present rebellion if we except a certain occurrence at New-Orleans hereafter to be mentioned; nor does any one question that they will stand the same test much longer after the rebellion closes. But these provisions of the constitution have no application to the case we have in hand, because the arrests complained of were not made for treason—that is, not for *the* treason defined in the constitution, and upon the conviction of which, the punishment is death—; nor yet were they made to hold persons to answer for any capital, or otherwise infamous crimes; nor were the proceedings following, in any constitutional or legal sense, "criminal prossecutions." The arrests were made on totally different grounds, and the proceedings following, accorded with the grounds of the arrests. Let us consider the real case with which we are dealing, and apply to it the parts of the constitution plainly made for such cases.

Prior to my instalation here it had been inculcated that any State had a lawful right to secede from the national Union; and that it would be expedient to exercise the right, whenever the devotees of the doctrine should fail to elect a President to their own liking. I was elected contrary to their liking; and accordingly, so far as it was legally possible, they had taken seven states out of the Union, had seized many of the United States Forts, and had fired upon the United States' Flag, all before I was inaugerated; and, of course, before I had done any official act whatever. The rebellion, thus began soon ran into the present civil war; and, in certain respects, it began on very unequal terms between the parties. The insurgents had been preparing for it more than thirty years, while the government had taken no steps to resist them. The former had carefully considered all the means which could be turned to their account. It undoubtedly was a well pondered reliance with them that in their own unrestricted effort to destroy Union, constitution, and law, all together, the government would, in great degree, be restrained by the same constitution and law, from arresting their progress. Their sympathizers pervaded all departments of the government, and nearly all communities of the people. From this material, under cover of "Liberty of speech" "Liberty of the press" and *"Habeas corpus"* they hoped to keep on foot amongst us a most efficient corps of spies, informers, supplyers, and aiders and abettors of their cause in a thousand ways. They knew that in times such as they were inaugerating, by the constitution itself, the "Habeas corpus" might be suspended; but they also knew they had friends who would make a question as to *who* was to suspend it; meanwhile their spies and others might remain at large to help on their cause. Or if, as has happened, the executive should suspend the writ, without ruinous waste of time, instances of arresting innocent persons might occur, as are always likely to occur in such cases; and then a clamor could be raised in regard to this, which might be, at least, of some service to the insurgent cause. It needed no very keen perception to discover this part of the enemies' programme, so soon as by open hostilities their machinery was fairly put in motion. Yet, thoroughly imbued with a reverence for the guarranteed rights of individuals, I was slow to adopt the strong measures, which by degrees I have been forced to regard as being within the exceptions of the constitution, and as indispensable to the public Safety. Nothing is better known to history than that courts of justice are utterly incompetent to such cases. Civil courts are organized chiefly for trials of individuals, or, at most, a few individuals acting in concert; and this in quiet times, and on charges of crimes well defined in the law. Even in times of peace, bands of horse-thieves and robbers frequently grow too numerous and powerful for the ordinary courts of justice. But what comparison, in numbers, have such bands ever borne to the insurgent sympathizers even in many of the loyal states? Again, a jury too frequently have at least one member, more ready to hang the panel than to hang the traitor. And yet again, he who dissuades one man from volunteering, or induces one soldier to desert, weakens the Union cause as much as he who kills a union soldier in battle. Yet this dissuasion, or inducement, may be so conducted as to be no defined crime of which any civil court would take cognizance.

Ours is a case of Rebellion—so called by the resolutions before me—in fact, a clear, flagrant, and gigantic case of Rebellion; and the provision of the constitution that "The previlege of the writ of Habeas Corpus shall not be suspended, unless when in cases of Rebellion or Invasion, the public Safety may require it" is *the* provision which specially applies to our present case. This provision plainly attests the understanding of those who made the constitution that ordinary courts of justice are inadequate to "cases of Rebellion"—attests their purpose that in such cases, men may be held in custody whom the courts acting on ordinary rules, would discharge. Habeas Corpus, does not discharge men who are proved to be guilty of defined crime; and its suspension is allowed by the constitution on purpose that, men may be arrested and held, who can not be proved to be guilty of defined crime, "when, in cases of Rebellion or Invasion the public Safety may require it." This is precisely our present case—a case of Rebellion, wherein the public Safety does require the suspension. Indeed, arrests by process of courts, and arrests in cases of rebellion, do not proceed altogether upon the same basis. The former is directed at the small per centage of ordinary and continuous perpetration of crime; while the latter is directed at sudden and extensive uprisings against the government, which, at most, will succeed or fail, in no great length of time. In the latter case, arrests are made, not so much for what has been done, as for what probably would be done. The latter is more for the preventive, and less for the vindictive, than the former. In such cases the purposes of men are much more easily understood, than in cases of ordinary crime. The man who stands by and says nothing, when the peril of his government is discussed, can not be misunderstood. If not hindered, he is sure to help the enemy. Much more, if he talks ambiguously—talks for his country with "buts" and "ifs" and "ands." . . . I think the time not unlikely to come when I shall be blamed for having made too few arrests rather than too many.

By the third resolution the meeting indicate their opinion that military arrests may be constitutional in localities where rebellion actually exists; but that such arrests are unconstitutional in localities where rebellion, or insurrection, does not actually exist. They insist that such arrests shall not be made "outside of the lines of necessary military occupation, and the scenes of insurrection" In asmuch, however, as the constitution itself makes no such distinction, I am unable to believe that there is any such constitutional distinction. I concede that the class of arrests complained of, can be constitutional only when, in cases of Rebellion or Invasion, the public Safety may require them; and I insist that in such cases, they are constitutional *wherever* the public safety does require them—as well in places to which they may prevent the rebellion extending, as in those where it may be already prevailing—as well where they may restrain mischievous interference with the raising and supplying of armies, to suppress the rebellion, as where the rebellion may actually be—as well where they may restrain the enticing men out of the army, as where they would prevent mutiny in the army—equally constitutional at all places where they will conduce to the public Safety, as against the dangers of Rebellion or Invasion.

Take the particular case mentioned by the meeting. It is asserted in substance that Mr. Vallandingham was by a military commander, seized and tried "for no other reason than words addressed to a public meeting, in criticism of the course of the administration, and in condemnation of the military orders of that general" Now, if there be no mistake about this—if this assertion is the truth and the whole truth—if there was no other reason for the arrest, then I concede that the arrest was wrong. But the arrest, as I understand, was made for a very different reason. Mr. Vallandigham avows his hostility to the war on the part of the Union; and his arrest was made because he was laboring, with some effect, to prevent the raising of troops, to encourage desertions from the army, and to leave the rebellion without an adequate military force to suppress it. He was not arrested because he was damaging the political prospects of the administration, or the personal interests of the commanding general; but because he was damaging the army, upon the existence, and vigor of which, the life of the nation depends. He was warring upon the military; and this gave the military constitutional jurisdiction to lay hands upon him. If Mr. Vallandigham was not damaging the military power of the country, then his arrest was made on mistake of fact, which I would be glad to correct, on reasonably satisfactory evidence.

I understand the meeting, whose resolutions I am considering, to be in favor of suppressing the rebellion by military force—by armies. Long experience has shown that armies can not be maintained unless desertion shall be punished by the severe penalty of death. The case requires, and the law and the constitution, sanction this punishment. Must I shoot a simple-minded soldier boy who deserts, while I must not touch a hair of a wiley agitator who induces him to desert? This is none the less injurious when effected by getting a father, or brother, or friend, into a public meeting, and there working upon his feelings, till he is persuaded to write the soldier boy, that he is fighting in a bad cause, for a wicked administration of a contemptable government, too weak to arrest and punish him if he shall desert. I think that in such a case, to silence the agitator, and save the boy, is not only constitutional, but, withal, a great mercy.

If I be wrong on this question of constitutional power, my error lies in believing that certain proceedings are constitutional when, in cases of rebellion or Invasion, the public Safety requires them, which would not be constitutional when, in absence of rebellion or invasion, the public Safety does not require them—in other words, that the constitution is not in it's application in all respects the same, in cases of Rebellion or invasion, involving the public Safety, as it is in times of profound peace and public security. The constitution itself makes the distinction; and I can no more be persuaded that the government can constitutionally take no strong measure in time of rebellion, because it can be shown that the same could not be lawfully taken in time of peace, than I can be persuaded that a particular drug is not good medicine for a sick man, because it can be shown to not be good food for a well one. Nor am I able to appreciate the danger, apprehended by the meeting, that the American people will, by means of military arrests during the rebellion, lose the right of public discussion, the liberty of speech and the press, the law of evidence, trial by jury, and Habeas corpus, throughout the indefinite peaceful future which I trust lies before them, any more than I am able to believe that a man could contract so strong an appetite for emetics during temporary illness, as to persist in feeding upon them through the remainder of his healthful life.

In giving the resolutions that earnest consideration which you request of me, I can not overlook the fact that the meeting speak as "Democrats." Nor can I, with full respect for their known intelligence, and the fairly presumed deliberation with which they prepared their resolutions, be permitted to suppose that this occurred by accident, or in any way other than that they preferred to designate themselves "democrats" rather than "American citizens." In this time of national peril I would have preferred to meet you upon a level one step higher than any party platform; because I am sure that from such more elevated position, we could do better battle for the country we all love, than we possibly can from those lower ones, where from the force of habit, the prejudices of the past, and selfish hopes of the future, we are sure to expend much of our ingenuity and strength, in finding fault with, and aiming blows at each other. But since you have denied me this, I will yet be thankful, for the country's sake, that not all democrats have done so. He on whose discretionary judgment Mr. Vallandigham was arrested and tried, is a democrat, having no old party affinity with me; and the judge who rejected the constitutional view expressed in these resolutions, by refusing to discharge Mr. V. on Habeas Corpus, is a democrat of better days than these, having received his judicial mantle at the hands of President Jackson. And still more, of all those democrats who are nobly exposing their lives and shedding their blood on the battle-field, I have learned that many approve the course taken with Mr. V. while I have not heard of a single one condemning it. I can not assert that there are none such. . . .

And yet, let me say that in my own discretion, I do not know whether I would have ordered the arrest of Mr. V. While I can not shift the responsibility from myself, I hold that, as a general rule, the commander in the field is the better judge of the necessity in any particular case. Of course I must practice a general directory and revisory power in the matter.

One of the resolutions expresses the opinion of the meeting that arbitrary arrests will have the effect to divide and distract those who should be united in suppressing the rebellion; and I am specifically called on to discharge Mr. Vallandigham. I regard this as, at least, a fair appeal to me, on the expediency of exercising a constitutional power which I think exists. In response to such appeal I have to say it gave me pain when I learned that Mr. V. had been arrested,—that is, I was pained that there should have seemed to be a necessity for arresting him—and that it will afford me great pleasure to discharge him so soon as I can, by any means, believe the public safety will not suffer by it. I further say, that as the war progresses, it appears to me, opinion, and action, which were in great confusion at first, take shape, and fall into more regular channels; so that the necessity for strong dealing with them gradually decreases. I have every reason to desire that it would cease altogether; and far from the least is my regard for the opinions and wishes of those who, like the meeting at Albany, declare their purpose to sustain the government in every constitutional and lawful measure to suppress the rebellion. Still, I must continue to do so much as may seem to be required by the public safety.

"Few things are so troublesome"

Letter to William Kellogg, June 29, 1863

The war created unprecedented business opportunities, and the problem of corruption in war contracts and other activities quickly overwhelmed the administration. One source of quick profits was the notorious cotton trade in the Mississippi Valley, in which northern speculators, armed with a military pass, purchased bales of cotton from southern planters behind the lines. William Kellogg, an Illinois congressman, had requested permission for a constituent to buy cotton and other articles in Arkansas. In denying this favor, Lincoln justifiably expressed concern about the baneful influence of this trade on the army.

Hon. Wm. Kellogg.   Executive Mansion, Washington

My dear Sir:

I have received, and read, your pencil note. I think you do not know how embarrassing your request is. Few things are so troublesome to the government as the fierceness with which the profits of trading in cotten are sought. The temptation is so great that nearly every body wishes to be in it; and when in, the question of profit controls all, regardless of whether the cotten seller is loyal or rebel, or whether he is paid in corn-meal or gun-powder. The officers of the army, in numerous instances, are believed to connive and share the profits, and thus the army itself is diverted from fighting the rebels to speculating in cotten; and steam-boats and wagons in the pay of the government, are set to gathering and carrying cotten, and the soldiers to loading cotten-trains and guarding them.

The matter deeply affects the Treasury and War Departments, and has been discussed again and again in the cabinet. What can, and what can not be done, has, for the time been settled, and it seems to me I can not safely break over it. I know it is thought that one case is not much, but how can I favor one and deny another. One case can not be kept a secret. The authority given would be utterly ineffectual until it is shown; and when shown, every body knows of it. The administration would do for you as much as for any other man; and I personally would do some more than for most others; but really I can not involve myself and the Government as this would do. Yours as ever

"You were right, and I was wrong"

Letter to Ulysses S. Grant, July 13, 1863

Lincoln's generosity in giving credit to others is demonstrated in this letter to Ulysses S. Grant, written shortly after the capture of Vicksburg. His remarks were prompted by the fact that Grant followed a different strategy than Lincoln had preferred in operating against the Confederate stronghold. Grant's success strengthened Lincoln's faith in the western commander.

Major General Grant   Executive Mansion, Washington

My dear General

I do not remember that you and I ever met personally. I write this now as a grateful acknowledgment for the almost inestimable service you have done the country. I wish to say a word further. When you first reached the vicinity of Vicksburg, I thought you should do, what you finally did—march the troops across the neck, run the batteries with the transports, and thus go below; and I never had any faith, except a general hope that you knew better than I, that the Yazoo Pass expedition, and the like, could succeed. When you got below, and took Port-Gibson, Grand Gulf, and vicinity, I thought you should go down the river and join Gen. Banks; and when you turned Northward East of the Big Black, I feared it was a mistake. I now wish to make the personal acknowledgment that you were right, and I was wrong. Yours very truly

"I am distressed immeasureably"

Letter to George G. Meade, July 14, 1863

Lincoln placed General George Meade in command of the Army of the Potomac only a few days before the Battle of Gettysburg. Meade's performance did not elicit the same praise from Lincoln that he extended to Grant. Meade had fought well at Gettysburg and forced Lee to abandon his northern invasion, but Lincoln was almost inconsolable that he allowed the Army of Northern Virginia to return to Virginia without serious resistance. Lincoln ultimately decided not to send his letter explaining his unhappiness, but his assessment fixed in his mind the conclusion that Meade lacked the aggressive qualities necessary to win the war. Though he would remain in command of the Army of the Potomac for the duration of the war, Meade never enjoyed Lincoln's confidence the way Grant did.

Major General Meade   Executive Mansion, Washington

I have just seen your despatch to Gen. Halleck, asking to be relieved of your command, because of a supposed censure of mine. I am very—very—grateful to you for the magnificent success you gave the cause of the country at Gettysburg; and I am sorry now to be the author of the slightest pain to you. But I was in such deep distress myself that I could not restrain some expression of it. I had been oppressed nearly ever since the battles at Gettysburg, by what appeared to be evidences that yourself, and Gen. Couch, and Gen. Smith, were not seeking a collision with the enemy, but were trying to get him across the river without another battle. What these evidences were, if you please, I hope to tell you at some time, when we shall both feel better. The case, summarily stated is this. You fought and beat the enemy at Gettysburg; and, of course, to say the least, his loss was as great as yours. He retreated; and you did not, as it seemed to me, pressingly pursue him; but a flood in the river detained him, till, by slow degrees, you were again upon him. You had at least twenty thousand veteran troops directly with you, and as many more raw ones within supporting distance, all in addition to those who fought with you at Gettysburg; while it was not possible that he had received a single recruit; and yet you stood and let the flood run down, bridges be built, and the enemy move away at his leisure, without attacking him. And Couch and Smith! The latter left Carlisle in time, upon all ordinary calculation, to have aided you in the last battle at Gettysburg; but he did not arrive. At the end of more than ten days, I believe twelve, under constant urging, he reached Hagerstown from Carlisle, which is not an inch over fiftyfive miles, if so much. And Couch's movement was very little different.

Again, my dear general, I do not believe you appreciate the magnitude of the misfortune involved in Lee's escape. He was within your easy grasp, and to have closed upon him would, in connection with our other late successes, have ended the war. As it is, the war will be prolonged indefinitely. If you could not safely attack Lee last monday, how can you possibly do so South of the river, when you can take with you very few more than two thirds of the force you then had in hand? It would be unreasonable to expect, and I do not expect you can now effect much. Your golden opportunity is gone, and I am distressed immeasureably because of it.

I beg you will not consider this a prossecution, or persecution of yourself. As you had learned that I was dissatisfied, I have thought it best to kindly tell you why.

"The same protection to all its soldiers"

Order, July 30, 1863

When the Union army began recruiting black soldiers, the Confederate government ordered that any captured black troops would be enslaved, and that any whites commanding them would be considered guilty of leading a slave insurrection (which carried the penalty of death). Lincoln responded with the following order, threatening retaliation if these soldiers were not treated as prisoners of war. The Confederacy generally did not enforce its announced policy, although there were examples, most notably at Fort Pillow, when captured black soldiers were summarily executed. Lincoln wished to avoid retaliatory practices, believing they were counterproductive.

Executive Mansion, Washington D.C.

It is the duty of every government to give protection to its citizens, of whatever class, color, or condition, and especially to those who are duly organized as soldiers in the public service. The law of nations and the usages and customs of war as carried on by civilized powers, permit no distinction as to color in the treatment of prisoners of war as public enemies. To sell or enslave any captured person, on account of his color, and for no offence against the laws of war, is a relapse into barbarism and a crime against the civilization of the age.

The government of the United States will give the same protection to all its soldiers, and if the enemy shall sell or enslave anyone because of his color, the offense shall be punished by retaliation upon the enemy's prisoners in our possession.

It is therefore ordered that for every soldier of the United States killed in violation of the laws of war, a rebel soldier shall be executed; and for every one enslaved by the enemy or sold into slavery, a rebel soldier shall be placed at hard labor on the public works and continued at such labor until the other shall be released and receive the treatment due to a prisoner of war.

"I can not consent to suspend the draft"

Letter to Horatio Seymour, August 7, 1863

In the wake of the antidraft riots in New York City in July 1863, Democratic Governor Horatio Seymour of New York called upon Lincoln to suspend the draft in the city until the Supreme Court ruled on its constitutionality. While agreeing to adjust the city's quota of men, Lincoln rejected the governor's proposal as dangerous and impractical. In fact, the Court never ruled on the validity of conscription during the war.

His Excellency Horatio Seymour　　　Executive Mansion, Washington
Governor of New-York

Your communication of the 3rd. Inst. has been received, and attentively considered.

I can not consent to suspend the draft in New-York, as you request, because, among other reasons, *time* is too important.

By the figures you send, which I presume are correct, the twelve Districts represented fall into two classes of eight, and four respectively. The disparity of the quotas for the draft, in these two classes is certainly very striking, being the difference between an average of 2200 in one class, and 4864 in the other. Assuming that the Districts are equal, one to another, in entire population, as required by the plan on which they were made, this disparity is such as to require attention. Much of it, however, I suppose will be accounted for by the fact that so many more persons fit for soldiers, are in the city than are in the country, who have too recently arrived from other parts of the United States and from Europe to be either included in the Census of 1860, or to have voted in 1862. Still, making due allowance for this, I am yet unwilling to stand upon it as an entirely sufficient explanation of the great disparity.

I shall direct the draft to proceed in all the Districts, drawing however, at first, from each of the four Districts, towit: the second, fourth, sixth, and eight, only 2200, being the average quota of the other class. After this drawing, these four Districts, and also the seventeenth and twentyninth, shall be carefully re-enrolled, and, if you please, agents of yours may witness every step of the process. Any deficiency which may appear by the new enrollment will be supplied by a special draft for that object, allowing due credit for volunteers who may be obtained from these Districts respectively, during the interval. And at all points, so far as consistent, with practical convenience, due credits will be given for volunteers; and your Excellency shall be notified of the time fixed for commencing a draft in each District.

I do not object to abide a decision of the United States Supreme Court, or of the judges thereof, on the constitutionality of the draft law. In fact, I should be willing to facilitate the obtaining of it; but I can not consent to lose the *time* while it is being obtained. We are contending with an enemy who, as I understand, drives every able bodied man he can reach, into his ranks, very much as a butcher drives bullocks into a slaughter-pen. No time is wasted, no argument is used. This produces an army which will soon turn upon our now victorious soldiers already in the field, if they shall not be sustained by recruits, as they should be. It produces an army with a rapidity not to be matched on our side, if we first waste time to re-experiment with the volunteer system, already deemed by congress, and palpably, in fact, so far exhausted, as to be inadequate; and then more time, to obtain a court decision, as to whether a law is constitutional, which requires a part of those not now in the service, to go to the aid of those who are already in it; and still more time, to determine with absolute certainty, that we get those, who are to go, in the precisely legal proportion, to those who are not to go.

My purpose is to be, in my action, just and constitutional; and yet practical, in performing the important duty, with which I am charged, of maintaining the unity, and the free principles of our common country. Your Obt. Servt.

"It works doubly"

Letter to Ulysses S. Grant, August 9, 1863

Following his decision to issue the Emancipation Proclamation, Lincoln coupled emancipation and the use of black troops as critical means to hasten the end of the war. Blacks were first used in combat in the summer of 1863, after which he intensified efforts to recruit former slaves for the army. The Mississippi Valley, a major slaveholding area, was the primary area for this effort. Grant fully supported this policy.

My dear General Grant: Executive Mansion, Washington

I see by a despatch of yours that you incline quite strongly towards an expedition against Mobile. This would appear tempting to me also, were it not that in view of recent events in Mexico, I am greatly impressed with the importance of re-establishing the national authority in Western Texas as soon as possible. I am not making an order, however. That I leave, for the present at least, to the General-in-Chief.

A word upon another subject. Gen. Thomas has gone again to the Mississippi Valley, with the view of raising colored troops. I have no reason to doubt that you are doing what you reasonably can upon the same subject. I believe it is a resource which, if vigorously applied now, will soon close the contest. It works doubly, weakening the enemy and strengthening us. We were not fully ripe for it until the river was opened. Now, I think at least a hundred thousand can, and ought to be rapidly organized along it's shores, relieving all the white troops to serve elsewhere.

Mr. Dana understands you as believing that the emancipation proclamation has helped some in your military operations. I am very glad if this is so. Did you receive a short letter from me, dated the 13th. of July? Yours very truly

"I am not watching you with an evil-eye"

Letter to William S. Rosecrans, August 10, 1863

As he had to do on so many occasions, Lincoln undertook to soothe the feelings of one of his generals, William S. Rosecrans, who resented pressure from Washington in the summer of 1863 to assume the offensive in Tennessee. Once again, Lincoln reiterated the importance he placed on occupying the Unionist region in eastern Tennessee.

My Dear General Rosecrans   Executive Mansion, Washington

Yours of the 1st was received two days ago. I think you must have inferred more than Gen Halleck has intended, as to any dissatisfaction of mine with you. I am sure you, as a reasonable man, would not have been wounded, could you have heard all my words and seen all my thoughts, in regard to you. I have not abated in my kind feeling for and confidence in you. I have seen most of your despatches to General Halleck—probably all of them. After Grant invested Vicksburg, I was very anxious lest Johnston should overwhelm him from the outside, and when it appeared certain that part of Bragg's force had gone, and was going to Johnston, it did seem to me, it was the exactly proper time for you to attack Bragg with what force he had left. In all kindness, let me say, it so seems to me yet. Finding from your despatches to General Halleck that your judgement was different, and being very anxious for Grant, I, on one occasion told Gen. Halleck, I thought he should direct you to decide at once, to immediately attack Bragg or to stand on the defensive, and send part of your force to Grant. He replied he had already so directed, in substance. Soon after, despatches from Grant abated my anxiety for him, and in proportion abated my anxiety about any movement of yours. When afterwards, however, I saw a despatch of yours arguing that the right time for you to attack Bragg was not before but would be after the fall of Vicksburg, it impressed me very strangely; and I think I so stated to the Secretary of War and General Halleck. It seemed no other than the proposition that you could better fight Bragg *when* Johnston should be at liberty to return and assist him, than you could *before* he could so return to his assistance.

Since Grant has been entirely relieved by the fall of Vicksburg, by which Johnston is also relieved, it has seemed to me that your chance for a stroke, has been considerably diminished, and I have not been pressing you directly or indirectly. True, I am very anxious for East Tennessee to be occupied by us; but I see and appreciate the difficulties you mention. The question occurs, Can the thing be done at all? Does preparation advance at all? Do you not consume supplies as fast as you get them forward? Have you more animals today than you had at the battle of Stone[s] River? and yet have not more been furnished you since then than your entire present stock? I ask the same questions as to your mounted force.

Do not misunderstand. I am not casting blame upon you. I rather think, by great exertion, you can get to East Tennessee. But a very important question is, "Can you stay there?" I make no order in the case —that I leave to General Halleck and yourself.

And now, be assured once more, that I think of you in all kindness and confidence: and that I am not watching you with an evil-eye. Yours very truly

"A fair specimen of what has occurred to me through life"

Letters to James H. Hackett, August 17, November 2, 1863

Lincoln had a deep fondness for Shakespeare's plays, particularly the tragedies, which he frequently read. He addressed the following letters to a famous American actor who had sent him a book of critical commentary on Shakespeare. When Hackett unexpectedly published Lincoln's initial letter, the opposition press mercilessly ridiculed the president's pretensions as a dramatic critic. Lincoln's second letter was written in response to Hackett's apologies for making his comments public.

My dear Sir: Executive Mansion, Washington

Months ago I should have acknowledged the receipt of your book, and accompanying kind note; and I now have to beg your pardon for not having done so.

For one of my age, I have seen very little of the drama. The first presentation of Falstaff I ever saw was yours here, last winter or spring. Perhaps the best compliment I can pay is to say, as I truly can, I am very anxious to see it again. Some of Shakespeare's plays I have never read; while others I have gone over perhaps as frequently as any unprofessional reader. Among the latter are Lear, Richard Third, Henry Eighth, Hamlet, and especially Macbeth. I think nothing equals Macbeth. It is wonderful. Unlike you gentlemen of the profession, I think the soliloquy in Hamlet commencing "O, my offence is rank" surpasses that commencing "To be, or not to be." But pardon this small attempt at criticism. I should like to hear you pronounce the opening speech of Richard the Third. Will you not soon visit Washington again? If you do, please call and let me make your personal acquaintance. Yours truly

PRIVATE

James H. Hackett   Executive Mansion, Washington

My dear Sir:

Yours of Oct. 22nd. is received, as also was, in due course, that of Oct. 3rd. I look forward with pleasure to the fulfilment of the promise made in the former.

Give yourself no uneasiness on the subject mentioned in that of the 22nd.

My note to you I certainly did not expect to see in print; yet I have not been much shocked by the newspaper comments upon it. Those comments constitute a fair of specimen of what has occurred to me through life. I have endured a great deal of ridicule without much malice; and have received a great deal of kindness, not quite free from ridicule. I am used to it. Yours truly

"The heaviest blow yet dealt to the rebellion"

Letter to James C. Conkling, August 26, 1863

Illinois Republicans scheduled a mass meeting in Springfield in early September 1863 to demonstrate support for the war and the Administration. The organizers invited Lincoln to speak at this meeting, and he was tempted to accept, since he had not been home in more than two years. But in the end he decided he could not leave Washington because of the military situation, so he instead sent a letter, addressed to his old friend James Conkling, vigorously defending his policies on emancipation and the use of black soldiers.

Hon. James C. Conkling   Executive Mansion, Washington

My Dear Sir.

Your letter inviting me to attend a mass-meeting of unconditional Union-men, to be held at the Capital of Illinois, on the 3d day of September, has been received.

It would be very agreeable to me, to thus meet my old friends, at my own home; but I can not, just now, be absent from here, so long as a visit there, would require.

The meeting is to be of all those who maintain unconditional devotion to the Union; and I am sure my old political friends will thank me for tendering, as I do, the nation's gratitude to those other noble men, whom no partizan malice, or partizan hope, can make false to the nation's life.

There are those who are dissatisfied with me. To such I would say: You desire peace; and you blame me that we do not have it. But how can we attain it? There are but three conceivable ways. First, to suppress the rebellion by force of arms. This, I am trying to do. Are you for it? If you are, so far we are agreed. If you are not for it, a second way is, to give up the Union. I am against this. Are you for it? If you are, you should say so plainly. If you are not for *force,* nor yet for *dissolution,* there only remains some imaginable *compromise.* I do not believe any compromise, embracing the maintenance of the Union, is now possible. All I learn, leads to a directly opposite belief. The strength of the rebellion, is its military—its army. That army dominates all the country, and all the people, within its range. Any offer of terms made by any man or men within that range, in opposition to that army, is simply nothing for the present; because such man or men, have no power whatever to enforce their side of a compromise, if one were made with them. To illustrate— Suppose refugees from the South, and peace men of the North, get together in convention, and frame and proclaim a compromise embracing a restoration of the Union; in what way can that compromise be used to keep Lee's army out of Pennsylvania? Meade's army can keep Lee's army out of Pennsylvania; and, I think, can ultimately drive it out of existence. But no paper compromise, to which the controllers of Lee's army are not agreed, can, at all, affect that army. In an effort at such compromise we should waste time, which the enemy would improve to our disadvantage; and that would be all. A compromise, to be effective, must be made either with those who control the rebel army, or with the people first liberated from the domination of that army, by the success of our own army. Now allow me to assure you, that no word or intimation, from that rebel army, or from any of the men controlling it, in relation to any peace compromise, has ever come to my knowledge or belief. All charges and insinuations to the contrary, are deceptive and groundless. And I promise you, that if any such proposition shall hereafter come, it shall not be rejected, and kept a secret from you. I freely acknowledge myself the servant of the people, according to the bond of service—the United States constitution; and that, as such, I am responsible to them.

But, to be plain, you are dissatisfied with me about the negro. Quite likely there is a difference of opinion between you and myself upon that subject. I certainly wish that all men could be free, while I suppose you do not. Yet I have neither adopted, nor proposed any measure, which is not consistent with even your view, provided you are for the Union. I suggested compensated emancipation; to which you replied you wished not to be taxed to buy negroes. But I had not asked you to be taxed to buy negroes, except in such way, as to save you from greater taxation to save the Union exclusively by other means.

You dislike the emancipation proclamation; and, perhaps, would have it retracted. You say it is unconstitutional—I think differently. I think the constitution invests its commander-in-chief, with the law of war, in time of war. The most that can be said, if so much, is, that slaves are property. Is there—has there ever been—any question that by the law of war, property, both of enemies and friends, may be taken when needed? And is it not needed whenever taking it, helps us, or hurts the enemy? Armies, the world over, destroy enemies' property when they can not use it; and even destroy their own to keep it from the enemy. Civilized belligerents do all in their power to help themselves, or hurt the enemy, except a few things regarded as barbarous or cruel. Among the exceptions are the massacre of vanquished foes, and non-combatants, male and female.

But the proclamation, as law, either is valid, or is not valid. If it is not valid, it needs no retraction. If it is valid, it can not be retracted, any more than the dead can be brought to life. Some of you profess to think its retraction would operate favorably for the Union. Why better *after* the retraction, than *before* the issue? There was more than a year and a half of trial to suppress the rebellion before the proclamation issued, the last one hundred days of which passed under an explicit notice that it was coming, unless averted by those in revolt, returning to their allegiance. The war has certainly progressed as favorably for us, since the issue of the proclamation as before. I know as fully as one can know the opinions of others, that some of the commanders of our armies in the field who have given us our most important successes, believe the emancipation policy, and the use of colored troops, constitute the heaviest blow yet dealt to the rebellion; and that, at least one of those important successes, could not have been achieved when it was, but for the aid of black soldiers. Among the commanders holding these views are some who have never had any affinity with what is called abolitionism, or with republican party politics; but who hold them purely as military opinions. I submit these opinions as being entitled to some weight against the objections, often urged, that emancipation, and arming the blacks, are unwise as military measures, and were not adopted, as such, in good faith.

You say you will not fight to free negroes. Some of them seem willing to fight for you; but, no matter. Fight you, then, exclusively to save the Union. I issued the proclamation on purpose to aid you in saving the Union. Whenever you shall have conquered all resistance to the Union, if I shall urge you to continue fighting, it will be an apt time, then, for you to declare you will not fight to free negroes.

I thought that in your struggle for the Union, to whatever extent the negroes should cease helping the enemy, to that extent it weakened the enemy in his resistance to you. Do you think differently? I thought that whatever negroes can be got to do as soldiers, leaves just so much less for white soldiers to do, in saving the Union. Does it appear otherwise to you? But negroes, like other people, act upon motives. Why should they do any thing for us, if we will do nothing for them? If they stake their lives for us, they must be prompted by the strongest motive—even the promise of freedom. And the promise being made, must be kept.

The signs look better. The Father of Waters again goes unvexed to the sea. Thanks to the great North-West for it. Nor yet wholly to them. Three hundred miles up, they met New-England, Empire, Key-Stone, and Jersey, hewing their way right and left. The Sunny South too, in more colors than one, also lent a hand. On the spot, their part of the history was jotted down in black and white. The job was a great national one; and let none be banned who bore an honorable part in it. And while those who have cleared the great river may well be proud, even that is not all. It is hard to say that anything has been more bravely, and well done, than at Antietam, Murfreesboro, Gettysburg, and on many fields of lesser note. Nor must Uncle Sam's Web-feet be forgotten. At all the watery margins they have been present. Not only on the deep sea, the broad bay, and the rapid river, but also up the narrow muddy bayou, and wherever the ground was a little damp, they have been, and made their tracks. Thanks to all. For the great republic—for the principle it lives by, and keeps alive—for man's vast future,—thanks to all.

Peace does not appear so distant as it did. I hope it will come soon, and come to stay; and so come as to be worth the keeping in all future time. It will then have been proved that, among free men, there can be no successful appeal from the ballot to the bullet; and that they who take such appeal are sure to lose their case, and pay the cost. And then, there will be some black men who can remember that, with silent tongue, and clenched teeth, and steady eye, and well-poised bayonet, they have helped mankind on to this great consummation; while, I fear, there will be some white ones, unable to forget that, with malignant heart, and deceitful speech, they have strove to hinder it.

Still let us not be over-sanguine of a speedy final triumph. Let us be quite sober. Let us diligently apply the means, never doubting that a just God, in his own good time, will give us the rightful result. Yours very truly

"Give up all footing upon constitution or law"

Letter to Salmon P. Chase, September 2, 1863

In his Emancipation Proclamation, Lincoln had exempted certain counties in Louisiana and Virginia from its terms, as they were under Union military control. When Secretary of the Treasury Salmon P. Chase subsequently urged the president to extend the proclamation to those counties, Lincoln justified his decision to exclude them.

Hon. S. P. Chase   Executive Mansion, Washington

My dear Sir:

Knowing your great anxiety that the emancipation proclamation shall now be applied to certain parts of Virginia and Louisiana which were exempted from it last January, I state briefly what appear to me to be difficulties in the way of such a step. The original proclamation has no constitutional or legal justification, except as a military measure. The exemptions were made because the military necessity did not apply to the exempted localities. Nor does that necessity apply to them now any more than it did then. If I take the step must I not do so, without the argument of military necessity, and so, without any argument, except the one that I think the measure politically expedient, and morally right? Would I not thus give up all footing upon constitution or law? Would I not thus be in the boundless field of absolutism? Could this pass unnoticed, or unresisted? Could it fail to be perceived that without any further stretch, I might do the same in Delaware, Maryland, Kentucky, Tennessee, and Missouri; and even change any law in any state? Would not many of our own friends shrink away appalled? Would it not lose us the elections, and with them, the very cause we seek to advance?

"An idea I have been trying to repudiate for quite a year"

Letter to Henry W. Halleck, September 19, 1863

In this letter to Henry Halleck, the Union's general-in-chief, Lincoln analyzed the military situation in Virginia in the fall of 1863. Concerned that the Virginia theater was becoming a military stalemate, he again stressed two of his main strategic ideas: that the Union army had to use its manpower advantage more effectively, and that Lee's army, not Richmond, was the true objective point of the Army of the Potomac.

Major General Halleck: Executive Mansion, Washington

By Gen. Meade's despatch to you of yesterday it appears that he desires your views and those of the government, as to whether he shall advance upon the enemy. I am not prepared to order, or even advise an advance in this case, wherein I know so little of particulars, and wherein he, in the field, thinks the risk is so great, and the promise of advantage so small. And yet the case presents matter for very serious consideration in another aspect. These two armies confront each other across a small river, substantially midway between the two Capitals, each defending it's own Capital, and menacing the other. Gen. Meade estimates the enemies infantry in front of him at not less than forty thousand. Suppose we add fifty per cent to this, for cavalry, artillery, and extra duty men stretching as far as Richmond, making the whole force of the enemy sixty thousand. Gen. Meade, as shown by the returns, has with him, and between him and Washington, of the same classes of well men, over ninety thousand. Neither can bring the whole of his men into a battle; but each can bring as large a per centage in as the other. For a battle, then, Gen. Meade has three men to Gen. Lee's two. Yet, it having been determined that choosing ground, and standing on the defensive, gives so great advantage that the three can not safely attack the two, the three are left simply standing on the defensive also. If the enemies sixty thousand are sufficient to keep our ninety thousand away from Richmond, why, by the same rule, may not forty thousand of ours keep their sixty thousand away from Washington, leaving us fifty thousand to put to some other use? Having practically come to the mere defensive, it seems to be no economy at all to employ twice as many men for that object as are needed. With no object, certainly, to misle[a]d myself, I can perceive no fault in this statement, unless we admit we are not the equal of the enemy man for man. I hope you will consider it.

To avoid misunderstanding, let me say that to attempt to fight the enemy slowly back into his intrenchments at Richmond, and there to capture him, is an idea I have been trying to repudiate for quite a year. My judgment is so clear against it, that I would scarcely allow the attempt to be made, if the general in command should desire to make it. My last attempt upon Richmond was to get McClellan, when he was nearer there than the enemy was, to run in ahead of him. Since then I have constantly desired the Army of the Potomac, to make Lee's army, and not Richmond, it's objective point. If our army can not fall upon the enemy and hurt him where he is, it is plain to me it can gain nothing by attempting to follow him over a succession of intrenched lines into a fortified city. Yours truly

"Quarrel not at all"

Letter to James M. Cutts, Jr., October 26, 1863

The recipient of this letter, who was a captain in the army, was the brother-in-law of Lincoln's longtime political adversary Stephen A. Douglas, who had died in 1861. Cutts had been convicted by a court martial of quarreling with another officer. Lincoln took an interest in the case out of his desire not to inflict any pain or embarrassment on Douglas's family. Lincoln may have delivered this gentle but wise reprimand in person.

Capt. James M. Cutts.   Executive Mansion, Washington

Although what I am now to say is to be, in form, a reprimand, it is not intended to add a pang to what you have already suffered upon the subject to which it relates. You have too much of life yet before you, and have shown too much of promise as an officer, for your future to be lightly surrendered. You were convicted of two offences. One of them, not of great enormity, and yet greatly to be avoided, I feel sure you are in no danger of repeating. The other you are not so well assured against. The advice of a father to his son "Beware of entrance to a quarrel, but being in, bear it that the opposed may beware of thee," is good, and yet not the best. Quarrel not at all. No man resolved to make the most of himself, can spare time for personal contention. Still less can he afford to take all the consequences, including the vitiating of his temper, and the loss of self-control. Yield larger things to which you can show no more than equal right; and yield lesser ones, though clearly your own. Better give your path to a dog, than be bitten by him in contesting for the right. Even killing the dog would not cure the bite.

In the mood indicated deal henceforth with your fellow men, and especially with your brother officers; and even the unpleasant events you are passing from will not have been profitless to you.

"Give me a tangible nucleus"

Letter to Nathaniel P. Banks, November 5, 1863

In the summer of 1863, Lincoln instructed Nathaniel Banks, the Union military commander in Louisiana, to begin the process of reconstruction in the occupied regions of the state. When Banks failed to take steps to organize a new loyal state government, Lincoln emphasized the urgency of prompt action. Lincoln was clear on the necessity of adopting emancipation but vague on the precise status of African Americans.

Major General Banks   Executive Mansion, Washington

Three months ago to-day I wrote you about Louisiana affairs, stating, on the word of Gov. Shepley, as I understood him, that Mr. Durant was taking a registry of citizens, preparatory to the election of a constitutional convention for that State. I sent a copy of the letter to Mr. Durant; and I now have his letter, written two months after, acknowledging receipt, and saying he is not taking such registry; and he does not let me know that he personally is expecting to do so. Mr. Flanders, to whom I also sent a copy, is now here, and he says nothing has yet been done. This disappoints me bitterly; yet I do not throw blame on you or on them. I do however, urge both you and them, to lose no more time. Gov. Shepley has special instructions from the War Department. I wish him—these gentlemen and others co-operating—without waiting for more territory, to go to work and give me a tangible nucleus which the remainder of the State may rally around as fast as it can, and which I can at once recognize and sustain as the true State government. And in that work I wish you, and all under your command, to give them a hearty sympathy and support. The instruction to Gov. Shepley bases the movement (and rightfully too) upon the loyal element. Time is important. There is danger, even now, that the adverse element seeks insidiously to pre-occupy the ground. If a few professedly loyal men shall draw the disloyal about them, and colorably set up a State government, repudiating the emancipation proclamation, and re-establishing slavery, I can not recognize or sustain their work. I should fall powerless in the attempt. This government, in such an attitude, would be a house divided against itself. I have said, and say again, that if a new State government, acting in harmony with this government, and consistently with general freedom, shall think best to adopt a reasonable temporary arrangement, in relation to the landless and homeless freed people, I do not object; but my word is out to be *for* and not *against* them on the question of their permanent freedom. I do not insist upon such temporary arrangement, but only say such would not be objectionable to me. Yours very truly

"A new birth of freedom"

Gettysburg Address, November 19, 1863

In November 1863 Lincoln traveled by train to Gettysburg, Pennsylvania, to participate in the dedication ceremonies for a national cemetery on part of the recent battlefield. The organizing committee asked the president to make a few appropriate remarks following those of the main speaker, Edward Everett of Massachusetts. Lincoln gave considerable thought to what he would say and carefully wrote out his remarks before he left Washington. In his address, which lasted only two minutes, Lincoln defined the purpose of the war in terms of the highest ideals of the American republic. Of particular importance was his dating of the country's birth with the Declaration of Independence and the connection he drew between the ideal of equality and emancipation. The text of Lincoln's enduring words is his final version.

Four score and seven years ago our fathers brought forth on this continent, a new nation, conceived in Liberty, and dedicated to the proposition that all men are created equal.

Now we are engaged in a great civil war, testing whether that nation, or any nation so conceived and so dedicated, can long endure. We are met on a great battle-field of that war. We have come to dedicate a portion of that field, as a final resting place for those who here gave their lives that that nation might live. It is altogether fitting and proper that we should do this.

But, in a larger sense, we can not dedicate—we can not consecrate—we can not hallow—this ground. The brave men, living and dead, who struggled here, have consecrated it, far above our poor power to add or detract. The world will little note, nor long remember what we say here, but it can never forget what they did here. It is for us the living, rather, to be dedicated here to the unfinished work which they who fought here have thus far so nobly advanced. It is rather for us to be here dedicated to the great task remaining before us—that from these honored dead we take increased devotion to that cause for which they gave the last full measure of devotion—that we here highly resolve that these dead shall not have died in vain—that this nation, under God, shall have a new birth of freedom—and that government of the people, by the people, for the people, shall not perish from the earth.

VI

"EVENTS HAVE CONTROLLED ME"

1863–1864

"The new reckoning"

Message to Congress, December 8, 1863

In his message to Congress in December 1863, Lincoln hailed the impact of emancipation on the Union war effort and pointed to the recent elections, in which the Republicans had done well, as evidence that public opinion had embraced the policy of emancipation. Looking ahead, he took up the problem of reconstruction.

When Congress assembled a year ago the war had already lasted nearly twenty months, and there had been many conflicts on both land and sea, with varying results.

The rebellion had been pressed back into reduced limits; yet the tone of public feeling and opinion, at home and abroad, was not satisfactory. With other signs, the popular elections, then just past, indicated uneasiness among ourselves, while amid much that was cold and menacing the kindest words coming from Europe were uttered in accents of pity, that we were too blind to surrender a hopeless cause. Our commerce was suffering greatly by a few armed vessels built upon and furnished from foreign shores, and we were threatened with such additions from the same quarter as would sweep our trade from the sea and raise our blockade. We had failed to elicit from European governments anything hopeful upon this subject. The preliminary emancipation proclamation, issued in September, was running its assigned period to the beginning of the new year. A month later the final proclamation came, including the announcement that colored men of suitable condition would be received into the war service. The policy of emancipation, and of employing black soldiers, gave to the future a new aspect, about which hope, and fear, and doubt contended in uncertain conflict. According to our political system, as a matter of civil administration, the general government had no lawful power to effect emancipation in any State, and for a long time it had been hoped that the rebellion could be suppressed without resorting to it as a military measure. It was all the while deemed possible that the necessity for it might come, and that if it should, the crisis of the contest would then be presented. It came, and as was anticipated, it was followed by dark and doubtful days. Eleven months having now passed, we are permitted to take another review. The rebel borders are pressed still further back, and by the complete opening of the Mississippi the country dominated by the rebellion is divided into distinct parts, with no practical communication between them. Tennessee and Arkansas have been substantially cleared of insurgent control, and influential citizens in each, owners of slaves and advocates of slavery at the beginning of the rebellion, now declare openly for emancipation in their respective States. Of those States not included in the emancipation proclamation, Maryland, and Missouri, neither of which three years ago would tolerate any restraint upon the extension of slavery into new territories, only dispute now as to the best mode of removing it within their own limits.

Of those who were slaves at the beginning of the rebellion, full one hundred thousand are now in the United States military service, about one-half of which number actually bear arms in the ranks; thus giving the double advantage of taking so much labor from the insurgent cause, and supplying the places which otherwise must be filled with so many white men. So far as tested, it is difficult to say they are not as good soldiers as any. No servile insurrection, or tendency to violence or cruelty, has marked the measures of emancipation and arming the blacks. These measures have been much discussed in foreign countries, and contemporary with such discussion the tone of public sentiment there is much improved. At home the same measures have been fully discussed, supported, criticised, and denounced, and the annual elections following are highly encouraging to those whose official duty it is to bear the country through this great trial. Thus we have the new reckoning. The crisis which threatened to divide the friends of the Union is past.

Looking now to the present and future, and with reference to a resumption of the national authority within the States wherein that authority has been suspended, I have thought fit to issue a proclamation, a copy of which is herewith transmitted. On examination of this proclamation it will appear, as is believed, that nothing is attempted beyond what is amply justified by the Constitution. True, the form of an oath is given, but no man is coerced to take it. The man is only promised a pardon in case he voluntarily takes the oath. The Constitution authorizes the Executive to grant or withhold the pardon at his own absolute discretion; and this includes the power to grant on terms, as is fully established by judicial and other authorities.

It is also proffered that if, in any of the States named, a State government shall be, in the mode prescribed, set up, such government shall be recognized and guarantied by the United States, and that under it the State shall, on the constitutional conditions, be protected against invasion and domestic violence. The constitutional obligation of the United States to guaranty to every State in the Union a republican form of government, and to protect the State, in the cases stated, is explicit and full. But why tender the benefits of this provision only to a State government set up in this particular way? This section of the Constitution contemplates a case wherein the element within a State, favorable to republican government, in the Union, may be too feeble for an opposite and hostile element external to, or even within the State; and such are precisely the cases with which we are now dealing.

An attempt to guaranty and protect a revived State government, constructed in whole, or in preponderating part, from the very element against whose hostility and violence it is to be protected, is simply absurd. There must be a test by which to separate the opposing elements, so as to build only from the sound; and that test is a sufficiently liberal one, which accepts as sound whoever will make a sworn recantation of his former unsoundness.

But if it be proper to require, as a test of admission to the political body, an oath of allegiance to the Constitution of the United States, and to the Union under it, why also to the laws and proclamations in regard to slavery? Those laws and proclamations were enacted and put forth for the purpose of aiding in the suppression of the rebellion. To give them their fullest effect, there had to be a pledge for their maintenance. In my judgment they have aided, and will further aid, the cause for which they were intended. To now abandon them would be not only to relinquish a lever of power, but would also be a cruel and an astounding breach of faith. I may add at this point, that while I remain in my present position I shall not attempt to retract or modify the emancipation proclamation; nor shall I return to slavery any person who is free by the terms of that proclamation, or by any of the acts of Congress. For these and other reasons it is thought best that support of these measures shall be included in the oath; and it is believed the Executive may lawfully claim it in return for pardon and restoration of forfeited rights, which he has clear constitutional power to withhold altogether, or grant upon the terms which he shall deem wisest for the public interest. It should be observed, also, that this part of the oath is subject to the modifying and abrogating power of legislation and supreme judicial decision.

The proposed acquiescence of the national Executive in any reasonable temporary State arrangement for the freed people is made with the view of possibly modifying the confusion and destitution which must, at best, attend all classes by a total revolution of labor throughout whole States. It is hoped that the already deeply afflicted people in those States may be somewhat more ready to give up the cause of their affliction, if, to this extent, this vital matter be left to themselves; while no power of the national Executive to prevent an abuse is abridged by the proposition.

The suggestion in the proclamation as to maintaining the political framework of the States on what is called reconstruction, is made in the hope that it may do good without danger of harm. It will save labor and avoid great confusion.

But why any proclamation now upon this subject? This question is beset with the conflicting views that the step might be delayed too long or be taken too soon. In some States the elements for resumption seem ready for action, but remain inactive, apparently for want for a rallying point—a plan of action. Why shall A adopt the plan of B, rather than B that of A? And if A and B should agree, how can they know but that the general government here will reject their plan? By the proclamation a plan is presented which may be accepted by them as a rallying point, and which they are assured in advance will not be rejected here. This may bring them to act sooner than they otherwise would.

The objections to a premature presentation of a plan by the national Executive consists in the danger of committals on points which could be more safely left to further developments. Care has been taken to so shape the document as to avoid embarrassments from this source. Saying that, on certain terms, certain classes will be pardoned, with rights restored, it is not said that other classes, or other terms, will never be included. Saying that reconstruction will be accepted if presented in a specified way, it is not said it will never be accepted in any other way.

The movements, by State action, for emancipation in several of the States, not included in the emancipation proclamation, are matters of profound gratulation. And while I do not repeat in detail what I have heretofore so earnestly urged upon this subject, my general views and feelings remain unchanged; and I trust that Congress will omit no fair opportunity of aiding these important steps to a great consummation.

In the midst of other cares, however important, we must not lose sight of the fact that the war power is still our main reliance. To that power alone can we look, yet for a time, to give confidence to the people in the contested regions, that the insurgent power will not again overrun them. Until that confidence shall be established, little can be done anywhere for what is called reconstruction. Hence our chiefest care must still be directed to the army and navy, who have thus far borne their harder part so nobly and well. And it may be esteemed fortunate that in giving the greatest efficiency to these indispensable arms, we do also honorably recognize the gallant men, from commander to sentinel, who compose them, and to whom, more than to others, the world must stand indebted for the home of freedom disenthralled, regenerated, enlarged, and perpetuated.

"A full pardon"

Proclamation of amnesty and reconstruction, December 8, 1863

At the same time that he submitted his annual message, Lincoln issued a proclamation outlining his program of reconstruction. In formulating his program, Lincoln emphasized future loyalty rather than past actions, since he wanted to encourage southern whites to return to their former loyalty as a way to speeed the end of the war. By not specifying what position former slaves would occupy under governments established by his program, Lincoln left himself flexibility on the race question, which was the most explosive issue raised by reconstruction.

Whereas, in and by the Constitution of the United States, it is provided that the President "shall have power to grant reprieves and pardons for offences against the United States, except in cases of impeachment;" and

Whereas a rebellion now exists whereby the loyal State governments of several States have for a long time been subverted, and many persons have committed and are now guilty of treason against the United States; and

Whereas, with reference to said rebellion and treason, laws have been enacted by Congress declaring forfeitures and confiscation of property and liberation of slaves, all upon terms and conditions therein stated, and also declaring that the President was thereby authorized at any time thereafter, by proclamation, to extend to persons who may have participated in the existing rebellion, in any State or part thereof, pardon and amnesty, with such exceptions and at such times and on such conditions as he may deem expedient for the public welfare; and

Whereas the congressional declaration for limited and conditional pardon accords with well-established judicial exposition of the pardoning power; and

Whereas, with reference to said rebellion, the President of the United States has issued several proclamations, with provisions in regard to the liberation of slaves; and

Whereas it is now desired by some persons heretofore engaged in said rebellion to resume their allegiance to the United States, and to reinaugurate loyal State governments within and for their respective States; therefore,

I, Abraham Lincoln, President of the United States, do proclaim, declare, and make known to all persons who have, directly or by implication, participated in the existing rebellion, except as hereinafter excepted, that a full pardon is hereby granted to them and each of them, with restoration of all rights of property, except as to slaves, and in property cases where rights of third parties shall have intervened, and upon the condition that every such person shall take and subscribe an oath, and thenceforward keep and maintain said oath inviolate; and which oath shall be registered for permanent preservation, and shall be of the tenor and effect following, to wit:

"I,——, do solemnly swear, in presence of Almighty God, that I will henceforth faithfully support, protect and defend the Constitution of the United States, and the union of the States thereunder; and that I will, in like manner, abide by and faithfully support all acts of Congress passed during the existing rebellion with reference to slaves, so long and so far as not repealed, modified or held void by Congress, or by decision of the Supreme Court; and that I will, in like manner, abide by and faithfully support all proclamations of the President made during the existing rebellion having reference to slaves, so long and so far as not modified or declared void by decision of the Supreme Court. So help me God."

The persons excepted from the benefits of the foregoing provisions are all who are, or shall have been, civil or diplomatic officers or agents of the so-called confederate government; all who have left judicial stations under the United States to aid the rebellion; all who are, or shall have been, military or naval officers of said so-called confederate government above the rank of colonel in the army, or of lieutenant in the navy; all who left seats in the United States Congress to aid the rebellion; all who resigned commissions in the army or navy of the United States, and afterwards aided the rebellion; and all who have engaged in any way in treating colored persons or white persons, in charge of such, otherwise than lawfully as prisoners of war, and which persons may have been found in the United States service, as soldiers, seamen, or in any other capacity.

And I do further proclaim, declare, and make known, that whenever, in any of the States of Arkansas, Texas, Louisiana, Mississippi, Tennessee, Alabama, Georgia, Florida, South Carolina, and North Carolina, a number of persons, not less than one-tenth in number of the votes cast in such State at the Presidential election of the year of our Lord one thousand eight hundred and sixty, each having taken the oath aforesaid and not having since violated it, and being a qualified voter by the election law of the State existing immediately before the so-called act of secession, and excluding all others, shall re-establish a State government which shall be republican, and in no wise contravening said oath, such shall be recognized as the true government of the State, and the State shall receive thereunder the benefits of the constitutional provision which declares that "The United States shall guaranty to every State in this union a republican form of government, and shall protect each of them against invasion; and, on application of the legislature, or the executive, (when the legislature cannot be convened,) against domestic violence."

And I do further proclaim, declare, and make known that any provision which may be adopted by such State government in relation to the freed people of such State, which shall recognize and declare their permanent freedom, provide for their education, and which may yet be consistent, as a temporary arrangement, with their present condition as a laboring, landless, and homeless class, will not be objected to by the national Executive. And it is suggested as not improper, that, in constructing a loyal State government in any State, the name of the State, the boundary, the subdivisions, the constitution, and the general code of laws, as before the rebellion, be maintained, subject only to the modifications made necessary by the conditions hereinbefore stated, and such others, if any, not contravening said conditions, and which may be deemed expedient by those framing the new State government.

To avoid misunderstanding, it may be proper to say that this proclamation, so far as it relates to State governments, has no reference to States wherein loyal State governments have all the while been maintained. And for the same reason, it may be proper to further say that whether members sent to Congress from any State shall be admitted to seats, constitutionally rests exclusively with the respective Houses, and not to any extent with the Executive. And still further, that this proclamation is intended to present the people of the States wherein the national authority has been suspended, and loyal State governments have been subverted, a mode in and by which the national authority and loyal State governments may be re-established within said States, or in any of them; and, while the mode presented is the best the Executive can suggest, with his present impressions, it must not be understood that no other possible mode would be acceptable.

"The jewel of liberty"

Letter to Michael Hahn, March 13, 1864

*In putting his reconstruction program into effect, Lincoln placed partic-
ular emphasis on Louisiana, which he wanted to serve as a model for
other southern states. In a private letter to the governor of the new loyal
government of Louisiana, Lincoln endorsed limited black suffrage but
did not require its adoption. Unlike Radicals, who wanted to completely
alter southern society, Lincoln had less sweeping aims and he was more
concerned than they were about southern white acquiescence.*

PRIVATE

Hon. Michael Hahn   Executive Mansion, Washington

My dear Sir:

I congratulate you on having fixed your name in history as the first-free-
state Governor of Louisiana. Now you are about to have a Convention
which, among other things, will probably define the elective franchise. I
barely suggest for your private consideration, whether some of the colored people may not be let in—as, for instance, the very intelligent, and
especially those who have fought gallantly in our ranks. They would
probably help, in some trying time to come, to keep the jewel of liberty
within the family of freedom. But this is only a suggestion, not to the
public, but to you alone. Yours truly

"If slavery is not wrong, nothing is wrong"

Letter to Albert G. Hodges, April 4, 1864

*In the spring of 1864, Lincoln met with several Kentucky Unionists to
discuss complaints about the army's interference with slavery in the
state. In the meeting, Lincoln made a statement tracing the evolution of
his policy on slavery. At the request of Albert Hodges, one of those present, he subsequently wrote out his remarks for use in influencing public
opinion in the state. The letter was Lincoln's most extended written
statement concerning his decision to adopt emancipation as a Union
war aim.*

A. G. Hodges, Esq   Executive Mansion, Washington
Frankfort, Ky.

My dear Sir: You ask me to put in writing the substance of what I ver-
bally said the other day, in your presence, to Governor Bramlette and
Senator Dixon. It was about as follows:

"I am naturally anti-slavery. If slavery is not wrong, nothing is
wrong. I can not remember when I did not so think, and feel. And yet I
have never understood that the Presidency conferred upon me an unrestricted right to act officially upon this judgment and feeling. It was in
the oath I took that I would, to the best of my ability, preserve, protect,
and defend the Constitution of the United States. I could not take the
office without taking the oath. Nor was it my view that I might take an
oath to get power, and break the oath in using the power. I understood,
too, that in ordinary civil administration this oath even forbade me to
practically indulge my primary abstract judgment on the moral question of slavery. I had publicly declared this many times, and in many
ways. And I aver that, to this day, I have done no official act in mere deference to my abstract judgment and feeling on slavery. I did understand
however, that my oath to preserve the constitution to the best of my
ability, imposed upon me the duty of preserving, by every indispensable
means, that government—that nation—of which that constitution was
the organic law. Was it possible to lose the nation, and yet preserve the
constitution? By general law life *and* limb must be protected; yet often a
limb must be amputated to save a life; but a life is never wisely given to
save a limb. I felt that measures, otherwise unconstitutional, might
become lawful, by becoming indispensable to the preservation of the
constitution, through the preservation of the nation. Right or wrong, I
assumed this ground, and now avow it. I could not feel that, to the best
of my ability, I had even tried to preserve the constitution, if, to save
slavery, or any minor matter, I should permit the wreck of government,
country, and Constitution all together. When, early in the war, Gen.
Fremont attempted military emancipation, I forbade it, because I did
not then think it an indispensable necessity. When a little later, Gen.
Cameron, then Secretary of War, suggested the arming of the blacks, I
objected, because I did not yet think it an indispensable necessity.
When, still later, Gen. Hunter attempted military emancipation, I again

forbade it, because I did not yet think the indispensable necessity had come. When, in March, and May, and July 1862 I made earnest, and successive appeals to the border states to favor compensated emancipation, I believed the indispensable necessity for military emancipation, and arming the blacks would come, unless averted by that measure. They declined the proposition; and I was, in my best judgment, driven to the alternative of either surrendering the Union, and with it, the Constitution, or of laying strong hand upon the colored element. I chose the latter. In choosing it, I hoped for greater gain than loss; but of this, I was not entirely confident. More than a year of trial now shows no loss by it in our foreign relations, none in our home popular sentiment, none in our white military force,—no loss by it any how or any where. On the contrary, it shows a gain of quite a hundred and thirty thousand soldiers, seamen, and laborers. These are palpable facts, about which, as facts, there can be no cavilling. We have the men; and we could not have had them without the measure.

And now let any Union man who complains of the measure, test himself by writing down in one line that he is for subduing the rebellion by force of arms; and in the next, that he is for taking these hundred and thirty thousand men from the Union side, and placing them where they would be but for the measure he condemns. If he can not face his case so stated, it is only because he can not face the truth.["]

I add a word which was not in the verbal conversation. In telling this tale I attempt no compliment to my own sagacity. I claim not to have controlled events, but confess plainly that events have controlled me. Now, at the end of three years struggle the nation's condition is not what either party, or any man devised, or expected. God alone can claim it. Whither it is tending seems plain. If God now wills the removal of a great wrong, and wills also that we of the North as well as you of the South, shall pay fairly for our complicity in that wrong, impartial history will find therein new cause to attest and revere the justice and goodness of God. Yours truly

"The world has never had a good definition of . . . liberty"

Address at Sanitary Fair, April 18, 1864

In 1864 Lincoln delivered a brief speech at a Sanitary Fair in Baltimore. Noting that no one had anticipated the changes the war would produce, he hailed the growing movement in Maryland to abolish slavery in the state and again pledged that the government would protect black men in the ranks.

Ladies and Gentlemen—Calling to mind that we are in Baltimore, we can not fail to note that the world moves. Looking upon these many people, assembled here, to serve, as they best may, the soldiers of the Union, it occurs at once that three years ago, the same soldiers could not so much as pass through Baltimore. The change from then till now, is both great, and gratifying. Blessings on the brave men who have wrought the change, and the fair women who strive to reward them for it.

But Baltimore suggests more than could happen within Baltimore. The change within Baltimore is part only of a far wider change. When the war began, three years ago, neither party, nor any man, expected it would last till now. Each looked for the end, in some way, long ere to-day. Neither did any anticipate that domestic slavery would be much affected by the war. But here we are; the war has not ended, and slavery has been much affected—how much needs not now to be recounted. So true is it that man proposes, and God disposes.

But we can see the past, though we may not claim to have directed it; and seeing it, in this case, we feel more hopeful and confident for the future.

The world has never had a good definition of the word liberty, and the American people, just now, are much in want of one. We all declare for liberty; but in using the same *word* we do not all mean the same *thing.* With some the word liberty may mean for each man to do as he pleases with himself, and the product of his labor; while with others the same word may mean for some men to do as they please with other men, and the product of other men's labor. Here are two, not only different, but incompatable things, called by the same name—liberty. And it follows that each of the things is, by the respective parties, called by two different and incompatable names—liberty and tyranny.

The shepherd drives the wolf from the sheep's throat, for which the sheep thanks the shepherd as a *liberator*, while the wolf denounces him for the same act as the destroyer of liberty, especially as the sheep was a black one. Plainly the sheep and the wolf are not agreed upon a definition of the word liberty; and precisely the same difference prevails today among us human creatures, even in the North, and all professing to love liberty. Hence we behold the processes by which thousands are daily passing from under the yoke of bondage, hailed by some as the advance of liberty, and bewailed by others as the destruction of all liberty. Recently, as it seems, the people of Maryland have been doing something to define liberty; and thanks to them that, in what they have done, the wolf's dictionary, has been repudiated.

It is not very becoming for one in my position to make speeches at great length; but there is another subject upon which I feel that I ought to say a word. A painful rumor, true I fear, has reached us of the massacre, by the rebel forces, at Fort Pillow, in the West end of Tennessee, on the Mississippi river, of some three hundred colored soldiers and white officers, who had just been overpowered by their assailants. There seems to be some anxiety in the public mind whether the government is doing it's duty to the colored soldier, and to the service, at this point. At the beginning of the war, and for some time, the use of colored troops was not contemplated; and how the change of purpose was wrought, I will not now take time to explain. Upon a clear conviction of duty I resolved to turn that element of strength to account; and I am responsible for it to the American people, to the christian world, to history, and on my final account to God. Having determined to use the negro as a soldier, there is no way but to give him all the protection given to any other soldier. The difficulty is not in stating the principle, but in practically applying it. It is a mistake to suppose the government is indiffe[re]nt to this matter, or is not doing the best it can in regard to it. We do not to-day *know* that a colored soldier, or white officer commanding colored soldiers, has been massacred by the rebels when made a prisoner. We fear it, believe it, I may say, but we do not *know* it. To take the life of one of their prisoners, on the assumption that they murder ours, when it is short of certainty that they do murder ours, might be too serious, too cruel a mistake. We are having the Fort-Pillow affair thoroughly investigated; and such investigation will probably show conclusively how the truth is. If, after all that has been said, it shall turn out that there has been no massacre at Fort-Pillow, it will be almost safe to say there has been none, and will be none elsewhere. If there has been the massacre of three hundred there, or even the tenth part of three hundred, it will be conclusively proved; and being so proved, the retribution shall as surely come. It will be matter of grave consideration in what exact course to apply the retribution; but in the supposed case, it must come.

"I wish not to obtrude any constraints . . . upon you"

Letter to Ulysses S. Grant, April 30, 1864

Once Ulysses S. Grant assumed command of the Union armies, Lincoln's supervision of military affairs became less constant and direct. Still, this letter to Grant, written as the 1864 spring campaign was about to begin, created a false impression of the president's subsequent involvement in military matters. After the fiasco of McClellan's tenure as commanding general, Lincoln never entirely entrusted direction of the war to any of his generals. Rather, Lincoln and Grant became partners in command in a way that had not been true of any of Grant's predecessors.

Lieutenant General Grant.   Executive Mansion, Washington

Not expecting to see you again before the Spring campaign opens, I wish to express, in this way, my entire satisfaction with what you have done up to this time, so far as I understand it. The particulars of your plans I neither know, or seek to know. You are vigilant and self-reliant; and, pleased with this, I wish not to obtrude any constraints or restraints upon you. While I am very anxious that any great disaster, or the capture of our men in great numbers, shall be avoided, I know these points are less likely to escape your attention than they would be mine. If there is anything wanting which is within my power to give, do not fail to let me know it.

And now with a brave Army, and a just cause, may God sustain you. Yours very truly

"Not best to swap horses when crossing streams"

Reply to delegation from the National Union League, June 9, 1864

Despite considerable grumbling about his leadership, Lincoln easily won renomination. He made the following reply to a delegation from the Union League, which had passed resolutions endorsing his renomination by the Union (Republican) National Convention.

Gentlemen: I can only say, in response to the kind remarks of your chairman, as I suppose, that I am very grateful for the renewed confidence which has been accorded to me, both by the convention and by the National League. I am not insensible at all to the personal compliment there is in this; yet I do not allow myself to believe that any but a small portion of it is to be appropriated as a personal compliment. The convention and the nation, I am assured, are alike animated by a higher view of the interests of the country for the present and the great future, and that part I am entitled to appropriate as a compliment is only that part which I may lay hold of as being the opinion of the convention and of the League, that I am not entirely unworthy to be intrusted with the place I have occupied for the last three years. I have not permitted myself, gentlemen, to conclude that I am the best man in the country; but I am reminded, in this connection, of a story of an old Dutch farmer, who remarked to a companion once that "it was not best to swap horses when crossing streams."

"Unprepared . . . to be inflexibly committed to any single plan"

Proclamation concerning reconstruction, July 8, 1864

After he pocket-vetoed the Wade–Davis reconstruction bill, which provided for a much more stringent program of reconstruction than he had established, Lincoln issued a proclamation outlining his objections to the bill. The bill and veto were part of larger struggle between the president and Congress over the control of reconstruction. Despite his objections to Congress's plan, Lincoln made it clear that he was not wedded to one plan and would modify his program if necessary. The bill's authors, Senator Benjamin F. Wade and Representative Henry Winter

Davis, responded with a harsh manifesto attacking the president and his reconstruction governments.

Whereas, at the late Session, Congress passed a Bill, "To guarantee to certain States, whose governments have been usurped or overthrown, a republican form of Government," a copy of which is hereunto annexed:

And whereas, the said Bill was presented to the President of the United States, for his approval, less than one hour before the *sine die* adjournment of said Session, and was not signed by him:

And whereas, the said Bill contains, among other things, a plan for restoring the States in rebellion to their proper practical relation in the Union, which plan expresses the sense of Congress upon that subject, and which plan it is now thought fit to lay before the people for their consideration:

Now, therefore, I, Abraham Lincoln, President of the United States, do proclaim, declare, and make known, that, while I am, (as I was in December last, when by proclamation I propounded a plan for restoration) unprepared, by a formal approval of this Bill, to be inflexibly committed to any single plan of restoration; and, while I am also unprepared to declare, that the free-state constitutions and governments, already adopted and installed in Arkansas and Louisiana, shall be set aside and held for nought, thereby repelling and discouraging the loyal citizens who have set up the same, as to further effort; or to declare a constitutional competency in Congress to abolish slavery in States, but am at the same time sincerely hoping and expecting that a constitutional amendment, abolishing slavery throughout the nation, may be adopted, nevertheless, I am fully satisfied with the system for restoration contained in the Bill, as one very proper plan for the loyal people of any State choosing to adopt it; and that I am, and at all times shall be, prepared to give the Executive aid and assistance to any such people, so soon as the military resistance to the United States shall have been suppressed in any such State, and the people thereof shall have sufficiently returned to their obedience to the Constitution and the laws of the United States,—in which cases, military Governors will be appointed, with directions to proceed according to the Bill.

"Will be received and considered"

Letter "To Whom it may concern," July 18, 1864

In the summer of 1864, the peace movement reached its peak strength on the northern home front, as countless Northerners blanched at the heavy losses Grant's 1864 offensive produced. As a result, Lincoln was under mounting pressure to seek a negotiated settlement with the Confederacy. Unlike northern peace advocates, Lincoln realized that Jefferson Davis would never accept reunion, but he recognized that the peace issue had to be neutralized in the 1864 election. After he drafted the following statement outlining his peace terms, Democrats bitterly assailed Lincoln for including emancipation, and thus his letter failed to silence the clamor in the North for peace.

To Whom it may concern: Executive Mansion, Washington

Any proposition which embraces the restoration of peace, the integrity of the whole Union, and the abandonment of slavery, and which comes by and with an authority that can control the armies now at war against the United States will be received and considered by the Executive government of the United States, and will be met by liberal terms on other substantial and collateral points; and the bearer, or bearers thereof shall have safe-conduct both ways.

"Not . . . an entirely impartial judge"

Letter to John McMahon, August 6, 1864

When a Pennsylvania man telegraphed Lincoln that white men were "class number one" and must govern blacks forever, Lincoln drafted a reply which his secretary, John Nicolay, copied and signed.

John McMahon   Washington, D.C.
Harmbrook, Bradford Co Penn.

The President has received yours of yesterday, and is kindly paying attention to it. As it is my business to assist him whenever I can, I will thank you to inform me, for his use, whether you are either a white man or black one, because in either case, you can not be regarded as an entirely impartial judge. It may be that you belong to a third or fourth class of *yellow* or *red* men, in which case the impartiality of your judgment would be more apparant.

"Hold on with a bull-dog gripe"

Telegram to Ulysses S. Grant, August 17, 1864

Throughout the summer of 1864, despite mounting Union casualties and his increasingly dire political situation, Lincoln was resolute in his determination to vigorously push the war effort, as this message to Grant starkly demonstrates.

"Cypher"
Lieut. Gen. Grant   Executive Mansion,
City Point, Va.   Washington

I have seen your despatch expressing your unwillingness to break your hold where you are. Neither am I willing. Hold on with a bull-dog gripe, and chew & choke, as much as possible.

"The curses of Heaven"

Letter to Charles D. Robinson, August 17, 1864

During the 1864 campaign, Democrats strenuously denounced Lincoln's "To whom it may concern letter" for stipulating emancipation as part of a peace settlement with the Confederacy. Lincoln wrote this letter to a Democratic editor in Wisconsin in response to the charge that he was prolonging the war merely to destroy slavery. Lincoln hoped through this letter to expose Jefferson Davis's unwillingness to consider reunion, but in the end he decided not to send it, concluding that it would create doubt and confusion among his supporters.

Hon. Charles D. Robinson   Executive Mansion, Washington

My dear Sir:
    Your letter of the 7th. was placed in my hand yesterday by Gov. Randall.

To me it seems plain that saying re-union and abandonment of slavery would be considered, if offered, is not saying that nothing *else* or *less* would be considered, if offered. But I will not stand upon the mere construction of language. It is true, as you remind me, that in the Greeley letter of 1862, I said: "If I could save the Union without freeing any slave I would do it; and if I could save it by freeing all the slaves I would do it; and if I could save it by freeing some, and leaving others alone I would also do that." I continued in the same letter as follows: "What I do about slavery and the colored race, I do because I believe it helps to save the Union; and what I forbear I forbear because I do not believe it would help to save the Union. I shall do less whenever I shall believe what I am doing hurts the cause; and I shall do more whenever I shall believe doing more will help the cause." All this I said in the utmost sincerety; and I am as true to the whole of it now, as when I first said it. When I afterwards proclaimed emancipation, and employed colored soldiers, I only followed the declaration just quoted from the Greeley letter that "I shall do *more* whenever I shall believe *doing* more will help the cause." The way these measures were to help the cause, was not to be by magic, or miracles, but by inducing the colored people to come bodily over from the rebel side to ours. On this point, nearly a year ago, in a letter to Mr. Conkling, made public at once, I wrote as follows: "But negroes, like other people, act upon motives. Why should they do anything for us if we will do nothing for them? If they stake their lives for us they must be prompted by the strongest motive—even the promise of freedom. And the promise, being made, must be kept." I am sure you will not, on due reflection, say that the promise being made, must be *broken* at the first opportunity. I am sure you would not desire me to say, or to leave an inference, that I am ready, whenever convenient, to join in re-enslaving those who shall have served us in consideration of our promise. As matter of morals, could such treachery by any possibility, escape the curses of Heaven, or of any good man? As matter of policy, to *announce* such a purpose, would ruin the Union cause itself. All recruiting of colored men would instantly cease, and all colored men now in our service, would instantly desert us. And rightfully too. Why should they give their lives for us, with full notice of our purpose to betray them? Drive back to the support of the rebellion the physical force which the colored people now give, and promise us, and neither the present, nor any coming administration, *can* save the Union. Take from us, and give to the enemy, the hundred and thirty, forty, or fifty thousand colored persons now serving us as soldiers, seamen, and laborers, and we can not longer maintain the contest. The party who could elect a President on a War & Slavery Restoration platform, would, of necessity, lose the colored force; and that force being lost, would be as powerless to save the Union as to do any other impossible thing. It is not a question of sentiment or taste, but one of physical force, which may be measured, and estimated as horse-power, and steam power, are measured and estimated. And by measurement, it is more than we can lose, and live. Nor can we, by discarding it, get a white force in place of it. There is a witness in every white mans bosom that he would rather go to the war having the negro to help him, than to help the enemy against him. It is not the giving of one class for another. It is simply giving a large force to the enemy, for *nothing* in return.

In addition to what I have said, allow me to remind you that no one, having control of the rebel armies, or, in fact, having any influence whatever in the rebellion, has offered, or intimated a willingness to, a restoration of the Union, in any event, or on any condition whatever. Let it be constantly borne in mind that no such offer has been made or intimated. Shall we be weak enough to allow the enemy to distract us with an abstract question which he himself refuses to present as a practical one? In the Conkling letter before mentioned, I said: "Whenever you shall have conquered all resistance to the Union, if I shall urge you to continue fighting, it will be an apt time *then* to declare that you will not fight to free negroes." I repeat this now. If Jefferson Davis wishes, for himself, or for the benefit of his friends at the North, to know what I would do if he were to offer peace and re-union, saying nothing about slavery, let him try me.

"Equal privileges in the race of life"

Speech to One Hundred Sixty-sixth Ohio Regiment, August 22, 1864

Lincoln addressed a few brief remarks to an Ohio regiment on its way home in the summer of 1864. Invoking the interest of future generations, he specifically linked saving of the Union to the preservation of opportunity in American society, which his own career exemplified.

I suppose you are going home to see your families and friends. For the service you have done in this great struggle in which we are engaged I present you sincere thanks for myself and the country. I almost always feel inclined, when I happen to say anything to soldiers, to impress upon them in a few brief remarks the importance of success in this contest. It is not merely for to-day, but for all time to come that we should perpetuate for our children's children this great and free government, which we have enjoyed all our lives. I beg you to remember this, not merely for my sake, but for yours. I happen temporarily to occupy this big White House. I am a living witness that any one of your children may look to come here as my father's child has. It is in order that each of you may have through this free government which we have enjoyed, an open field and a fair chance for your industry, enterprise and intelligence; that you may all have equal privileges in the race of life, with all its desirable human aspirations. It is for this the struggle should be maintained, that we may not lose our birthright—not only for one, but for two or three years. The nation is worth fighting for, to secure such an inestimable jewel.

"This Administration will not be re-elected"

Memorandum, August 23, 1864

As the summer wore on without a decisive Union military victory, Lincoln became convinced that he would be defeated. In the gloom of late August, shortly after receiving a bleak assessment of his prospects from Henry J. Raymond, the party's national chairman, Lincoln drafted a statement and sealed it in an envelope, which he had his cabinet members sign without telling them its contents. Only after the election did Lincoln open the envelope and read to his advisers the memorandum inside.

This morning, as for some days past, it seems exceedingly probable that this Administration will not be re-elected. Then it will be my duty to so co-operate with the President elect, as to save the Union between the election and the inauguration; as he will have secured his election on such ground that he can not possibly save it afterwards.

"Go far towards losing the whole Union cause"

Letter to William T. Sherman, September 19, 1864

Union soldiers voted strongly Republican, and Lincoln was anxious to maximize their participation in the 1864 elections. Unlike most northern states, Indiana did not authorize its soldiers to vote in the field. A skilled operator of the political machine, Lincoln asked General William Tecumseh Sherman to furlough Indiana troops in his army so they could go home and vote. When the state's Republican governor subsequently requested that the furloughed troops remain until the presidential election, Lincoln declined to intervene.

Major General Sherman,   Executive Mansion, Washington, D.C.

The State election of Indiana occurs on the 11th. of October, and the loss of it to the friends of the Government would go far towards losing the whole Union cause. The bad effect upon the November election, and especially the giving the State Government to those who will oppose the war in every possible way, are too much to risk, if it can possibly be avoided. The draft proceeds, notwithstanding its strong tendency to lose us the State. Indiana is the only important State, voting in October, whose soldiers cannot vote in the field. Any thing you can safely do to let her soldiers, or any part of them, go home and vote at the State election, will be greatly in point. They need not remain for the Presidential election, but may return to you at once. This is, in no sense, an order, but is merely intended to impress you with the importance, to the army itself, of your doing all you safely can, yourself being the judge of what you can safely do. Yours truly

"I am struggling to maintain the government, not to overthrow it"

Response to a serenade, October 19, 1864

During the 1864 campaign Lincoln delivered a brief impromptu address to a group of serenaders who were celebrating Maryland's adoption of a constitution abolishing slavery. He took the occasion to emphasize the importance of sustaining the constitutional system regardless of the outcome of the election.

Friends and Fellow-citizens:

I am notified that this is a compliment paid me by the loyal Maryland-ers, resident in this District. I infer that the adoption of the new consti-tution for the State, furnishes the occasion; and that, in your view, the extirpation of slavery constitutes the chief merit of the new constitu-tion. Most heartily do I congratulate you, and Maryland, and the nation, and the world, upon the event. I regret that it did not occur two years sooner, which I am sure would have saved to the nation more money than would have met all the private loss incident to the measure. But it has come at last, and I sincerely hope it's friends may fully realize all their anticipations of good from it; and that it's opponents may, by it's effects, be agreeably and profitably, disappointed.

A word upon another subject.

Something said by the Secretary of State in his recent speech at Auburn, has been construed by some into a threat that, if I shall be beaten at the election, I will, between then and the end of my constitu-tional term, do what I may be able, to ruin the government.

Others regard the fact that the Chicago Convention adjourned, not *sine die*, but to meet again, if called to do so by a particular individual, as the intimation of a purpose that if their nominee shall be elected, he will at once seize control of the government. I hope the good people will permit themselves to suffer no uneasiness on either point. I am struggling to maintain government, not to overthrow it. I am struggling especially to prevent others from overthrowing it. I therefore say, that if I shall live, I shall remain President until the fourth of next March; and that whoever shall be constitutionally elected therefor in November, shall be duly installed as President on the fourth of March; and that in the interval I shall do my utmost that whoever is to hold the helm for the next voyage, shall start with the best possible chance to save the ship.

This is due to the people both on principle, and under the constitu-tion. Their will, constitutionally expressed, is the ultimate law for all. If they should deliberately resolve to have immediate peace even at the loss of their country, and their liberty, I know not the power or the right to resist them. It is their own business, and they must do as they please with their own. I believe, however, they are still resolved to preserve their country and their liberty; and in this, in office or out of it, I am resolved to stand by them.

I may add that in this purpose to save the country and it's liberties, no classes of people seem so nearly unanamous as the soldiers in the field and the seamen afloat. Do they not have the hardest of it? Who should quail while they do not?

God bless the soldiers and seamen, with all their brave commanders.

"The election was a necessity"

Response to a serenade, November 10, 1864

Lincoln delivered these remarks, which he had written out in advance, to a group of well-wishers who came to the White House to celebrate his recent reelection. Emphasizing the benefits of the election, he urged unity to finish the war.

It has long been a grave question whether any government, not *too* strong for the liberties of its people, can be strong *enough* to maintain its own existence, in great emergencies.

On this point the present rebellion brought our republic to a severe test; and a presidential election occurring in regular course during the rebellion added not a little to the strain. If the loyal people, *united*, were put to the utmost of their strength by the rebellion, must they not fail when *divided*, and partially paralized, by a political war among themselves?

But the election was a necessity.

We can not have free government without elections; and if the rebellion could force us to forego, or postpone a national election, it might fairly claim to have already conquered and ruined us. The strife of the election is but human-nature practically applied to the facts of the case. What has occurred in this case, must ever recur in similar cases. Human-nature will not change. In any future great national trial, compared with the men of this, we shall have as weak, and as strong; as silly and as wise; as bad and good. Let us, therefore, study the incidents of this, as philosophy to learn wisdom from, and none of them as wrongs to be revenged.

But the election, along with its incidental, and undesirable strife, has done good too. It has demonstrated that a people's government can sustain a national election, in the midst of a great civil war. Until now it has not been known to the world that this was a possibility. It shows also how *sound*, and how *strong* we still are. It shows that, even among candidates of the same party, he who is most devoted to the Union, and most opposed to treason, can receive most of the people's votes. It shows also, to the extent yet known, that we have more men now, than we had when the war began. Gold is good in its place; but living, brave, patriotic men, are better than gold.

But the rebellion continues; and now that the election is over, may not all, having a common interest, re-unite in a common effort, to save our common country? For my own part I have striven, and shall strive to avoid placing any obstacle in the way. So long as I have been here I have not willingly planted a thorn in any man's bosom.

While I am deeply sensible to the high compliment of a re-election; and duly grateful, as I trust, to Almighty God for having directed my countrymen to a right conclusion, as I think, for their own good, it adds nothing to my satisfaction that any other man may be disappointed or pained by the result.

May I ask those who have not differed with me, to join with me, in this same spirit towards those who have?

And now, let me close by asking three hearty cheers for our brave soldiers and seamen and their gallant and skilful commanders.

VII

"TO BIND UP THE NATION'S WOUNDS," 1864–1865

"So costly a sacrifice upon the altar of Freedom"

Letter to Lydia Bixby, November 21, 1864

When he was informed that Lydia Bixby, who was a Boston widow, had lost five sons in the war, Lincoln wrote one of his most effective letters, which was widely published. It turned out that Lincoln had been misinformed. Of Mrs. Bixby's five sons, only two died in the service; a third, who was captured, may have died while a prisoner. That he was mistaken does not detract from her personal loss or the beauty of Lincoln's language. Some scholars maintain that John Hay, one of Lincoln's secretaries, wrote the letter, but Hay himself pronounced it genuine.

Executive Mansion, Washington

Dear Madam,—I have been shown in the files of the War Department a statement of the Adjutant General of Massachusetts, that you are the mother of five sons who have died gloriously on the field of battle.

I feel how weak and fruitless must be any words of mine which should attempt to beguile you from the grief of a loss so overwhelming. But I cannot refrain from tendering to you the consolation that may be found in the thanks of the Republic they died to save.

I pray that our Heavenly Father may assuage the anguish of your bereavement, and leave you only the cherished memory of the loved and lost, and the solemn pride that must be yours, to have laid so costly a sacrifice upon the altar of Freedom. Yours, very sincerely and respectfully,

"An issue which can only be . . . decided by victory"

Message to Congress, December 6, 1864

In his last annual message, Lincoln surveyed the Union's military situation and noted that the North had the manpower and resources to continue the war indefinitely. In the long closing section below, Lincoln devoted most of his attention to the problem of reconstruction.

The war continues. Since the last annual message all the important lines and positions then occupied by our forces have been maintained, and our arms have steadily advanced; thus liberating the regions left in rear, so that Missouri, Kentucky, Tennessee and parts of other States have again produced reasonably fair crops.

The most remarkable feature in the military operations of the year is General Sherman's attempted march of three hundred miles directly through the insurgent region. It tends to show a great increase of our relative strength that our General-in-Chief should feel able to confront and hold in check every active force of the enemy, and yet to detach a well-appointed large army to move on such an expedition. The result not yet being known, conjecture in regard to it is not here indulged.

Important movements have also occurred during the year to the effect of moulding society for durability in the Union. Although short of complete success, it is much in the right direction, that twelve thousand citizens in each of the States of Arkansas and Louisiana have organized loyal State governments with free constitutions, and are earnestly struggling to maintain and administer them. The movements in the same direction, more extensive, though less definite in Missouri, Kentucky and Tennessee, should not be overlooked. But Maryland presents the example of complete success. Maryland is secure to Liberty and Union for all the future. The genius of rebellion will no more claim Maryland. Like another foul spirit, being driven out, it may seek to tear her, but it will woo her no more.

At the last session of Congress a proposed amendment of the Constitution abolishing slavery throughout the United States, passed the Senate, but failed for lack of the requisite two-thirds vote in the House of Representatives. Although the present is the same Congress, and nearly the same members, and without questioning the wisdom or patriotism of those who stood in opposition, I venture to recommend the reconsideration and passage of the measure at the present session. Of course the abstract question is not changed; but an intervening election shows, almost certainly, that the next Congress will pass the measure if this does not. Hence there is only a question of *time* as to when the proposed amendment will go to the States for their action. And as it is to so go, at all events, may we not agree that the sooner the better? It is not claimed that the election has imposed a duty on members to change their views or their votes, any further than, as an additional element to be considered, their judgment may be affected by it. It is the voice of the people now, for the first time, heard upon the question. In a great national crisis, like ours, unanimity of action among those seeking a common end is very desirable—almost indispensable. And yet no approach to such unanimity is attainable, unless some deference shall be paid to the will of the majority, simply because it is the will of the majority. In this case the common end is the maintenance of the Union; and, among the means to secure that end, such will, through the election, is most clearly declared in favor of such constitutional amendment.

The most reliable indication of public purpose in this country is derived through our popular elections. Judging by the recent canvass and its result, the purpose of the people, within the loyal States, to maintain the integrity of the Union, was never more firm, nor more nearly unanimous, than now. The extraordinary calmness and good order with which the millions of voters met and mingled at the polls, give strong assurance of this. Not only all those who supported the Union ticket, so called, but a great majority of the opposing party also, may be fairly claimed to entertain, and to be actuated by, the same purpose. It is an unanswerable argument to this effect, that no candidate for any office whatever, high or low, has ventured to seek votes on the avowal that he was for giving up the Union. There have been much impugning of motives, and much heated controversy as to the proper means and best mode of advancing the Union cause; but on the distinct issue of Union or no Union, the politicians have shown their instinctive knowledge that there is no diversity among the people. In affording the people the fair opportunity of showing, one to another and to the world, this firmness and unanimity of purpose, the election has been of vast value to the national cause.

The election has exhibited another fact not less valuable to be known—the fact that we do not approach exhaustion in the most important branch of national resources—that of living men. While it is melancholy to reflect that the war has filled so many graves, and carried mourning to so many hearts, it is some relief to know that, compared with the surviving, the fallen have been so few. While corps, and divisions, and brigades, and regiments have formed, and fought, and dwindled, and gone out of existence, a great majority of the men who composed them are still living. The same is true of the naval service. . . . The important fact remains demonstrated, that we have *more* men *now* than we had when the war *began*; that we are not exhausted, nor in process of exhaustion; that we are *gaining* strength, and may, if need be, maintain the contest indefinitely. This as to men. Material resources are now more complete and abundant than ever.

The national resources, then, are unexhausted, and, as we believe, inexhaustible. The public purpose to re-establish and maintain the national authority is unchanged, and, as we believe, unchangeable. The manner of continuing the effort remains to choose. On careful consideration of all the evidence accessible it seems to me that no attempt at negotiation with the insurgent leader could result in any good. He would accept nothing short of severance of the Union—precisely what we will not and cannot give. His declarations to this effect are explicit and oft-repeated. He does not attempt to deceive us. He affords us no excuse to deceive ourselves. He cannot voluntarily reaccept the Union; we cannot voluntarily yield it. Between him and us the issue is distinct, simple, and inflexible. It is an issue which can only be tried by war, and decided by victory. If we yield, we are beaten; if the Southern people fail him, he is beaten. Either way, it would be the victory and defeat following war. What is true, however, of him who heads the insurgent cause, is not necessarily true of those who follow. Although he cannot reaccept the Union, they can. Some of them, we know, already desire peace and reunion. The number of such may increase. They can, at any moment, have peace simply by laying down their arms and submitting to the national authority under the Constitution. After so much, the government could not, if it would, maintain war against them. The loyal people would not sustain or allow it. If questions should remain, we would adjust them by the peaceful means of legislation, conference, courts, and votes, operating only in constitutional and lawful channels. Some certain, and other possible, questions are, and would be, beyond the Executive power to adjust; as, for instance, the admission of members into Congress, and whatever might require the appropriation of money. The Executive power itself would be greatly diminished by the cessation of actual war. Pardons and remissions of forfeitures, however, would still be within Executive control. In what spirit and temper this control would be exercised can be fairly judged of by the past.

A year ago general pardon and amnesty, upon specified terms, were offered to all, except certain designated classes; and, it was, at the same time, made known that the excepted classes were still within contemplation of special clemency. During the year many availed themselves of the general provision, and many more would, only that the signs of bad faith in some led to such precautionary measures as rendered the practical process less easy and certain. During the same time also special pardons have been granted to individuals of the excepted classes, and no voluntary application has been denied. Thus, practically, the door has been, for a full year, open to all, except such as were not in condition to make free choice—that is, such as were in custody or under constraint. It is still so open to all. But the time may come—probably will come— when public duty shall demand that it be closed; and that, in lieu, more rigorous measures than heretofore shall be adopted.

In presenting the abandonment of armed resistance to the national authority on the part of the insurgents, as the only indispensable condition to ending the war on the part of the government, I retract nothing heretofore said as to slavery. I repeat the declaration made a year ago, that "while I remain in my present position I shall not attempt to retract or modify the emancipation proclamation, nor shall I return to slavery any person who is free by the terms of that proclamation, or by any of the Acts of Congress." If the people should, by whatever mode or means, make it an Executive duty to re-enslave such persons, another, and not I, must be their instrument to perform it.

In stating a single condition of peace, I mean simply to say that the war will cease on the part of the government, whenever it shall have ceased on the part of those who began it.

"The honor is all yours"

Letter to William T. Sherman, December 26, 1864

Following his successful March to the Sea, Sherman captured the city of Savannah, which in a famous dispatch he presented to the president as "a Christmas gift." Lincoln sent the following letter saluting Sherman's accomplishment. One of Lincoln's strengths as a war leader was his willingness to give generous credit to his commanders for their successes. The letter also revealed his growing confidence in the Union's top military leadership and his diminished role in directing the war effort.

Executive Mansion, Washington

My dear General Sherman.

Many, many, thanks for your Christmas-gift—the capture of Savannah.

When you were about leaving Atlanta for the Atlantic coast, I was *anxious*, if not fearful; but feeling that you were the better judge, and remembering that "nothing risked, nothing gained" I did not interfere. Now, the undertaking being a success, the honor is all yours; for I believe none of us went farther than to acquiesce. And, taking the work of Gen. Thomas into the count, as it should be taken, it is indeed a great success. Not only does it afford the obvious and immediate military advantages; but, in showing to the world that your army could be divided, putting the stronger part to an important new service, and yet leaving enough to vanquish the old opposing force of the whole— Hood's army—it brings those who sat in darkness, to see a great light. But what next? I suppose it will be safer if I leave Gen. Grant and yourself to decide.

Please make my grateful acknowledgments to your whole army, officers and men. Yours very truly

"*Time* . . . is more important than ever before"

Letter to Edwin Stanton, January 5, 1865

In January Secretary of War Stanton went to Savannah to confer with Sherman about military movements. In this letter, Lincoln emphasized the importance of Sherman quickly resuming the offensive. It was prompted by a communication from Sherman indicating that he needed to carefully prepare before moving forward again, which no doubt revived memories for Lincoln of his repeated frustration over his earlier commanders' unwillingness to move until everything was perfect. Sherman, however, proved to be a much different kind of general.

Hon. Sec. of War   Executive Mansion, Washington

Dear Sir,

Since parting with you, it has occurred to me to say that while Gen. Sherman's *"get a good ready"* is appreciated, and is not to be overlooked, *time*, now that the enemy is wavering, is more important than ever before. Being on the down-hill, & some what confused, keeping him going. Please say so much to Genl. S. Yours truly

"My son . . . wishes to see something of the war"

Letter to Ulysses S. Grant, January 19, 1865

Lincoln's oldest son, Robert Todd Lincoln, was a student at Harvard when the war began. When he graduated, Robert wanted to enlist. Having already lost two of their four sons, Lincoln worried that if his eldest son were killed, his wife would lose her mental balance entirely, so he wrote the following letter to Grant, seeking to satisfy his son's desire to be part of the war. Appointed captain, Robert joined Grant's staff and served for four months.

Lieut. General Grant: Executive Mansion, Washington

Please read and answer this letter as though I was not President, but only a friend. My son, now in his twenty second year, having graduated at Harvard, wishes to see something of the war before it ends. I do not wish to put him in the ranks, nor yet to give him a commission, to which those who have already served long, are better entitled, and better qualified to hold. Could he, without embarrassment to you, or detriment to the service, go into your Military family with some nominal rank, I, and not the public, furnishing his necessary means? If no, say so without the least hesitation, because I am as anxious, and as deeply interested, that you shall not be encumbered as you can be yourself. Yours truly

"Three things are indispensable"

Letter to William H. Seward, January 31, 1865

Early in 1865 Jefferson Davis appointed three commissioners to discuss peace with the United States. In his instructions to Secretary of State William Henry Seward, Lincoln reiterated the main conditions for peace that he had specified during the 1864 campaign. At the last moment, Lincoln decided to join Seward for the discussions at Hampton Roads, Virginia. The Confederate commissioners, however, were not authorized to accept reunion, and the peace talks ended in failure, as Lincoln had anticipated.

Hon. William H. Seward   Executive Mansion, Washington
Secretary of State

You will proceed to Fortress-Monroe, Virginia, there to meet, and informally confer with Messrs. Stephens, Hunter, and Campbell, on the basis of my letter to F. P. Blair, Esq., on Jan. 18, 1865, a copy of which you have.

You will make known to them that three things are indispensable, towit:

1. The restoration of the national authority throughout all the States.

2. No receding, by the Executive of the United States on the Slavery question, from the position assumed thereon, in the late Annual Message to Congress, and in preceding documents.

3. No cessation of hostilities short of an end of the war, and the disbanding of all forces hostile to the government.

You will inform them that all propositions of theirs not inconsistent with the above, will be considered and passed upon in a spirit of sincere liberality. You will hear all they may choose to say, and report it to me.

You will not assume to definitely consummate anything. Yours &c.

"A King's cure for all the evils"

Response to a serenade, February 1, 1865

Lincoln delivered these remarks following passage a day earlier of the proposed Thirteenth Amendment abolishing slavery by the House of Representatives (the Senate had approved the amendment in 1864). To Lincoln, the amendment was a fitting consummation of the war.

The President said he supposed the passage through Congress of the Constitutional amendment for the abolishment of Slavery throughout the United States, was the occasion to which he was indebted for the honor of this call. The occasion was one of congratulation to the country and to the whole world. But there is a task yet before us—to go forward and consummate by the votes of the States that which Congress so nobly began yesterday. He had the honor to inform those present that Illinois had already to-day done the work. Maryland was about half through; but he felt proud that Illinois was a little ahead. He thought this measure was a very fitting if not an indispensable adjunct to the winding up of the great difficulty. He wished the reunion of all the States perfected and so effected as to remove all causes of disturbance in the future; and to attain this end it was necessary that the original disturbing cause should, if possible, be rooted out. He thought all would bear him witness that he had never shrunk from doing all that he could to eradicate Slavery by issuing an emancipation proclamation. But that proclamation falls far short of what the amendment will be when fully consummated. A question might be raised whether the proclamation was legally valid. It might be added that it only aided those who came into our lines and that it was inoperative as to those who did not give themselves up, or that it would have no effect upon the children of the slaves born hereafter. In fact it would be urged that it did not meet the evil. But this amendment is a King's cure for all the evils. It winds the whole thing up. He would repeat that it was the fitting if not indispensable adjunct to the consummation of the great game we are playing. He could not but congratulate all present, himself, the country and the whole world upon this great moral victory.

"With charity for all"

Second Inaugural Address, March 4, 1865

Lincoln delivered his second inaugural only a few weeks before the end of the war. He chose the occasion, however, not to celebrate the Union army's accomplishments or his own political leadership, but to discuss the origins and meaning of the war. The speech, which was rich with religious overtones, displayed a profound understanding of the depths of the tragedy the nation had experienced. Lincoln ended with an eloquent plea for a generous peace.

[Fellow Countrymen:]

At this second appearing to take the oath of the presidential office, there is less occasion for an extended address than there was at the first. Then a statement, somewhat in detail, of a course to be pursued, seemed fitting and proper. Now, at the expiration of four years, during which public declarations have been constantly called forth on every point and phase of the great contest which still absorbs the attention, and engrosses the enerergies of the nation, little that is new could be presented. The progress of our arms, upon which all else chiefly depends, is as well known to the public as to myself; and it is, I trust, reasonably satisfactory and encouraging to all. With high hope for the future, no prediction in regard to it is ventured.

On the occasion corresponding to this four years ago, all thoughts were anxiously directed to an impending civil-war. All dreaded it—all sought to avert it. While the inaugeral address was being delivered from this place, devoted altogether to *saving* the Union without war, insurgent agents were in the city seeking to *destroy* it without war—seeking to dissol[v]e the Union, and divide effects, by negotiation. Both parties deprecated war; but one of them would *make* war rather than let the nation survive; and the other would *accept* war rather than let it perish. And the war came.

One eighth of the whole population were colored slaves, not distributed generally over the Union, but localized in the Southern part of it. These slaves constituted a peculiar and powerful interest. All knew that this interest was, somehow, the cause of the war. To strengthen, perpetuate, and extend this interest was the object for which the insurgents would rend the Union, even by war; while the government claimed no right to do more than to restrict the territorial enlargement of it. Neither party expected for the war, the magnitude, or the duration, which it has already attained. Neither anticipated that the *cause* of the conflict might cease with, or even before, the conflict itself should cease. Each looked for an easier triumph, and a result less fundamental and astounding. Both read the same Bible, and pray to the same God; and each invokes His aid against the other. It may seem strange that any men should dare to ask a just God's assistance in wringing their bread from the sweat of other men's faces; but let us judge not that we be not judged. The prayers of both could not be answered; that of neither has been answered fully. The Almighty has His own purposes. "Woe unto the world because of offences! for it must needs be that offences come; but woe to that man by whom the offence cometh!" If we shall suppose that American Slavery is one of those offences which, in the providence of God, must needs come, but which, having continued through His appointed time, He now wills to remove, and that He gives to both North and South, this terrible war, as the woe due to those by whom the offence came, shall we discern therein any departure from those divine attributes which the believers in a Living God always ascribe to Him? Fondly do we hope—fervently do we pray—that this mighty scourge of war may speedily pass away. Yet, if God wills that it continue, until all the wealth piled by the bond-man's two hundred and fifty years of unrequited toil shall be sunk, and until every drop of blood drawn with the lash, shall be paid by another drawn with the sword, as was said three thousand years ago, so still it must be said "the judgments of the Lord, are true and righteous altogether."

With malice toward none; with charity for all; with firmness in the right, as God gives us to see the right, let us strive on to finish the work we are in; to bind up the nation's wounds; to care for him who shall have borne the battle, and for his widow, and his orphan—to do all which may achieve and cherish a just, and a lasting peace, among ourselves, and with all nations.

"A truth which I thought needed to be told"

Letter to Thurlow Weed, March 15, 1865

*When Thurlow Weed, a prominent New York Republican leader, con-
gratulated Lincoln on his second inaugural address, Lincoln noted that
while the speech had not been universally praised, he expected it to have
lasting significance.*

Thurlow Weed, Esq   Executive Mansion, Washington

My dear Sir.

Every one likes a compliment. Thank you for yours on my little notifi-
cation speech, and on the recent Inaugeral Address. I expect the latter to
wear as well as—perhaps better than—any thing I have produced; but I
believe it is not immediately popular. Men are not flattered by being
shown that there has been a difference of purpose between the Almighty
and them. To deny it, however, in this case, is to deny that there is a God
governing the world. It is a truth which I thought needed to be told; and
as whatever of humiliation there is in it, falls most directly on myself, I
thought others might afford for me to tell it. Yours truly

"Let the *thing* be pressed"

Telegram to Ulysses S. Grant, April 7, 1865

*Shortly before Lee surrendered, Lincoln sent the following telegram
instructing Grant to keep up his relentless pressure on Lee's army.*

Head Quarters Armies of the United States, City-Point

Lieut Gen. Grant.

Gen Sheridan says "If the thing is pressed I think that Lee will surrender." Let the *thing* be pressed.

"No exclusive, and inflexible plan can safely be prescribed"

Speech, April 11, 1865

Lincoln's last speech dealt with the subject of reconstruction. He deliv-
ered it from a window in the White House to a crowd that had come to
celebrate Lee's surrender. In the speech Lincoln called for limited black
suffrage in the South as part of reconstruction, his first public endorse-
ment of a position he had assumed privately a year earlier. Among those
in the audience was John Wilkes Booth, the famous actor. When he
heard Lincoln sanction black suffrage in the postwar South, he decided
to kill the president.

We meet this evening, not in sorrow, but in gladness of heart. The evacuation of Petersburg and Richmond, and the surrender of the principal
insurgent army, give hope of a righteous and speedy peace whose joyous
expression can not be restrained. In the midst of this, however, He, from
Whom all blessings flow, must not be forgotten. A call for a national
thanksgiving is being prepared, and will be duly promulgated. Nor must
those whose harder part gives us the cause of rejoicing, be overlooked.
Their honors must not be parcelled out with others. I myself, was near
the front, and had the high pleasure of transmitting much of the good
news to you; but no part of the honor, for plan or execution, is mine. To
Gen. Grant, his skilful officers, and brave men, all belongs. The gallant
Navy stood ready, but was not in reach to take active part.

By these recent successes the re-inauguration of the national authority—reconstruction—which has had a large share of thought from the
first, is pressed much more closely upon our attention. It is fraught with
great difficulty. Unlike the case of a war between independent nations,
there is no authorized organ for us to treat with. No one man has
authority to give up the rebellion for any other man. We simply must
begin with, and mould from, disorganized and discordant elements. Nor
is it a small additional embarrassment that we, the loyal people, differ
among ourselves as to the mode, manner, and means of reconstruction.

As a general rule, I abstain from reading the reports of attacks upon
myself, wishing not to be provoked by that to which I can not properly
offer an answer. In spite of this precaution, however, it comes to my

knowledge that I am much censured for some supposed agency in setting up, and seeking to sustain, the new State Government of Louisiana. In this I have done just so much as, and no more than, the public knows. In the Annual Message of Dec. 1863 and accompanying Proclamation, I presented *a* plan of re-construction (as the phrase goes) which, I promised, if adopted by any State, should be acceptable to, and sustained by, the Executive government of the nation. I distinctly stated that this was not the only plan which might possibly be acceptable; and I also distinctly protested that the Executive claimed no right to say when, or whether members should be admitted to seats in Congress from such States. This plan was, in advance, submitted to the then Cabinet, and distinctly approved by every member of it. One of them suggested that I should then, and in that connection, apply the Emancipation Proclamation to the theretofore excepted parts of Virginia and Louisiana; that I should drop the suggestion about apprenticeship for freed-people, and that I should omit the protest against my own power, in regard to the admission of members to Congress; but even he approved every part and parcel of the plan which has since been employed or touched by the action of Louisiana. The new constitution of Louisiana, declaring emancipation for the whole State, practically applies the Proclamation to the part previously excepted. It does not adopt apprenticeship for freed-people; and it is silent, as it could not well be otherwise, about the admission of members to Congress. So that, as it applies to Louisiana, every member of the Cabinet fully approved the plan. The Message went to Congress, and I received many commendations of the plan, written and verbal; and not a single objection to it, from any professed emancipationist, came to my knowledge, until after the news reached Washington that the people of Louisiana had begun to move in accordance with it. From about July 1862, I had corresponded with different persons, supposed to be interested, seeking a reconstruction of a State government for Louisiana. When the Message of 1863, with the plan before mentioned, reached New-Orleans, Gen. Banks wrote me that he was confident the people, with his military co-operation, would reconstruct, substantially on that plan. I wrote him, and some of them to try it; they tried it, and the result is known. Such only has been my agency in getting up the Louisiana government. As to sustaining it, my promise is out, as before stated. But, as bad promises are better broken than kept, I shall treat this as a bad promise, and break it, whenever I shall be convinced that keeping it is adverse to the public interest. But I have not yet been so convinced.

I have been shown a letter on this subject, supposed to be an able one, in which the writer expresses regret that my mind has not seemed to be definitely fixed on the question whether the seceded States, so called, are in the Union or out of it. It would perhaps, add astonishment to his regret, were he to learn that since I have found professed Union men endeavoring to make that question, I have *purposely* forborne any public expression upon it. As appears to me that question has not been, nor yet is, a practically material one, and that any discussion of it, while it thus remains practically immaterial, could have no effect other than the mischievous one of dividing our friends. As yet, whatever it may hereafter become, that question is bad, as the basis of a controversy, and good for nothing at all—a merely pernicious abstraction.

We all agree that the seceded States, so called, are out of their proper practical relation with the Union; and that the sole object of the government, civil and military, in regard to those States is to again get them into that proper practical relation. I believe it is not only possible, but in fact, easier, to do this, without deciding, or even considering, whether these states have even been out of the Union, than with it. Finding themselves safely at home, it would be utterly immaterial whether they had ever been abroad. Let us all join in doing the acts necessary to restoring the proper practical relations between these states and the Union; and each forever after, innocently indulge his own opinion whether, in doing the acts, he brought the States from without, into the Union, or only gave them proper assistance, they never having been out of it.

The amount of constituency, so to speak, on which the new Louisiana government rests, would be more satisfactory to all, if it contained fifty, thirty, or even twenty thousand, instead of only about twelve thousand, as it does. It is also unsatisfactory to some that the elective franchise is not given to the colored man. I would myself prefer that it were now conferred on the very intelligent, and on those who serve our cause as soldiers. Still the question is not whether the Louisiana government, as it stands, is quite all that is desirable. The question is "Will it be wiser to take it as it is, and help to improve it; or to reject, and disperse it?" "Can Louisiana be brought into proper practical relation with the Union *sooner* by *sustaining*, or by *discarding* her new State Government?"

Some twelve thousand voters in the heretofore slave-state of Louisiana have sworn allegiance to the Union, assumed to be the rightful political power of the State, held elections, organized a State government, adopted a free-state constitution, giving the benefit of public schools equally to black and white, and empowering the Legislature to confer the elective franchise upon the colored man. Their Legislature has already voted to ratify the constitutional amendment recently passed by Congress, abolishing slavery throughout the nation. These twelve thousand persons are thus fully committed to the Union, and to perpetual freedom in the state—committed to the very things, and nearly all the things the nation wants—and they ask the nations recognition, and it's assistance to make good their committal. Now, if we reject, and spurn them, we do our utmost to disorganize and disperse them. We in effect say to the white men "You are worthless, or worse— we will neither help you, nor be helped by you." To the blacks we say "This cup of liberty which these, your old masters, hold to your lips, we will dash from you, and leave you to the chances of gathering the spilled and scattered contents in some vague and undefined when, where, and how." If this course, discouraging and paralyzing both white and black, has any tendency to bring Louisiana into proper practical relations with the Union, I have, so far, been unable to perceive it. If, on the contrary, we recognize, and sustain the new government of Louisiana the converse of all this is made true. We encourage the hearts, and nerve the arms of the twelve thousand to adhere to their work, and argue for it, and proselyte for it, and fight for it, and feed it, and grow it, and ripen it to a complete success. The colored man too, in seeing all united for him, is inspired with vigilance, and energy, and daring, to the same end. Grant that he desires the elective franchise, will he not attain it sooner by saving the already advanced steps toward it, than by running backward over them? Concede that the new government of Louisiana is only to what it should be as the egg is to the fowl, we shall sooner have the fowl by hatching the egg than by smashing it? Again, if we reject Louisiana, we also reject one vote in favor of the proposed amendment to the national constitution. To meet this proposition, it has been argued that no more than three fourths of those States which

have not attempted secession are necessary to validly ratify the amendment. I do not commit myself against this, further than to say that such
a ratification would be questionable, and sure to be persistently questioned; while a ratification by three fourths of all the States would be
unquestioned and unquestionable.

I repeat the question. "Can Louisiana be brought into proper practical relation with the Union *sooner* by *sustaining* or by *discarding* her new
State Government?"

What has been said of Louisiana will apply generally to other States.
And yet so great peculiarities pertain to each state; and such important
and sudden changes occur in the same state; and, withal, so new and
unprecedented is the whole case, that no exclusive, and inflexible plan
can safely be prescribed as to details and colatterals. Such exclusive, and
inflexible plan, would surely become a new entanglement. Important
principles may, and must, be inflexible.

In the present *"situation"* as the phrase goes, it may be my duty to
make some new announcement to the people of the South. I am considering, and shall not fail to act, when satisfied that action will be proper.

CHRONOLOGY OF ABRAHAM LINCOLN

1809	February 12	Born in Hardin County, Kentucky
1816	December	Family moves to Indiana
1818	October 5	Mother, Nancy Hanks Lincoln, dies
1819	December 2	Father marries Sarah Bush Johnson
1830	March	Family moves to Illinois
1831	late July	Arrives in New Salem
1832	April–July	Serves in Black Hawk War
	August 6	Defeated for legislature in first political race
1834	August 4	Elected to state legislature
	Autumn	Begins studying law
1836	August 1	Reelected to legislature
	September 9	Receives law license
1837	March 3	First public declaration against slavery
	April 15	Moves to Springfield, joins law partnership with John T. Stuart
1838	August 6	Reelected to legislature

1840	August 3	Reelected to legislature
	Fall–Winter	Engaged to Mary Todd; breaks engagement
1841	March	Forms legal partnership with Stephen T. Logan
1842	November 4	Marries Mary Todd
1843	August 1	Son Robert Todd Lincoln born
1844	December	Forms legal partnership with William Herndon
1846	March 10	Son Edward Baker (Eddie) Lincoln born
	August 3	Elected to Congress
1847–	December 3–	Serves in Congress
1849	March 4	
1850	February 1	Son Eddie dies
	December 21	Son William Wallace (Willie) Lincoln born
1851	January 17	Father, Thomas, dies
1853	April 4	Son Thomas (Tad) Lincoln born
1854	August 26	Delivers first speech against the Kansas–Nebraska Act
	November 7	Elected to the legislature; resigns to seek U.S. Senate seat
1855	February 8	Defeated for senator
1856	February 22	Affiliates with Republican party
	June 19	Finishes second in balloting for Republican vice-presidential nomination
	Fall	Campaigns for Republican ticket
1858	June 16	Nominated for senator by Republican convention
	August 21– October 15	Lincoln–Douglas debates
	November 4	State election foreshadows defeat for Senate
1859	January 5	Defeated for senator
1860	May 18	Nominated for president
	November 6	Elected president
	December 20	South Carolina secedes

CIVIL WAR

1860–1861	December–March	Opposes compromise

1861	January–February	Six remaining states of the Deep South secede
	February 11	Leaves Springfield to go to Washington
	March 4	Inaugurated
	April 12	Fort Sumter bombarded
	April 15	Calls for 75,000 volunteers
	April 19	Institutes blockade
	April 27	Suspends writ of habeas corpus in Maryland
	July 21	Battle of Bull Run
	July 26	McClellan takes command of the army at Washington
	September 12	Revokes Frémont's emancipation proclamation
	November 1	Appoints McClellan commanding general

1862	February 20	Son Willie dies
	March–July	Peninsula Campaign
	May 19	Revokes Hunter's emancipation proclamation
	June 26–July 2	Seven Days' Battles
	July 12	Meets with border state representatives
	July 22	Circulates draft of emancipation proclamation to cabinet
	July 23	Names Halleck general-in-chief (serves until March 9, 1864)
	August 30	Second Battle of Bull Run
	September 17	Battle of Antietam
	September 22	Issues preliminary Emancipation Proclamation
	September 24	Suspends writ of habeas corpus throughout the North
	October–November	Democrats gain in fall elections
	November 5	Removes McClellan from command

1863	January 1	Issues final Emancipation Proclamation
	January 25	Hooker appointed commander of the Army of the Potomac
	May 6	Vallandigham arrested
	June 7	Black troops fight at Battle of Milliken's Bend
	June 28	Names Meade commander of the Army of the Potomac
	July 1–3	Battle of Gettysburg
	July 4	Vicksburg captured

	July 13–16	New York City draft riots
	October–November	Democrats suffer severe defeats in state elections
	November 19	Gettysburg Address
	December 8	Announces reconstruction program
1864	March 9	Names Grant commanding general
	May–June	Grant's offensive in Virginia
	June 8	Renominated
	July 4	Pocket-vetoes Wade–Davis bill
	September 2	Sherman captures Atlanta
	November 8	Reelected
1865	January 31	Thirteenth Amendment passes Congress
	March 4	Second inauguration
	April 9	Lee surrenders
	April 11	Last speech on reconstruction
	April 14	Shot at Ford's Theater by John Wilkes Booth; dies the next morning
	May 4	Burial in Springfield

SELECTED BIBLIOGRAPHY

PRIMARY SOURCES

Basler, Roy P., Marian Dolores Pratt, and Lloyd A. Dunlap, eds. *The Collected Works of Abraham Lincoln*. 8 vols. New Brunswick, N.J.: Rutgers University Press, 1953.

Burlingame, Michael, ed. *At Lincoln's Side: John Hay's Civil War Correspondence and Selected Writings*. Carbondale: Southern Illinois University Press, 2000.

———. *An Oral History of Abraham Lincoln: John G. Nicolay's Interviews and Essays*. Carbondale: Southern Illinois University Press, 1996.

———. *With Lincoln in the White House: Letters, Memoranda, and Other Writings of John G. Nicolay, 1860–1865*. Carbondale: Southern Illinois University Press, 2000.

Burlingame, Michael, and John R. Turner Ettinger, eds. *Inside Lincoln's White House: The Complete Civil War Diary of John Hay*. Carbondale: Southern Illinois University Press, 1997.

Fehrenbacher, Don E., and Virginia Fehrenbacher, eds. *Recollected Words of Abraham Lincoln*. Stanford, Calif.: Stanford University Press, 1996.

Holzer, Harold, ed. *The Lincoln–Douglas Debates: The First Complete, Unexpurgated Text*. New York: HarperCollins, 1993.

Johannsen, Robert W., ed. *The Lincoln–Douglas Debates of 1858*. New York: Oxford University Press, 1965.

Segal, Charles M., ed. *Conversations with Lincoln*. New York: G. P. Putnam's Sons, 1961.

Wilson, Douglas L. and Rodney O. Davis, eds. *Herndon's Informants: Letters, Interviews, and Statements about Abraham Lincoln*. Urbana: University of Illinois Press, 1998.

REFERENCE WORKS AND COLLECTIONS OF ESSAYS

Boritt, Gabor, ed. *The Lincoln Enigma*. New York: Oxford University Press, 2001.

Current, Richard N. *The Lincoln Nobody Knows*. New York: McGraw-Hill, 1958.

Donald, David. *Lincoln Reconsidered: Essays on the Civil War.* New York: Alfred A. Knopf, 1956.

Fehrenbacher, Don E. *Lincoln in Text and Context: Collected Essays.* Stanford, Calif.: Stanford University Press, 1987.

McPherson, James M., ed. *"We Cannot Escape History": Lincoln and the Last Best Hope of Earth.* Urbana: University of Illinois Press, 1995.

Miers, Earl S., William E. Baringer, and C. Percy Powell, eds. *Lincoln Day by Day: A Chronology.* 3 vols. Washington: Lincoln Sesquicentennial Association, 1960.

Neely, Mark E., Jr. *The Abraham Lincoln Encyclopedia.* New York: McGraw-Hill, 1982.

Schwartz, Thomas F., ed. *"For a Vast Future Also": Essays from the Journal of the Abraham Lincoln Association.* New York: Fordham University Press, 1999.

Wilson, Douglas. *Lincoln Before Washington: New Perspectives on the Illinois Years.* Urbana: University of Illinois Press, 1997.

Zall, Paul, ed. *Abe Lincoln Laughing.* Knoxville: University of Tennessee Press, 1995.

BIOGRAPHIES

Charnwood, Godfrey Rathbone, Baron. *Abraham Lincoln.* New York: Henry Holt and Company, 1917.

Donald, David. *Lincoln.* New York: Simon and Schuster, 1995.

Herndon, William, and Jesse E. Weik. *Herndon's Life of Lincoln.* Edited by Paul Angle. Cleveland: World Publishing Company, 1942.

Neely, Mark E. *The Last Best Hope of Earth: Abraham Lincoln and the Promise of America.* Cambridge: Harvard University Press, 1993.

Randall, James G. *Lincoln the President.* 4 vols. New York: Dodd, Mead, 1945–1955.

Thomas, Benjamin. *Abraham Lincoln: A Biography.* New York: Alfred A. Knopf, 1952.

THE PRE–CIVIL WAR YEARS

Baker, Jean Harvey. *Mary Todd Lincoln.* New York: W. W. Norton and Co., 1987.

Baringer, William E. *Lincoln's Rise to Power.* Boston: Little, Brown and Company, 1937.

———. *A House Dividing: Lincoln as President Elect.* Springfield, Ill.: Abraham Lincoln Association, 1945.

Boritt, Gabor S. *Lincoln and the Economics of the American Dream.* Memphis, Tenn.: Memphis State University Press, 1978.

Burlingame, Michael. *The Inner World of Abraham Lincoln.* Urbana: University of Illinois Press, 1994.

Current, Richard N. *Lincoln and the First Shot.* Philadelphia: J. B. Lippincott Co., 1963.

Duff, John A. *A. Lincoln: Prairie Lawyer.* New York: Rinehart and Co., 1960.

Fehrenbacher, Don E. *Prelude to Greatness: Lincoln in the 1850s.* Stanford, Calif.: Stanford University Press, 1962.

Findley, Paul. *A. Lincoln: The Crucible of Congress.* New York: Crown Publishers, 1979.

Forgie, George B. *Patricide in the House Divided: A Psychological Interpretation of Lincoln and His Age.* New York: W. W. Norton, 1979.

Franklin, John Hope. *The Emancipation Proclamation*. Garden City, N.Y.: Doubleday and Co., 1963.

Jaffa, Harry V. *Crisis of the House Divided: An Interpretation of the Issues in the Lincoln–Douglas Debates*. Garden City, N.Y.: Doubleday and Co., 1959.

———. *A New Birth of Freedom: Abraham Lincoln and the Coming of the Civil War*. Lanham, Md.: Rowman and Littlefield, 2000.

Johannsen, Robert W. *Lincoln, the South, and Slavery*. Baton Rouge: Louisiana State University Press, 1991.

Riddle, Donald W. *Congressman Abraham Lincoln*. Westport, Conn.: Greenwood Press, 1979.

Simon, Paul. *Lincoln's Preparation for Greatness: The Illinois Legislative Years*. Norman: University of Oklahoma Press, 1965.

Strozier, Charles P. *Lincoln's Quest for Union: Public and Private Meanings*. New York: Basic Books, 1982.

Thomas, Benjamin P. *Lincoln's New Salem*. New York: Alfred A. Knopf, 1954.

Walsh, John Evangelist. *Moonlight: Abraham Lincoln and the Almanac Trial*. New York: St. Martin's Press, 2000.

Warren, Louis A. *Lincoln's Youth: Indiana Years, 1816–1830*. Indianapolis: Indiana Historical Society, 1959.

Wilson, Douglas. *Honor's Voice: The Transformation of Abraham Lincoln*. New York: Alfred A. Knopf, 1998.

THE CIVIL WAR YEARS

Belz, Herman. *Abraham Lincoln, Constitutionalism, and Equal Rights in the Civil War Era*. New York: Fordham University Press, 1998.

Boritt, Gabor, ed. *Lincoln's Generals*. New York: Oxford University Press, 1994.

Bruce, Robert. *Lincoln and the Tools of War*. Indianapolis: Bobbs-Merrill, 1956.

Cox, LaWanda. *Lincoln and Black Freedom: A Study in Presidential Leadership*. Columbia: University of South Carolina Press, 1981.

Guelzo, Allen C. *Abraham Lincoln: Redeemer President*. Grand Rapids, Mich.: William B. Eerdmans Publishing Co., 1999.

Harris, William C. *With Charity for All: Lincoln and the Restoration of the Union*. Lawrence: University Press of Kansas, 1997.

Hesseltine, William B. *Lincoln and the War Governors*. New York: Alfred A. Knopf, 1955.

Long, David E. *The Jewel of Liberty: Abraham Lincoln's Re-election and the End of Slavery*. Mechanicsburg, Pa.: Stackpole Books, 1994.

Neely, Mark E., Jr. *The Fate of Liberty: Abraham Lincoln and Civil Liberties*. New York: Oxford University Press, 1991.

Paludan, Phillip S. *The Presidency of Abraham Lincoln*. Lawrence: University Press of Kansas, 1994.

Peterson, Merrill D. *Lincoln in American Memory*. New York: Oxford University Press, 1994.

Schwartz, Barry. *Abraham Lincoln and the Forge of National Memory.* Chicago: University of Chicago Press, 2000.

Williams, T. Harry. *Lincoln and His Generals.* New York: Alfred A. Knopf, 1952.

Wills, Garry. *Lincoln at Gettysburg: The Words that Remade America.* New York: Simon and Schuster, 1992.

Wolf, William J. *The Almost Chosen People: A Study of the Religion of Abraham Lincoln.* Garden City, N.Y.: Doubleday and Co., 1959.